THE CUT OF HIS COAT

Temptation.

BRENT SHANNON

The Cut of His Coat

Men, Dress, and Consumer Culture in Britain, 1860–1914

Ohio University Press   Athens

Ohio University Press, Athens, Ohio 45701
www.ohio.edu/oupress
© 2006 by Ohio University Press

Ohio University Press books are printed on acid-free paper ∞ ™

13 12 11 10 09 08 07 06   5 4 3 2 1

Frontispiece: "Temptation." Cartoon reprinted in Maurice Baren, *Victorian Shopping* (London: Michael O'Mara, 1998), 74.

Library of Congress Cataloging-in-Publication Data

Shannon, Brent Alan, 1970–
  The cut of his coat : men, dress, and consumer culture in Britain, 1860–1914 / Brent Alan Shannon.
      p. cm.
  Includes bibliographical references (p.   ) and index.
  ISBN-13: 978-0-8214-1702-7 (acid-free paper)
  ISBN-10: 0-8214-1702-9 (acid-free paper)
  ISBN-13: 978-0-8214-1703-4 (pbk. : acid-free paper)
  ISBN-10: 0-8214-1703-7 (pbk. : acid-free paper)
  1. Male consumers—Great Britain—History. 2. Men's clothing—England—History.
3. Social classes—England—History. 4. Masculinity—England—History. 5. Consumption (Economics)—England—History. I. Title.
  HC260.C6S52 2006
  306.30941'09034—dc22

                                                                    2006017471

To Sophia

Contents

Figures

Acknowledgments

I'd like to thank my former colleagues at the University of Kentucky—Virginia Blum, Susan Bordo, Joseph Gardner of the English department, and Ellen Furlough and Philip Harling of the history department—for their invaluable suggestions, questions, and advice.

Lisa Collins of the University of Kentucky for supporting my research through extensive travel funding to both London and New York.

The Reverend Leslie and Margaret Griffiths of Wesley's Chapel and Leysian Center, London, for their warm hospitality during my lengthy research trip.

Helen Walasek and Brigitte Istim of the *Punch* Archives, London, for generously allowing me unlimited access to their overwhelming cartoon library.

Sebastian Wormell of the Harrods Archives, London, for his seemingly inexhaustible knowledge of Harrods and for granting me permission to use several one-of-a-kind images.

Brian Baker, customer liaison officer of Liberty's, London, for his colorful, fascinating guided tour of the amazing department store.

Shawn Livingston and Bonnie Jean Cox of the University of Kentucky's W. T. Young Library for their assistance and willingness to purchase a microfilm of the entire run of *Fashion*, which was vital to my project.

Janet Layman, Carolyn Tassie, and the entire interlibrary loan staffs at both the University of Kentucky and Transylvania University for filling my seemingly neverending requests and hunting down innumerable hard-to-find materials.

David Stone for granting me permission to use materials from his exhaustive Gilbert and Sullivan collection.

Ivan Kreilkamp and Jennifer M. Salrin of *Victorian Studies* for guiding my revision of a portion of chapter 2 for publication, which subsequently strengthened the entire book.

David Sanders, Nancy Basmajian, Jean Cunningham, and John Morris and the editorial staff at Ohio University Press for working diligently to bring my project to print.

Dear friends and colleagues Jeff Birkenstein, Ann Ciasullo, Chris Dixon, Jessica Hollis, Valerie Johnson, Samantha Jones, Meg Marquis, and Darren Shannon for conversation, suggestions, and patience over the years.

My mentor, colleague, and friend Ellen Rosenman for her untiring guidance and generous support throughout the original project that led to this book.

An earlier version of portions of chapters 2, 3, and 4 was published as "ReFashioning Men: Fashion, Masculinity, and the Cultivation of the Male Consumer in Britain, 1860–1914" in *Victorian Studies* 46, no. 4 (Summer 2004): 597–630.

Introduction

Man's earthly interests are all hooked and buttoned together, and held up, by Clothes.

 —Thomas Carlyle, *Sartor Resartus*

Costly thy habit as thy purse can buy: for the apparel oft proclaims the man.

 —*Hamlet* (This quotation hung in the new hat and tailoring department of
 Sydney W. Knight's of London, 1910)

Why, in the choice of the pattern of a man's trousers you may see something of the
"internal quality of his soul!" It is for this reason that our novelists always insist so
strongly on the *dress* of their heroes and heroines; they feel that the mind influences
the apparel; that a lady's temper betrays itself in her bonnet, and a man's disposition
in the cut of his coat.

 —*The Glass of Fashion*

*I*N MAY 1904, THE LONDON MEN'S MONTHLY *Fashion* REPRINTED
in full a letter written to the *Irish Independent* by a frustrated tailor and closet reader
of popular fiction. "I wonder what it is that the writers of fiction pay so little attention to the costuming of their male characters," the letter began; "Of course,
nobody expects a man's clothes to be as interesting as a woman's, but they certainly deserve more space than they get in novels, particularly the novels of women."
The tailor cautiously admitted that he had lately begun to read a great deal of fiction, "not because I like it, but because I was anxious to find out how real heroes
dressed. I didn't learn much. Judging by the scant courtesy accorded the apparel
of mankind in literature, they don't do much dressing." The tailor noted that Jane
Austen, George Eliot, Dinah Mulock Craik, Mrs. Humphry Ward, Edith Whar-
ton, Frances Hodgson Burnett, and Lucas Malet "seldom, except in cases of character study, . . . go into details of dress" regarding their male protagonists and vil-
lains and most often "discreetly leave their tailoring to our imagination." "It isn't
fair to us tailors," he concluded; "Dressmakers get a good write-up on almost every
page of the popular novels, but the tailor is cut down to about six lines in the
whole book" ("Men's Fashions," 23).

At first glance, the tailor's comments appear to be the trivial complaints of a
rather eccentric reader whose appreciation of literature is amusingly dependent

on how closely it relates to his calling. Yet the tailor stumbles upon a curious over-sight in Victorian texts. While nineteenth- and early-twentieth-century commentary on women's fashion is abundant, men's sartorial habits seem hardly to have been noticed. Victorian British fiction reflects an implicit disregard for men's dress, and novelists and their male protagonists regularly insist on an ignorance of, and a conscious distancing from, any deep understanding of fashion. The costume and physical appearance of male characters of the middle and upper classes are rarely described in any detail, and many authors consistently rely on vague—albeit loaded—adjectives such as *neat, clean, simple, understated, subtle,* and *effortless* to characterize "proper" male dress. For example, in *The Way We Live Now* (1875), Anthony Trollope tells us that the young aristocratic cad Sir Felix Carbury "had been clever enough to dress himself always with simplicity and to avoid the appearance of thought about his outward man" (18). Trollope himself is reluctant to appear too knowledgeable about clothing, admitting only that Mrs. Hurtle's dress is made of "a fabric which the milliners I think call grenadine" (258–59). One might presume that Trollope would know what his own characters were wearing, yet overt self-awareness, conscious self-display, conspicuous consumption, or a manifestation of any deep knowledge of fashion by male characters (or by their creators) was immediately stigmatized and constantly repressed within Victorian literature. Thus, men's roles as consumers and as class performers through fashion and appearance seemingly exist only as an absent presence in nineteenth-century fiction.

This lack of interest—feigned or real—is curious considering England's emerging dominance over the world of men's fashion at that time. By the second half of the nineteenth century, English dressmakers—and particularly tailors—had usurped their French counterparts as the leaders in high fashion, a process that had begun with the "Anglomania" of the 1770s in France and had gained strength after Wellington's victory over Napoleon in 1815 (Chenoune, 31). "The Parisians do not lead the field in men's fashions," declared the *Pall Mall Gazette* in 1889; "All the ideas come from England for men's fashions" ("Round," 7). The conduct manual *Best Dressed Man* (1892) maintained that while Englishwomen still "slavishly follow[ed]" "*la mode Parisienne,*" Englishmen preferred homegrown styles (26–27). Certainly after the fall of the Second Empire in 1870, France had permanently lost its sartorial preeminence, as English society in ever-greater numbers opted to patronize London's tailors and dressmakers rather than make the once-customary annual trip to Paris. In 1896, the trade publication *Tailor and Cut-*

ter asserted, "At the present time the eyes of the world are fixed on the fashions of London. . . . Much beautiful work is turned out in Paris but their day as leaders of [male] fashions, is past" (quoted in Cunnington and Cunnington, 310). By the close of the century, London had defined for the Western world the masculine ideal of the "gentleman," an image that symbolized English aristocratic refinement and imperial might. The fin de siècle essayist and dandy Max Beerbohm concluded that the English costume and overall style of presentation (of simplicity and sobriety), first promoted by Regency-era dandy Beau Brummell, had reemerged to gain global acceptance (22–23).

Britain's sartorial dominance was one reflection of its overall economic prosperity during the Victorian age. The booming capitalist economy and relative peace enjoyed by Britons in the mid- to late nineteenth century paved the way for the dawn of modern consumer culture. Dramatic developments in industrial production, the importing of new goods and raw materials from Britain's vast empire, the rise of the modern metropolis, and the continued growth of the middle classes created a vigorous economy of consumption. The population of England and Wales surged during the nineteenth century, rising from 17.9 million in 1851 to 32.5 million by 1901 (Cook, 111). Much of the population was concentrated in the cities, as nearly 77 percent lived in urban areas of ten thousand or more inhabitants by the turn of the century, with over five million in London alone (Fraser, 7). Britain's populace was an increasingly affluent one as well, as real wages increased and white-collar professionals grew steadily in numbers. All this meant more people with more purchasing power who were more willing to spend rather than save as they had previously. Enterprising retailers zealously chased after these new consumers by abandoning conservative early-Victorian sales practices and adopting increasingly aggressive and sophisticated techniques of advertising, display, and promotion. Beginning in the 1860s, the small haberdashery shops gave way to large-scale urban department stores, with fixed, clearly marked prices; a greater diversity of products; and high turnover that increased sales volume. By the 1890s, British department stores—including Whiteley's, Swan and Edgar, D. H. Evans, Derry and Toms, Barker's, Harrods, and Liberty's—had developed not only in Britain's major cities but also in provincial towns to an extent not equaled in France and the United States.[1] The evolution of the department store, the development of mass-produced clothing and ready-made items, and innovations in product promotion and display all increased the sheer number of products that consumers could buy and, for the first time, made these goods available and affordable for many among the working and middle classes. With much greater ease than ever before, working-class and bourgeois consumers could affect the fashions, pursuits, and luxuries of the wealthy, and many consumers aspired to buy their way into the upper classes, as the age-old qualifications of lineage and land were eclipsed by money, conduct, and outward appearance.

The enormous changes rendered by what Peter Mathias calls the "Retailing Revolution" on the economic, cultural, and psychological lives of Britain's consumers cannot be underestimated, yet their effects on male consumption and the social construction of masculinity have yet to be examined thoroughly (Winstanley, 34). Having been effectively hidden—even pathologized—by most Victorian popular and professional literature, men's gender and class performance via men's fashion, grooming, and consumer habits have been largely overlooked or ignored by historians and cultural critics (Paoletti, 121). Overshadowed by an abundance of readily available and visually arresting primary texts documenting the popular cultural history of women's fashion and shopping, men's fashionable consumption has been further obscured by long-held, though overly reductive, historical and theoretical apparatuses that construct clothing, display, and shopping as exclusively feminine pursuits (thereby removing men completely from the act of consumption) and that dismiss men's fashion as plain, utilitarian, and static. Contemporary historians' and critics' overreliance on notions of a "separate spheres" ideology that imagines men as producers and women as consumers and of a "Great Masculine Renunciation," in which nineteenth-century middle-class Englishmen adopted sober, unadorned business-oriented dress in an attempt to gain sociopolitical legitimacy, have prevented us from discerning men's significant interest in dress and consumption during the Victorian age.

Moreover, fashion and consumption have been consistently gendered as the exclusive domains of women. Western society has long accepted the axiom that women are interested in shopping and clothes, and that men are not. The iconography of shopping—including its spaces (grand department stores, tony urban boutiques, supermarkets) and its goods (dresses, cosmetics, groceries)—as well as the act of shopping are consistently encoded as feminine. Consumption is readily linked to adornment and beautification of the body and therefore has historically been associated with the feminine and female vanity (Nixon, "Have," 151).[2] "Women are supposed to care very much about fashion, 'vanity,' looking good, and may be seen as unfeminine, man-hating, or lesbian if they don't," Susan Bordo asserts. "The reverse goes for men. The man who cares about his looks the way a woman does, self-esteem on the line, ready to be shattered at the slightest insult or weight gain, is unmanly, sexually suspect" (200). Responding to the familiar axiom "clothes make the man," fashion theorist Antony Shugaar writes, "Men aren't even supposed to know what makes the man. They are supposed to be men and deeply unaware of it. Men are supposed to be ignorant of clothing, even if they somehow dress well. The only true male elegance, then, would be an unconscious understanding of clothing, an instinctive selection of one look rather than another" (64). Men are believed to exhibit little interest in decoration or style, dressing instead for comfort and utility. If a man's costume is acknowledged to perform a further symbolic purpose, it is that it enables him to "dress for success"—that is, to enhance his professional career. Menswear—epitomized by the development and the endurance of the men's three-piece business suit—has long been regarded by fashion historians as both uniform and *a* uniform, reflecting men's desire to adopt a standardized, fixed, and practical costume that affords little room for ornamental flair or personal expression.[3] For these reasons, Victorian and turn-of-the-century fashion and shopping have conventionally been read only in terms of their effects on female consumers; recent historical and critical studies, including Lori Anne Loeb's *Consuming Angels,* Elizabeth Langland's *Nobody's Angels,* and Erika Diane Rappaport's *Shopping for Pleasure* have explored the influence of consumer culture on femininity and the ways in which commerce and consumerism were culturally gendered as feminine during the nineteenth century.[4]

What needs to be recovered is the substantial evidence that ornament, ostentation, and overt forms of sartorial flamboyance did not vanish from the male figure, nor did mid- to late-Victorian men renounce their desire for personal expression or self-display through their clothing choices. Even a cursory look at the fashion record of the nineteenth century reveals countless popular trends and ever-changing modes that contradict the idea of a near-total disavowal of men's interest in sartorial display and of a slow, virtually unchanging progression of men's attire. Indeed, at the very same time that the Great Masculine Renunciation was purportedly shifting into full gear, England experienced a "rage for fashion," and one French fashion magazine noted that "as women become more straightforward in their dress, young men are becoming more clothes-conscious" (Chenoune, 31, 35). The 1830s and '40s neckcloth, the immediate forerunner of the necktie, was worn so high and starched that wearers supposedly could not move their heads (fig. i.1). Stiff, soaring collars were so popular then, and again in the 1890s and 1900s, that stories (apocryphal or no) widely circulated of men cutting their ears

WHICH THE GREATER TORTURE—
THE 1837 STOCK OR THE 1897 COLLAR?

Figure i.1. High stocks and high collars. Cartoon by C. Harrison (*Punch*, 18 December 1897, 285)

on the corners of their shirt collars and of burning their chins in an attempt to iron the bows of their neckcloths after these were tied (Cole, 80).[5]

Contrary to the familiar images of grave-looking Victorian gentlemen dressed in a drab palette of blacks and grays, color did not disappear from the male wardrobe. The popularity of men's colored silk neckties during the 1840s reflected the decade's general air of flamboyance and vibrant hues accenting ordinary dress (Byrde, 118). The *Gazette of Fashion and Cutting-Room Companion*'s 1853 issues herald the "resumption of coloured cloths for light overcoats and morning-coats" and remark that "coloured and medley cloths have now become to a certain extent established" (June 1853, 10; August 1853, 23). Stripes, checks, and other broad and striking patterns appeared with great regularity in men's fashion plates from the 1850s onward. Bright blues and purples were also acceptable colors for menswear, particularly for celebratory occasions. The introduction of aniline dyes in 1859 had an enormous impact on men's sartorial choices, making available a vibrant spectrum of often crude and garish hues and color combinations that were particularly in vogue in the 1860s and early '70s (Adburgham, *Shops*, 179). Men's legwear also proved to be a constantly changing medium for fashionable expression. The popularity of striped and checkered pants began in the 1840s and gained force in the '50s, as a rage for Scottish culture, fueled in part by Sir Walter Scott's novels, inspired tartan trousers. That same decade saw military stripes and piping down trouser seams. Fashion plates in the May 1853 issue of *Gazette of Fashion* depict several unexpected patterns on trousers, including stripes, plaids, and alternating stripes and plaids at the waist and leg cuffs (figs. i.2 and i.3); the journal notes in July of that same year that "transversal stripes" are "one of the leading novelties of the present season" (17). Peg-top trousers—cut very full at the top and tapering sharply at the ankle—were popular in the late 1850s to mid-'60s and again in the 1890s (Walkley and Foster, 129). Moreover, many among Britain's male populace were indeed concerned with the display of the body throughout the nineteenth century. The Beau Brummell–era dandies were not the only ones who occupied themselves with cutting a physically attractive figure, for Victorian men in large numbers wore corsets and other body-shaping undergarments, widely advertised in newspapers and periodicals.

Such evidence of men indulging in fashionable display in the nineteenth century is admittedly anecdotal and in some cases represents perhaps only extremes in fashion adopted by a small minority. However, it nevertheless demonstrates that the full variety of middle-class men's engagement with fashion—as well as the fabric, style, and color options available to them—cannot be accurately characterized by the reductive image of the grim-faced Victorian patriarch clad in dark frock coat and thick boots. As in all facets of Victorian social history, it is important to make careful distinctions between the cultural ideals promoted in popular discourse and real-life practice. Fashion historian Christopher Breward notes, "Restrictive modes of social and sexual organisation should be viewed as models fit for negotiation, rather than immovable edicts" (*Hidden*, 7).

Figure i.2. Color fashion plate illustrating patterned trousers, from *Gazette of Fashion and Cutting-Room Companion* (October 1853, n.p.)

Figure i.3. Color fashion plate illustrating patterned trousers, from *Gazette of Fashion and Cutting-Room Companion* (May 1853, n.p.)

What remains to be acknowledged and examined in detail is how modern consumer capitalism sought to radically transform Victorian men's clothing and consumption as well as constructions of masculinity and male class identity. The scarcity of surviving men's garments from the period,[6] the relative lack of primary materials that openly acknowledge men's active interest in fashion,[7] and the wholesale acceptance of a popular Victorian rhetoric that privileges female consumption have led to problematic scholarship that replicates rather than analyzes Victorian ideologies regarding men's fashion and consumption. Further, the attention paid to the well-documented lifestyle of upper-class gentlemen as well as to transgressive, borderline figures of male consumption such as the dandy has tended to obscure the facts, distract our attention, and prevent us from perceiving more common, more middle-class, more mainstream social and commercial discourses on nineteenth-century men's fashion and male consumption. Consequently, the Victorian middle-class man has become what Breward refers to as the "hidden consumer." Thorough, nuanced scholarship on male fashion, grooming, and buying habits within the burgeoning culture of city shops, department stores, and fashionable spaces barely exists as yet. Despite the importance of costume in communicating gender, very little research has focused on the link between clothing styles and sex roles. Studies specifically on dress and masculinity are scarcer still, and no proper theoretical framework has been established by which to apprehend the full breadth of men's consumption in the nineteenth century (Paoletti, 124).

In *The Cut of His Coat*, I examine the costume, grooming habits, and consumer practices of Britain's middle-class urban males in the decades surrounding the turn of the twentieth century, thereby reevaluating long-overlooked changes in male sartorial and consumer habits to discern why the Victorians seem heavily invested in denying men's relationship to consumption. I contend that the public discourse on men's engagement with fashion and consumption was far greater, far more dynamic, and far more complicated than has been generally acknowledged. Men's direct relationship with shopping was not as socially stigmatized as a cursory examination of popular Victorian texts suggests, nor were men's sartorial codes nearly as static, uniform, and unchanging as fashion historians have claimed. Men in fact were invited to participate vigorously in fashion and in the public display of their masculinity, sexuality, and class status through their clothing and other purchases throughout the nineteenth century. Rapid changes in styles and cuts of jackets, trousers, shirts, neckties, shoes, and hair—seldom recognized by historians—suggest that many men were just as preoccupied with fashionable consumption as women were. Men's interest in fashionable display and their participation in consumption increased substantially in the late Victorian age, assisted by the development of the apparatuses of commodity culture, including advertising and the department store.

Rather than cultivating female markets exclusively, the public discourse of the burgeoning consumer culture industries actively sought to transform men into consumers and make the act of shopping safe and appealing to men during the second half of the nineteenth century. The emerging department stores and urban shopping centers did not take long to recognize men's consumer potential and to aggressively cultivate the once-dormant male market. I do not mean to suggest that Victorian men were merely passive dupes of the consumer industry's manipulations; rather, England's middle-class males used the new availability of products to assert class status and expand definitions of acceptable masculinity. Through the growth both in variety and in availability of goods, bourgeois male consumers reappropriated and transformed formerly "effeminate" or "deviant" male consumer practices and public display via clothing and accessories into normative masculine behavior. By the turn of the century, male self-display, conspicuous consumption, and the sexual objectification of men had indeed become more culturally accepted. And through pioneering the adoption of ready-made garments, the business lounge suit, and casual sports-inspired dress, young men of the middle classes—rather than their upper-class peers—had become innovators and leaders of fashion in Britain.

Finally, in this book I argue that the new accessibility and affordability of clothing and accessories once available only to the elite blurred class distinctions and reconfigured the markers of class belonging. As the middle classes acquired the goods that formerly distinguished elite status, the satirical figure of the dandy, formerly a caricature of upper-class male sartorial excess, gradually shifted downward in the form of the "masher" to become a negative stereotype of lower- and middle-class males' clumsy aping of aristocratic costume and pursuits. At the same time, however, many men among the middle classes abandoned social emulation to assert their own sartorial aesthetic, which reflected the modern lifestyle of the emerging bourgeoisie. By the end of the Victorian age, the socioeconomic transformations wrought by mass production and consumer culture had led to at least a partial reversal of the class- and gender-specific ideologies (namely, the "stove-pipe severity" of the middle-class male) that had begun the century and which inform most contemporary scholarship on the entire era.

A single, linear trajectory of male costume, characterized by the dominant fashions of the elite and the clumsy belated knock-offs of the middle and working classes, fails to account for the full spectrum of late-nineteenth-century male sartorial history. Multiple, even contradictory trends in menswear—influenced by class, competing masculinities, the department store—coexisted at the turn of the century. Ultimately, *The Cut of His Coat* is an examination of what new ideologies of manhood were constructed through new kinds of mass-produced clothes, through new kinds of sartorial markers, and through new kinds of consumer values. It serves to help decode the social semiotics of male dress in literature in terms of what they mean regarding the changing Victorian constructions of masculinity in the later half of the nineteenth century.

The Cut of His Coat is an attempt to recover the roles of middle-class men as active participants in the birth of modern consumer culture from 1860 to the turn of the twentieth century. Ultimately, the conclusion that women exclusively were consumers or that male consumers appeared only in "deviant" forms such as the dandy is too reductive. Because commodity culture and gender identities were and are produced together, historians must seek evidence of the involvement of men in nineteenth-century consumerism in terms of their identity as males. Without a clear recognition of the relationship between male shoppers and the emerging machinery of nineteenth-century consumer capitalism, there is a danger that the historiography of the period will replicate the familiar gender dichotomies of the Victorian era. Without an investigation of the complexities and nuances of male consumption, we risk understanding consumerism in Victorian Britain as having been solely about women and femininity. The relatively recent growth in scholarship in consumer culture as well as the emergence of men's studies afford us an opportunity to look at the socioeconomic changes brought about by the late-nineteenth-century development of mass production, ready-made clothing, and the department store from a more informed perspective.

Further, this book demonstrates that the kinds of transformations in the construction of masculinity wrought by consumer culture began at a much earlier date than has typically been assumed. Most recent critical work has identified the transformation of men's fashionable consumption by consumer culture during the interwar years. For example, Laura Ugolini has examined fashion among male Oxford students in the 1930s, noting, "The emphasis in recent fashion histories has been on the relative 'relaxation' of men's clothing after the First World War, with the abandonment of the stiff formality of the frock coat and of starched collars, in favor of the adoption—at least outside 'business hours'—of lighter materials and the more relaxed style of lounge suits, pullovers and soft collars" (429). Jill Greenfield, Sean O'Connell, and Chris Reid have explored how the advent of British men's lifestyle magazines in the 1920s and '30s, specifically *Men Only*, cultivated men's gender fantasies and anxieties to generate male consumer desire. And Kathy Peiss's fascinating work *Hope in a Jar*, while primarily about the social history of the American cosmetics industry, takes time to mention unsuccessful attempts to develop a men's cosmetics market in the 1930s (158–66). Lengthier, more in-depth studies of men's consumption have concentrated almost exclusively on the postwar years, as histories of consumerism have tended to focus on the feminization of consumer culture in the nineteenth century and recognize major male consumer trends only after World War II. Most fashion historians locate men's open embrace of fashionable consumption among the emergence of youth movements, alternative subcultures, and the swinging Carnaby Street boutiques of the '60s. Andrew Wernick's *Promotional Culture*, for example, claims that the targeting of men as consumers began in the 1960s, and Jon Stratton's *Desirable Body* (1996) acknowledges a "prehistory" of male consumption only as far back as Britain's working-class "teddy boys" of the 1950s (179). Both sociologist Frank Mort's *Cultures of Consumption* and Tim Edwards's *Men in the Mirror* are groundbreaking studies of the effects of consumer culture on modern (English) masculinity, men's consumption, and commercial representations of the male body, but their insights are confined to the 1980s and '90s.[8]

In this book I trace the Victorian origins of many of the current trends in consumer culture and masculinity and examine the early era of the masculinization of commodities and the commodification of masculinities. In doing so, I elucidate the vital connection between cultural constructions of gender and commercial goods in an effort to retrieve and reevaluate the long-overlooked changes in male sartorial and consumer habits in late-nineteenth-century Britain—to examine, in Edwards's words, "the reconstruction of masculinity through looking, through sexuality, and through consumption" during the nineteenth-century beginnings of modern consumer culture (53). I have chosen to concentrate on a roughly fifty-year period beginning in 1860 and ending with the advent of the First World War in 1914,[9] an era many historians identify as "crucial to the development of a modern consumer society" (Breward, *Hidden*, 20). While there is no precise date that we can point to as the start of modern Western consumer culture, historians argue that many of the elements of a commercial capitalism and a sophisticated consumer society—including social emulation of the wealthy by the lower and middle classes, the development of a market for fashionable rather than utilitarian goods, and a growing availability of store-bought (rather than homemade) goods—were in place by the seventeenth and eighteenth centuries.[10] However, much of the machinery vital to the ascent of a modernized, mechanized capitalist culture of consumption—the large-scale urban department store, sophisticated advertising and marketing strategies, the mass production of affordable ready-made items—was not possible until the technological and commercial advances of the machine age and did not truly take off until the second half of the nineteenth century. These included developments in building materials such as iron, steel, plate glass, and reinforced concrete (which made possible the soaring, cathedral-like show palaces of the urban department stores) as well as the introduction of mail order (first introduced in department stores in the 1870s), the telephone (1876), electric lighting (1878), elevators and escalators (1898), three-dimensional mannequins (1890s), and illustrated advertisements that in various ways made goods more visible, more accessible, and more desirable (Pasdermadjian, 25–26; Ferry, 213; Lancaster, 51). By 1860 most of Britain's most influential department stores had been established (though many would not achieve the stature of full-fledged grand stores until the 1870s, '80s, and '90s)[11] and had begun to transform urban commercial geographies and to attract the attention of male consumers. The First World War serves as an obvious conclusion for this study not only because it arguably marks the "true" beginning of the twentieth century but also, and more importantly, because the decades immediately following the war have already been well documented by historians who incorrectly identify the interwar years as the first significant emergence of men's fashionable consumption, owing to the emergence of men's fashion magazines, men's stores, and the explosive popularity of the cinema.

The focus of this study is limited primarily to the examination of late-Victorian men's consumption of clothing and grooming items. To be sure, other forms of consumption enjoyed by men (particularly those related to leisure, such as theatergoing, sporting events, and activities centered on alcohol and tobacco) also increased between 1860 and 1914,[12] but because of limits of space and time, I have elected to confine this discussion to the consumption of commodifiable goods, such as clothing, regularly and familiarly purchased in shops and stores. Dress is the most publicly visible, most portable, and arguably most personal manifestation of one's relationship with consumer culture; clothing is the good with which we are most physically intimate and which is most directly related to our self-expression. Carlyle believed that clothes were "unspeakably significant" because they were "emblematic" of our true selves (51). Likewise, I regard fashion neither as a superficial and frivolous concern nor as high art and haute couture, but rather as a sociocultural phenomenon that reflects the values of a specific time and place. "Clothes are social phenomena," declares Anne Hollander in *Sex and Suits* (1994); "Changes in dress *are* social changes" (4). Examining seemingly superficial alterations in men's appearance and purchasing habits allows us to identify much larger and significant transformations in social constructions of Victorian masculinity wrought by the development of a massive and sophisticated consumer culture machine—a force so powerful that it succeeded in luring men to take up formerly "effeminate" and "deviant" dress and consumer behaviors and to reassert them as appropriate and even attractive masculinity. Ultimately, zealous adherence to a long-held ideology regarding normative masculine behavior and dress was overturned by the even greater forces of capitalism. Thus, the serious study of men's relation to fashion and clothing must be undertaken as a "microcosm of the macrocosm of men, masculinity and society" (Edwards, 3–4).

Further, because goods have cultural meaning, fashion—both as clothing and as a commodity—can be regarded as one of the fundamental signifiers in a complicated gender and cultural sign system.[13] Mary Douglas and Baron C. Isherwood argue that goods "are the visible part of culture"; they are "a means of making visible and stable the basic categories by which we classify people in society" (66). Goods serve as conveyors of social identity, and clothing acts as a symbolic visual code by which individuals communicate to others their membership in a particular social group. Therefore, fashion is the most integral component of both class and gender performance. If, as Judith Butler asserts, "gender is always a doing," then it is done most visibly through our dress (25). What we have only begun to acknowledge is that masculinity is as much a performance, a spectacle, a deliberate self-fashioning as femininity is, and even normative masculinity requires the maintenance of a constant, uninterrupted performance to a real or imagined audience (Adams, 11).

The Cut of His Coat actively embraces a multidisciplinary historical-cultural studies reading of Victorian nonfiction popular and professional texts in tandem with canonical literary works. That men's fashionable consumption was not widely discussed, was even hidden, is both the major premise and the major challenge of this work. Because *The Cut of His Coat* is looking at an "absent presence," substantial primary evidence from the nineteenth century is often difficult to find. Obviously, market research and demographic studies were unheard of in the Victorian age. Statistical information regarding the number of male customers who patronized department stores, what they bought, and how frequently they bought it would be invaluable to any thorough reconstruction of men's purchasing habits during the Victorian era, but such data either no longer exist or, in most cases, were simply never recorded in the first place.[14] As a literary scholar, I naturally turn first to the novels of the period. The nineteenth century, declares John Harvey, was "the great century of the novel—of the novel as the record of social life. The novel recorded unceasingly manners and appearances, and endlessly 'read' the meaning of manners" (133). Fictional representations can reflect the social realities of a particular time; in *The Cut of His Coat*, therefore, I examine depictions of men's consumer and sartorial habits in traditional literary texts by George Eliot, Anthony Trollope, George Grossmith, Thomas Hughes, Wilkie Collins, Arnold Bennett, and H. G. Wells. However, this investigation centers in large part on nineteenth-century discussions, descriptions, and prescriptions of men's consumption, fashion, grooming habits, and public appearance found in popular conduct literature, journals of the tailoring trade, advertising, cartoons, and fashion plates of the period 1860–1914. These visual and textual materials—what Breward calls the "ephemera, the visual and aural 'urban noise'" of the age—provide invaluable insight into the influences that affected the sartorial and consumer choices of the late-nineteenth-century middle-class Englishman (*Hidden*, 154).

While the main emphasis of this book is social constructions of gender, such constructions blur in inseparable ways with issues of class. Leonore Davidoff and Catherine Hall argue that "gender and class always operate together" (13). The construction of sexual difference always affects class formation. Since *The Cut of His Coat* looks at men's costume and consumption as markers of both class and gender performance, I follow contemporary gender theorist Judith Butler's work on the performativity of gender, as well as the approach of social historians Davidoff and Hall (and others), who assert that gender identity is central to the formation of class consciousness and that sexual difference always influences class belonging. I do this in part to challenge the popular notion that as the social function of dress shifted from distinguishing the classes in the eighteenth century to distinguishing the sexes in the nineteenth (a change discussed in chapter 1), men rapidly distanced themselves from the fashionable display now exclusively associated with females and retreated into social and sartorial conservatism

(Steele, 53). For years scholars have been at work dismantling the long-held myth of a buttoned-up and sexually repressed Victorian age, and certainly this myth has been served by the image of the conservatively dressed middle-class Victorian man. This study offers a revised portrait of a middle-class manhood that was not nearly so conservative, reserved, obsessed with rules, and preoccupied with appearing upper class as it has been painted previously. The shift to a gender-based sartorial matrix meant that men's costume became increasingly important in defining and reflecting their masculine identity. Recent scholarship has eschewed outmoded approaches that regard men as the *un*marked sex, acknowledging men as gendered subjects. Careful men's histories closely examine the social construction of masculinity and the socioeconomic forces that keep idealized notions of manhood in constant flux. Dress serves, in Jo Barraclough Paoletti's words, as "an artificial secondary sex characteristic," revealing how a given culture or time imagines femininity and masculinity (123–24).

I therefore align this project with recent theorists who have offered more nuanced and complex takes on masculinity. In the past ten to fifteen years, a number of historians and critics have begun challenging reductive Victorian class and gender notions such as "separate spheres" ideology as accurate descriptions of behavior, presenting these notions instead as ideological wishful thinking.[15] However, much of the geography of masculine experience once obscured by these outmoded approaches still remains unexplored. Social geographer Peter Jackson notes, "The experience of men *as men* has scarcely yet been addressed" (209). Christopher Breward's work in particular has reevaluated old readings of the Great Masculine Renunciation and introduced closer historical examinations of working- and middle-class men's engagement with consumer culture in the nineteenth century. My scholarship is also informed by modern gender theorists including John Tosh, Anthony Rotundo, Michael Kimmel, and Susan Bordo, whose work has offered more balanced reevaluations of formerly reductive, monolithic understandings of masculinity, patriarchy, and separate sexual spheres ideology. These critical approaches stress the recognition of multiple masculinities and push for "a different set of languages to speak about masculinity—languages which grasp masculinity as process rather than as static and unchanging" (Mort, "Boy's," 196).

Rather than overturning everything historians and critics have contended before, *The Cut of His Coat* is intended to redraw the markers of middle-classness and masculinity for mainstream male bourgeoisie in the late Victorian era. Social historians and cultural critics must attend closely to exactly how women and men are characterized by given commentators at given times, and to what purpose. The book serves as an examination of the sartorial codes outlined by popular literature, conduct books, and fashion periodicals and the ideological function they perform. Determining what men "really" wore during this period is perhaps an impossible task. Instead, the primary goal is to uncover and explore what was invested in the various and often competing discursive codes regarding male clothing and consumption. This study is thus a sketch of what kinds of dress, consumption, and class performance were privileged as "proper" and what were pathologized as "deviant." It aims to complicate, problematize, and thereby enhance our understanding of Victorian masculinity through a closer examination of the complex and sometimes contradictory trends in men's fashion at turn of the century. Although the department store's ready-made items enabled many middle-class men to ape the affectations and clothing of the rich (to a certain extent), many rejected aristocratic tastes to create their own class "uniform." It is true that the dark business suit (with jacket, trousers, and vest all made of the same fabric) was universally adopted, but at the same time, men's fashion options and accessories became more elaborate and expressive. While Englishmen may have had more "freedom" of self-display, this freedom faced new forms of containment.

The Cut of His Coat is divided into five chapters that explore the middle-class male's relationship to dress and consumption in late-Victorian and early-twentieth-century Britain. Chapter 1 reviews how and why men's consumption and sartorial habits were "hidden" in Victorian culture. Men's interest in fashion and consumption did not decline during the Victorian age, despite popular notions of a "Great Masculine Renunciation" that presumed a nonexistent male consumer and a "separate spheres" ideology that assigned women the task of shopping and served to obscure men's consumption and fashion. Men continued to purchase goods and care about their appearance, but their relationship with fashion was often complicated by increasingly byzantine social and sartorial rules, and they often enacted their own consumer desires through female or servant surrogates. Chapter 2 reveals how the new apparatuses of the emerging commodity culture courted male buyers and whetted their interest in fashionable consumption. Through an examination of advertising and department store architecture, this study shows how male shopping grew more socially acceptable and the male body became a decorated and eroticized medium of the public display of masculinity. Chapter 3 examines *Fashion*, a London monthly that appeared between 1898 and 1905, which I believe to be the first fashion journal for a general male audience, antedating other men's fashion and lifestyle magazines by at least twenty years. Through a close analysis of the magazine's layout, features, and rhetoric, this chapter explores how *Fashion* legitimated men's interest in costume and self-display, not by aggressively asserting that such behaviors were masculine, but rather by insisting that men had as much right and responsibility as women to care for their appearance. Chapter 4 turns to issues of class to examine how the negative characteristics of the Regency-era "dandy"—his love of clothing and narcissistic self-display—were ultimately absorbed through the expanding consumer practices of normative mainstream middle-class males. At the same time, the "masher" emerged as a satirical figure of working- and middle-class masculinity, a flashily dressed poseur who unsuccessfully emulated the fashions and lifestyle of upper-class gentlemen. The final chapter continues to focus on intersections of late-Victorian class and gender identities to reveal that many of the new fashions adopted by the middle-class male were not rooted in social emulation of the elite at all. While the upper classes developed increasingly complex fashion rules and occasion-specific clothing to distinguish themselves from the rising bourgeoisie, the middle classes sought not (solely) to emulate the elite, but rather to develop (also) their own class-distinctive style and uniform through the business suit, which emerged as *the* popular image of the British male.

The Cut of His Coat deals exclusively with British masculinity and fashionable consumption between 1860 and 1914. However, the book's discoveries provide a striking parallel to the dramatic rise in the sexualization and commercialization of masculinity and men's bodies that began in the final decades of the twentieth century on both sides of the Atlantic and has only recently been recognized by scholars. Since World War II, unprecedented economic prosperity and relative peace in the West, alongside a gradual relaxation of the sexual division of labor, have enabled men's active engagement with commodities to grow rapidly (Bocock, 96). Mort argues that beginning slowly in the 1950s, men's interest in individual expression and narcissistic self-display through body posture, hairstyle, clothing, and other consumer goods has increased. By the 1980s, advertisers and marketers had begun to respond to this change, promoting a sexualization of the male body through men's fashion lines, boutiques, and print and television ads. The modern young man has come to exist in a highly visual culture of glances, poses, and immediate impressions—a culture celebrated by the flood of successful men's lifestyle magazines that emerged in the 1990s. And the aggressively macho lifestyle idealized by these publications—one of "sex, sports, beer, gadgets, and fitness," to quote the advertising slogan of one such magazine—is underwritten to a great extent by the expanding market of high-fashion menswear and men's grooming products, including aftershaves and colognes, hair gels and hair coloring, body lotions and foundation creams (Sharkey, 177).

Admittedly, the scale of male consumption between 1860 and 1914 cannot compare to the massive consumer machinery that has emerged since World War II. Moreover, the number of men affected by and participating in the changes I am discussing—that is, single, middle-class males between the ages of fifteen and thirty-four residing in London (roughly fifty thousand in 1901)[16]—represents a decidedly small minority of the 32.5 million living in England and Wales at that time (Cook, 111). This book deals with the small beginnings of consumer behaviors and sexual display, which did not explode into full bloom until much later. What I describe is the production of an environment and a shift in cultural attitudes that would make male fashionable consumption more attractive, normative, socially acceptable. There is little that is genuinely new about the current recognition and marketing of masculine narcissism—epitomized by the media celebrity of the "metrosexual"—at the turn of the twenty-first century. To be sure, the tools of today's manufacture, advertising, and display are far more sophisticated, efficient, and effective, but they were already in place by the concluding decades of the nineteenth century. Writing of male Londoners in the 1980s and '90s, Mort declares, "Young men are being sold images which rupture traditional icons of masculinity. They are stimulated to look at themselves—and other men—as objects of consumer desire. They are getting pleasures previously branded taboo and feminine. A new bricollage of masculinity is the noise coming from the fashion house, the marketplace and the street," but the same could be said about male Londoners in the 1880s and '90s as well ("Boy's," 194).

In our own time, when social theorists and cultural critics increasingly turn their focus on the potential dangers and consequences of our highly commercial, media-saturated, image-conscious, beauty-obsessed mall culture, it is especially useful to look back at the origins of consumer culture and the ways it shaped the social, sexual, and class identities of the Victorians. The dramatic shifts of Victorian constructions of masculinity wrought by the emergence of commodity culture that this study traces are not dissimilar to the trends that Frank Mort, Sean Nixon, and Tim Edwards identify as taking place in the London of the 1980s and '90s. Further, the recent "discovery" and commodification of the male body within popular culture (as explored by Susan Bordo and again Nixon) and the sudden proliferation of men's plastic surgery, "body-sculpting" underwear, hair products, cosmetics, and men's vitamins points to heightened recognition of men as consumers and objects of consumption by the fashion and beauty industries and the rapid acceleration of gender, social, and economic phenomena begun over a century earlier. The changes begun in the late nineteenth century in men's sartorial display, in consumer habits, and in men's construction of their identity as males attributable to the emergence of mass production and consumer culture served to shape the socioeconomic phenomena that drove twentieth-century— and continue to drive twenty-first-century—understandings of class, gender, and consumption. They therefore invite, even demand, a careful second look.

"IT CANNOT BE SUPPOSED THAT MEN
MAKE NO STUDY OF DRESS"

The "Disappearance" of Men's Fashion and Consumption in Victorian Britain

> Of course it will be thought that there cannot be much to say about men's toilets, since they are supposed never to think about dress, nor talk about it, and rarely to change their fashion.
>
> —Lady Gertrude Elizabeth Campbell, *Etiquette of Good Society*

> The man who consciously pays no heed to fashion accepts its form just as much as the dude does, only he embodies it in another category, the former in that of exaggeration, the latter in that of negation. Indeed, it occasionally happens that it becomes fashionable in whole bodies of a large class to depart altogether from the standards set by fashion.
>
> —Georg Simmel, "Fashion"

> The human race, to my mind, is seen to dire disadvantage when admiring itself. Man is admirable only when unconscious. Exhibited in top-hatted and frock-coated droves, he suggests to the student of biology the dismal lowness of his origin. A few are aware of this and avoid the cake-walk; but those who have persuaded themselves that they are the best-dressed in London, enjoy themselves and their clothes at least as much as the prettiest girls in the most original gowns.
> "Do you like fancy waistcoats?" my observant aunt inquired.
> "Not at all," said I.
> "I'm not so sure," she replied.
>
> —Percy White, *The West End*

*I*N AUGUST 1898, THE MEN'S MONTHLY *Fashion* PRINTED AN editorial by an anonymous female contributor pondering over the mysterious silence cast over the topic of fashion among men. "It cannot be supposed that men make no study of dress," it began; "London society makes it quite apparent that they do study it pretty exhaustively. A man cannot be well dressed simply by going to a good tailor. He must abet the efforts of the tailor himself by exercising a careful choice of all the adjuncts of his costume. And yet men do not talk about dress— at least, in public. No woman overhears men in omnibuses and railway carriages discussing their ideas for a frock coat or their preferences in spats; whereas the public conveyances ring with women's talk on a cognate theme" ("Queen," 7).[1]

This anonymous writer is not mistaken in her belief that men of the Victorian age did indeed study their clothing and appearance "pretty exhaustively." But like the men she describes, the existing Victorian record is remarkably mute on the issue of men's engagement with fashion, particularly when compared to the extensive writings that resound with breathless descriptions of women's costume. The popular social norms of the era promoted a middle-class masculinity defined in direct contrast to the flamboyant sartorial display and profligate consumer habits of the frivolous aristocracy, women, and dandies. The Victorian notion of a "Great Masculine Renunciation," in which middle-class males abandoned ornamentation and sartorial display for a sober, plain costume, idealized a practical, business-minded manhood immune to vanity and unconcerned with outward appearance. Further, the notion of "separate spheres"—which constructed men as producers and assigned women exclusively the task of shopping and household management—presumed that men were uninterested in clothing and fashionable consumption. Operating in tandem, these two social ideas sought to define a middle-class masculinity through the institution of stronger sanctions and taboos on male fashionable display and consumer desire. The ideals of the Great Masculine Renunciation and separate spheres were so ubiquitous in Victorian Britain, promoted endlessly by social commentators and the authors of conduct literature, that men's real relationship with fashion and consumption has been rendered nearly invisible.

While the Great Masculine Renunciation and separate spheres are social constructs now widely subject to debate, they nevertheless continue to obscure men's fashionable consumption from contemporary historians who have all but ignored it, turning their attention instead to the much more well-documented and visually striking fashion and consumer practices of Victorian women. The seemingly monolithic nature of the renunciation has proven problematic for contemporary historians attempting to recover the social and consumer habits of the era and has hindered a nuanced, rigorous examination of nineteenth-century middle-class male engagement with clothing and shopping. Yet the ideals that Victorian advice literature and the popular press profess are not necessarily accurate reflections of the attitudes and behaviors of most middle-class Englishmen. Middle-class males' participation in fashion and consumption did not disappear during the nineteenth century. Men continued to attend to their clothing and fuss over their appearance; they continued to purchase many goods and to desire others. And the existing evidence suggests that many did so with great eagerness.

The Great Masculine Renunciation

Most conventional histories posit that between 1800 and World War II, men's consumption was suppressed and their sartorial display muted because of dramatic changes in societal concepts of both class and gender formation. In 1930, the psychologist J. C. Flugel popularized the theory of the "Great Masculine Renunciation," a radical shift to sober male attire during the late eighteenth and early nineteenth centuries, which he saw as having arisen from the sociopolitical upheavals of the French Revolution. The magnificent figure of the ancien régime aristocrat—decked out in lacy cuffs and collar, powdered wig and rouged face, delicate stockings and slippers—became distasteful to the new male revolutionaries and their democratic ideals (Flugel, 111–12). The revolution's emphasis on the brotherhood of man promoted a uniformity of dress, intended to abolish those distinctions that separated wealthy from poor and to advance a simplification of dress that suggested democratic, plebeian values. As the revolution made labor respectable, work (or business) clothes became the new uniform of the new democratic man (112).

More contemporary readings of the social and sartorial history of the age by David Kuchta, Valerie Steele, and Leonore Davidoff and Catherine Hall have generally adhered to Flugel's description of the Great Masculine Renunciation. Kuchta, however, contends that the renunciation had much earlier English roots, originating as a struggle for political superiority between aristocratic and middle-class men who linked both the new image of a more modest and sober masculinity and the repudiation of conspicuous luxury to their political legitimacy beginning in 1688 and continuing into the early nineteenth century (62, 71). To critics and supporters of the aristocracy alike, the issue of consumption was central to the idea of political legitimacy, and thus the notion of what Kuchta calls "inconspicuous consumption" became central to the Great Masculine Renunciation, as aristocratic and middle-class men attempted to outdo each other's attempts at displaying frugality, economic virtue, and a "well-regulated spirit of manliness and humility" (71). Steele asserts that extravagant and modish male attire in England came to be associated with "tyranny, political and moral corruption, and a 'degenerate exotic effeminacy'" of the aristocracy, while plainer and soberer dress became increasingly associated with bourgeois notions of "liberty, patriotism, virtue, enterprise, and manliness" (52–53). The French Revolution only helped solidify these connotations, and the new sartorial ideals in the form of the plain frock coat—the direct ancestor of the modern man's business suit—quickly proliferated through English, French, and American society (52–53). Though the ideology of "modest masculinity" may have first been employed by early-eighteenth-century aristocrats in an effort to justify their claims to speak on behalf of the nation, middle-class reformers had by the early nineteenth century turned this ideology against the elite by appropriating it for themselves and, simply put, by playing the part better (Kuchta, 70–71). Around the turn of the nineteenth century, this "democratization of clothing" manifested itself through the radical adoption of simpler, darker, more conservative male dress (Steele, 52; Kuchta, 55). Davidoff and Hall explain that within a time span of only thirty years, ornamental and effeminate hose, form-fitting breeches, powdered wigs, ruffles, lace, silk, and jewelry were replaced by drab colors, stiff collars, and loose-fitting trousers (410–12). Gradually, all male adornments and accessories were abandoned, save for the middle-class businessman's ever-present pocket watch (412). Foster remarks that men's clothing grew "increasingly standardized" during the nineteenth century, and by midcentury, men of the upper, middle, and even urban working classes had all begun to dress in the same uniform: a plain and somber coat and waistcoat, trousers, shirt, underclothes, and some kind of hat or cap (Foster, 12; Steele, 53).

The Great Masculine Renunciation is widely understood to be a reflection of the triumph and dominance of conservative middle-class ideals during the Victorian age. A life based around labor and commerce rather than idle luxury called for a utilitarian uniform that reflected hard work, sobriety, and business-mindedness. "The gentleman becomes an essentially reforming concept, a middle-class call to seriousness which challenged the frivolity of fashionable life," observes Robin Gilmour. "Gentlemanliness is on the side of decency, the values of family life, social responsibility, the true respectability of innate worth as opposed to the sham respectability of fashionable clothes" (11). Middle-class reformers and moralists successfully waged war against the powdered extravagances of the Georgian aristocrats and the starched fastidiousness of the Beau Brummell dandies of the 1810s and '20s. By midcentury, asserts James Laver, "the whole world of men, aristocrats as well as merchant bankers, had settled down to a drab uniformity of attire in which every manifestation of personal eccentricity was condemned as bad form" (*Dandies*, 80). It was this plain uniform symbolizing the middle-class man's "devotion to the principles of duty, of renunciation, and of self-control" that emerged as the dominant idealized form of middle-class dress in the nineteenth century and that has endured more or less intact well through the twentieth and into the twenty-first century (Flugel, 113).

Significantly, the Great Masculine Renunciation also purportedly marks a major shift from a sartorial system based on distinctions of class to one based primarily on distinctions of gender. Previously, differences in sartorial display served to distinguish one class from another, as the brightly colored silks, lace trimmings, powdered wigs, and delicate slippers of the eighteenth century were common to both men and women of the upper classes. In their efforts to secure political participation and legitimacy, however, middle-class men disavowed luxury, vanity, and flamboyant self-display and reassigned them to the aristocracy and women. By midcentury, bright colors had been relegated mainly to women's dress, while "most men wore some version of the plain, dark, uniform three-piece suit," with all pieces fashioned from the same material and color (Steele, 52). For men, color, decoration, and fittedness remained only in military and evening wear (57). The straight lines, practical fabrics, dark tones, and loose fit of men's dress—juxtaposed against the flowing lines, rich materials, fine detail, and constricting forms of women's dress—had become a powerful sign system of gender segregation.

Many scholars therefore also popularly regard the Great Masculine Renunciation as a renunciation of men's physicality—of a male sexual, visual self—in favor of what Anne Hollander and Davidoff and Hall identify as a "utilitarian male body" devoted to work rather than pleasure. Flugel famously asserts that beginning in the early decades of the nineteenth century, "man abandoned his claim to be considered beautiful. He henceforth aimed at being only useful" (11). The baggy fit, boxy shape, and tubelike jacket sleeves and trouser legs of the ordinary man's suit "tended to conceal any possible physical attractions or evidence of physical strength, other than sheer size and bulk" (Steele, 59). The baggy three-piece suit standardized men's bodies in that it hid both muscles and paunches and obliterated the visible expression of the powerful, aggressive male body. This drabness and uniformity of men's clothing eventually grew so normalized, according to Laver, as to suggest that "there was something morally reprehensible in a man who paid too much attention to his own clothes" (*Dandies*, 80). Thus, through the prescription of a sober, business-oriented male costume, the popular sartorial codes of the age defined legitimate bourgeois masculinity. The nineteenth-century middle-class male uniform both conveyed sobriety, pragmatism, frugality, and conservatism and consciously distinguished itself from that of the frivolous and idle aristocracy, coquettish and materialistic womanhood, and the vain and effeminate dandy whose preoccupation with his outer appearance represented both class and gender transgressions.

This chapter is not intended to suggest that the premise of the Great Masculine Renunciation is a purely twentieth-century construct. Unquestionably, between 1750 and 1850 men's dress did indeed radically and permanently change, as powdered wigs, lace, knee breeches, and stockings gave way to dark frock coats, corduroy trousers, and thick boots. And, indeed, many late-Victorian sources acknowledged a major shift in male clothing arriving in the early decades of the nineteenth century.[2] The renunciation could never have brought about a complete disappearance of men's fashion; after all, even antifashion—even nudity—is a fashion statement. Yet the dominance of the Great Masculine Renunciation in popular Victorian literature has effected a seeming disappearance of men's very significant interest and participation in fashion from the historical record. However, the renunciation was merely an ideology, which, though extremely popular, did not necessarily reflect the actual sartorial behaviors of all or even most Englishmen. I argue that many middle-class men negotiated around the Great Masculine Renunciation, actively—even aggressively—pursuing fashion. What I wish to examine now is how the popular public discourse of Victorian prose and advice literature advanced a general repudiation of men's interest and participation in fashion and how the renunciation's ambiguities and paradoxes simultaneously complicated masculine ideals and made available certain avenues of male fashionable display.

Fine Lines: The Performativity of Male Sartorial Renunciation

The ideals of the renunciation were promoted endlessly throughout the era by social commentators both in the popular press and in conduct books. Widely successful in the seventeenth and eighteenth centuries, the advice literature genre disappeared in the early decades of the nineteenth century,[3] only to find during the Victorian age a renewed popularity that lasted well into the twentieth century. Its significant role in promulgating and maintaining dominant social constructs of femininity has been well documented,[4] yet conduct manuals, often tiny and slim enough not to ruin the smooth line of a coat and to be consulted on the sly during potential social dilemmas, were also instrumental in promoting the bourgeois ideals of gentlemanly reserve that drove the ethos of the Great Masculine Renunciation. What most distinctly defined a true gentleman in Victorian eyes was his behavior, and the era's conduct book authors consistently stressed a male deportment based on a combination of reserved understatement and relaxed effortlessness. Advice commentators increasingly emphasized the proper gentleman's complete absence of self-consciousness. Apparently oblivious to the paradox their advice created, they regularly urged their readers to make a conscious, concerted, premeditated effort to be natural, artless, and unaffected. The author of *The Art of Conversing* (1897), for example, strongly emphasized naturalness and a total lack of self-consciousness in conversation—despite the fact that the book is primarily composed of conversation models and recommended responses for all occasions and settings.

How anxious male readers between 1860 and 1914 grappled with such confounding tenets is unclear, as with modern hindsight the dilemma seems at best vexing and at worst preposterously illogical. This paradox naturally crossed over into advice regarding dress as well. The connection between proper masculine behavior and proper masculine dress was an obvious one for etiquette authors, as a man's dress was a visible, outward reflection of his inner qualities. One's manly reserve extended to all elements of dress, and the ideals of self-control and sobriety, so vital to Victorian middle-class notions of sociopolitical power, manifested themselves in the popular promotion of a discreet "natural" elegance that became the very ethic of nineteenth-century costume. The contradictions, fine lines, and double binds inherent in conduct literature's ambiguous instruction regarding men's dress forced the middle-class man to walk an ever-narrowing gauntlet of supposed sartorial threats to both his gender and his class status.

Conduct literature of the period 1860–1914 recited that the sartorial understatement characteristic of the proper gentleman was best achieved through the dark fabrics and muted colors familiarly associated with the Great Masculine Renunciation. Advice writers repeatedly instructed middle-class male readers to select sober shades described as "quiet" and therefore not liable to draw the improper attention eagerly sought by the upper-class dandy and the working-class masher. *The Glass of Fashion*, a conduct manual of 1881, advises, "Do not indulge in violent colours; let your walking-dress be a 'quiet' tweed uniform shade, with a tie of neutral tint and a black hat" (176), while Mrs. Burton Kingsland's *Etiquette for All Occasions* (1901) claims, "The best dressed men are only conspicuous because of the extreme quietness of their attire" (343).[5] Another conduct book allows that colored shirts could be worn only in the morning, though "they should be small in pattern and quiet in colour. Fancy cloths of conspicuous patterns are exceedingly objectionable" (*Mixing*, 129). Historian John Harvey notes that muted, dark, and especially black dress provided "good cover" for the upwardly mobile middle-class man who hoped to rise, in part unobserved, into the elite classes (147). This notion of an understated, discreet, inconspicuous male uniform became the ideal of gentlemanly dress for the countless advice authors and journalists writing in the nineteenth century. Adam Blenkinsop's 1850 conduct manual, *A Shilling's-Worth of Advice on Manners, Behaviour and Dress,* instructs that "a gentleman is always freely and easily dressed" (13). The sentiment is echoed fifty years later in Mrs. Kingsland's *Etiquette:* "A true gentleman is simple, unpretending, natural" (337). *The London Tailor* chimes in by declaring, "Let it not be said of a man, 'What a well-dressed person he is,' but 'How gentlemanly he dresses'" ("Hints on Dress," 28).[6] And *The Glass of Fashion* goes even further, asserting that it is best "to dress so as to call forth no remark at all. . . . Men and women endeavour to attract notice by their dress only when they are aware there is nothing attractive in themselves" (172–73).

Simply put, men were to wear clothes that made the wearing of clothes "invisible." Readers of conduct books were instructed that the gentleman distinguished himself by, above all, being inconspicuous, offending no one by anything extreme in the order of his appearance. One of the general maxims of the celebrated Regency dandy Beau Brummell was that to attract attention by his outward appearance was "the severest mortification which a gentleman could incur" (Moers, 34).[7] Brummell was famously reported to have declared, "If John Bull turns to look after you, you are not well dressed," and this tenet was repeated over and over again in conduct manuals throughout the remainder of the century (quoted in McDowell, 60). The popular etiquette manual *Routledge's Etiquette for Gentlemen,* first published in 1864 and reprinted in multiple forms and under various titles and authors for over forty years, declares:

> A gentleman should always be so well dressed that his dress shall never
> be observed at all. Does this sound like an enigma? It is not meant for
> one. It only implies that perfect simplicity is perfect elegance, and that
> the true test of dress in the toilet of a gentleman is its entire harmony,
> unobtrusiveness and becomingness. If any friend should say to you,

"What a handsome waistcoat you have on!" you may depend that a less handsome waistcoat would be in better taste. If you hear it said that Mr. So-and-So wears superb jewellery, you may conclude beforehand that he wears too much. Display, in short, is ever to be avoided, especially in matters of dress.[8] (39–40)

The key to this sartorial invisibility, according to conduct manuals, was never to appear too fashionable, too fitted, too well dressed. Advice writers consistently warned against overdressing, far more zealously than underdressing. The *Habits of Good Society* asserts that the gentleman must avoid "all extravagance, all splendour, and all profusion" (140). Chasing the recherché or striving to remain ever on the cutting edge of fashion was not the proper business of reserved masculinity. Samuel Beeton, author of *Beeton's Manners of Polite Society* (1879), instructs that "a well-dressed man will never be the first to set a new fashion, he will allow others to hazard the innovation, and decline the questionable honour of being the first to advertise a novelty" (28). A true gentleman was to wear his clothing somewhat loosely and to avoid the overstarched neckcloth, stuffed shirt, and skin-tight trousers that belied the overreaching counterfeit. *The Hand-Book of Etiquette* (1860) urges readers to "be particular to have your things made to fit well, but not to fit tightly. In fact, the loose, easy fit, is in accordance with the good taste of the fashions of the present day" (16).[9] This advice against overdone fastidiousness was apparently standard throughout even the highest classes of respectable society, as is evident in a list of rules of conduct and dress that Prince Albert wrote to his son Albert Edward (later Edward VII) in the 1850s:

> The appearance, deportment and dress of a gentleman consists perhaps more in the absence of certain offences against good taste, and in careful avoidance of vulgarities and exaggerations of any kind, however generally they may be the fashion of the day, than in the adherence to any rules which can be exactly laid down. . . . In dress, with scrumptious attention to neatness and good taste, he will never give in to the unfortunately loose and slang style which predominates at the present day. He will borrow nothing from the fashions of the groom or the gamekeeper, and whilst avoiding the frivolity and foolish vanity of Dandyism, will take care that his clothes are of the best quality, well-made and suitable to his rank and position. (Quoted in Duke of Windsor, 13–14)

What Prince Albert and the conduct manual authors make clear is that a gentleman is discerned not so much by what he wears as by what he does not wear. Popular advice literature consciously defined the male sartorial ideal as a renunciation of the fashionable dress favored by individuals who were regarded as exhibiting the values counter to normative masculinity. Women served as the most obvious diametric touchstone from which to gauge proper manliness, and conventional middle-class wisdom held that the luxurious pleasures of dress and the toilette were "the domain of the fair sex" (*Routledge's Etiquette*, 39–40). *Routledge's Etiquette for Gentlemen*, for example, advises, "Let a wise man leave its graces and luxuries to his wife, daughters, or sisters, and seek to be himself appreciated for something of higher worth than the embroidery upon his shirt front, or the trinkets on his chain" (39–40).[10] Social commentators also regularly warned against the transgressive dress of effeminate dandies and flashy youth. Like women, dandies and college-age boys were popularly believed to be preoccupied with outward appearance, eagerly adopting the latest and the loudest that fashion had to offer. And all three groups were often implicitly equated by conduct books and popular fiction as representing an undesirable vain effeminacy that stood in direct opposition to the prescribed ideals of masculine reserve. *Etiquette for Gentlemen* (1864) declares that only young men and fops—"those who have no other claim to distinction"—sought attention and status through extreme dress: "A servile submission to the capricious goddess betrays a weak intellect and paucity of ideas" (17).[11] Similarly, *Routledge's Etiquette for Gentlemen* exhorts, "To be fitted *too* well is to look like a tailor's assistant. This is the great fault which we have to find in the style of even the best bred Frenchmen. They look as if they had just stepped out of a fashion-book, and lack the careless ease which makes an English gentleman look as if his clothes belonged to him, and not he to his clothes" (40).

Cautioning the male reader that such dress would cause him to resemble a dandy—or worse yet, a Frenchman (!)—might seem sufficient threat to warn him against such sartorial predilections. But many conduct books, such as the *Habits of Good Society*, went even further, pathologizing fashion, particularly for men, as a seductive and ruinous evil. "Dress and sin came in together, and have kept good fellowship ever since," *Habits* declares; "The love of dress, take it as you will, can only arise from one of two closely allied sins, vanity and pride" (129, 130). The love of fashion was portrayed as the path to decadence and degradation, as it led to a perverse preoccupation with one's own beauty and outward, physical self: "The best dressers of every age have always been the worst men and women. . . .

No life can be more contemptible than one of which the Helicon is a tailor's shop, and its paradise the Park; no man more truly wretched than he whose mind is only a mirror of his body, and whose soul can fly no higher than a hat or a neck-tie; who strangles ambition with a yard-measure, and suffocates glory in a boot. But this puny peacockism always brings its own punishment. The fop ruins himself by his vanity, and ends a sloven" (130).

A preoccupation with fashion threatened to distract men from their duty, emasculate them, and render them consumers rather than producers. Near the turn of the century, English society grew increasingly sensitive to the necessary distance between proper masculinity and the deviant fopperies of devout fashion worship. The popular emphasis on athleticism, physical and nutritional health, and "rugged masculinity" in both Britain and the United States (having evolved in part out of the "Muscular Christianity" movement begun in England in the 1850s) was intended as an antidote to the dangerous overrefinement and over-civilizing effects of feminine influence that had reputedly weakened British and American men and further underscored the importance of a male sartorial ideal distinct from the cultivated and fastidiously "put-together" look of women and dandies. The sense of understatement, subtlety, and effortlessness—of display-ing oneself as if *not* on display—heavily promoted in conduct literature was per-haps best expressed as an overarching indifference to personal appearance. Too much neatness, care, and attention to dress was considered unmasculine—real men did not want to look as if they spent hours on their toilette—and certainly by the turn of the century, a charming, slightly rumpled or tousled look was regarded as decidedly manly.[12] According to American fashion historian Jo Barraclough Pao-letti, "Neatness was desirable, but not really expected, as it seems to have been be-lieved to run contrary to masculine nature. As American women were reminded in *Good Housekeeping* [in 1909]: 'All-round capable, wholesome men—men who can be depended upon in every business venture, who are sincere in all they profess, etc . . .—are often very distinguished by a deplorable carelessness in taste'" (127). While this carelessness might initially seem antithetical to the emphasis on dis-cretion and propriety mentioned earlier, this sort of "anti-deportment" was every bit as much a premeditated construct—a fiction—as was meticulous sartorial re-serve. Here again, men had to carefully tread a fine line, as this studied indiffer-ence was always in danger of falling into genuinely indifferent, sloppy dress.

All this is not to say that etiquette books indiscriminately spoke against fol-lowing fashion's decrees in all forms. Indeed, an unexpected paradox of conduct literature is that despite repeated acknowledgments that fashion was a vain, silly, and even wicked pursuit, nineteenth-century commentators nevertheless insisted that it was an essential social convention to which meticulous attention had to be paid. *Best Dressed Man* explains that while dress is an "insignificant thing," it is still an "object worthy of very careful attention, whatever may be said to the contrary. It is unquestionably a thing of consequence in the polite world" (62–63). The reasoning in some conduct manuals was, "if you can't beat 'em, join 'em." For example, *Habits of Good Society* resignedly declares, "Fashion is called a despot; but if men . . . are willing, nay, eager to be its slaves, we cannot, and ought not, to upbraid fashion. Its crowning is, in short, nothing more than the confession that vanity makes of its own weakness. We must be vain; we *are* weak; all we ask is to be guided in our vanity" (129). *The Manual of Etiquette for Ladies and Gentlemen* (1907), however, took a different approach by defending fashion philosophically: "If persons are inclined to rail against fashion and denounce it, let them remember that there is a fashion in everything. In thought, in politics, in physic, in art, in architecture, in science, in speech, in language, and even in religion we find fashion to have a guiding and governing power" (141). It was, after all, reminded *The Glass of Fashion*, a social responsibility to conform—within reason—to popularly accepted conventions, a "duty we owe to others as well as to ourselves to make the best of our personal appearance" (166). Failing to do so meant risking social stigma. Etiquette writers repeatedly stressed the importance of keeping abreast of popular trends and adhering to current fashions and warned of the humiliation that resulted from sartorial faux pas. In 1902, G. R. M. Devereaux clearly laid out the stakes:

> Nothing in the world is easier than to sneer at those who follow fashion, and expend time and thought and money on the subject of dress. But such sneers do not alter the fact that some attention should and must be paid to the prevailing fashions.
>
> Looking at it, too, from another point of view, if you have a certain number of friends, and receive a certain amount of attention from them in the way of invitations, &c., it is your duty to go to their houses and their parties suitably attired; if you do not you will quickly find yourself excluded. (19)

Devereaux suggests the way in which concern over fashion could be artfully transformed into a positive, masculine quality. Men's interest in fashion and personal appearance, their vigorous efforts to keep up with current fashions while conveying the proper sartorial image of middle-class reserve, could be justified to ensure male professional success. Moreover, the Devereaux passage illustrates how conduct authors and other social commentators increasingly relied on threats of social ridicule to persuade both flashy and slovenly middle-class male readers to adopt the proper sartorial uniform. Contemporary social historians have long acknowledged fear of ridicule as a primary driving force of fashion conformity.[13] Such sartorial anxieties apparently operated quite effectively to regulate proper dress, at least among certain professions in Victorian London. The author of *Best Dressed Man* quotes at length from a (most likely fictitious) stock-brokering friend who describes how peer pressure and ridicule maintained a code of proper dress at the Stock Exchange:

> In the matter of Dress, we have our unwritten but well-recognised law within "the House," which tends to check any propensity to snobbishness or vulgarity. If a member offends the eye by any incongruity or extravagance of custom, we are down upon him in a jiffy. "Deerstalkers" or "bowlers," for example, are held to be "not-exactly-the-thing" in business hours. If a man invites criticism by appearing thus covered in "the House" he subjects himself to the attacks of scoffers. "Hi! Hi!" they shout, "outside boat to Margate!"—a suggestive invitation to go elsewhere. The obnoxious hat is quickly removed, or is liable to be knocked off the head that wears it. . . .
>
> . . . It requires a very strong man to introduce any startling innovation in the way of dress on the Stock Exchange and expect to see it adopted. (41–42)

Here the brokers supposedly maintained a normative sartorial ideal by policing and regulating one another's dress. Indeed, many conduct books employed similar discursive strategies to promote conformity of male dress, particularly within the business-oriented City. *The Glass of Fashion* urges, "Let your head-covering resemble as nearly as possible that of other men," and John Wanamaker insists, "The well-dressed man . . . wears the same style of garment that every other man in his set is wearing. He distrusts anything noticeable and looks askance at anything startling" (*Glass*, 176; Wanamaker, 2). Several etiquette writers admonish male readers to avoid display and outshining others, by scrupulously trying to match others' appearance.

In his valuable study *Men in Black,* Harvey traces the rise of "professional black" in the nineteenth century, arguing that as many age-old trades evolved into respectable, middle-class "professions," black dress was employed to convey the proper sense of legitimacy and gravitas (140, 146). Through black dress, middle-class men "were able, with increasing confidence and dignity, to assert their importance *as* professionals, wearing smart dark clothes which showed their respect for what they were" (144). Black became the standard color for many a banker and stockbroker and was the basic uniform for those who worked in the City: "A man in black is a man you can trust. He is a man, to come to the bottom line, whom you can trust with your money" (147).[14] In this way, men's interest in fashion was recast. True, no longer was it about ornament (as ostentatious display had come to be associated with women, the aristocracy, and dandies), but the sobriety, understatement, and rugged minimalism necessary for professional success demanded an equal level of commitment. By the end of the period covered in this study, advice literature—as well as the fashion industry—insisted that a man's careful maintenance of his sartorial image was vital to his professional success. As Pope and Bradley's 1912 clothing catalogue asserts, "It savours very much of cant and hypocrisy for any man to say that he does not study dress in one form or another. It is absolutely imperative for a man nowadays to study his appearance. As a business, a professional or a social asset it is a very potent factor, and it is the privilege only of the millionaire and the pauper to be able to dress badly" (Bradley, 55). "Renunciation" was, after all, just another fashion. By conforming to it, middle-class men hoped to assert their social membership and to secure their professional legitimacy.

The dictates of the renunciation promoted by conduct literature pressed the middle-class male reader into negotiating always-changing dictates of fashion to maintain social acceptance, but not so devoutly as to risk making himself conspicuous as a vain and affected dandy—a daunting challenge issued over and over again by conduct authors. *Etiquette of Modern Society* (1882) asserts, "Fashion demands a discreet but not servile observance" (12). Fashion should be honored and obeyed, but only to a point, and it was essential that male readers understood where to draw the line:

> The creed of some persons in respect to dress may be expressed as consisting in a conviction of the necessity of "following the fashion." But this is not the gentleman's view of the question. He, indeed, "follows the

fashion" to an extent, because it is an affectation and a vulgarism to outrage it; but he follows it "with a difference." That is to say, he does not hasten to seize on every caprice, and to identify himself with every extravagance. He concedes only to the limits of good taste, and always with an eye to his age, position, and individual peculiarities. (15)

An essential difference—instinctively and effortlessly understood by the true gentleman[15]—existed, therefore, between his tasteful conformity to society's currently acceptable sartorial conventions and the effeminate dandy's or crude masher's fanatical aping of the latest mode from Paris's preposterous haute couture. "There is a happy medium to be observed," *Modern Etiquette in Private and Public* (1870) declares, "between being over-dressed and under-dressed," but precisely what should be considered too much or too little remains unclear here, as elsewhere (40). Where that "happy medium" lay was never clearly pinpointed—such advice was always confoundingly ambiguous on specifics, in part, certainly, because the rules that governed fashionable society were in constant flux.

In any case, renouncing fashion entirely was not an option offered to men by late-nineteenth-century commentators. In fact, many conduct books even assert that those who rejected fashion were just as guilty of vanity as were fashion's slaves. This too, after all, was a form of sartorial singularity that made one's physical self conspicuously and inappropriately visible. The *Habits of Good Society* offers this admonition, plagiarized whole cloth thirty years later in 1888 by the *Gentleman's Magazine of Fashion*:[16] "The man who rebels against fashion, is even more open to the imputation of vanity than he who obeys it, because he makes himself conspicuous, and practically announces that he is wiser than his kind. There cannot be greater vulgarity than an affectation of superior simplicity. Between the two it is left to the man of sense and modesty only to follow fashion so far as not to make himself peculiar by opposing it" (129).

The concern expressed by conduct writers was not so much that a man who rebelled against fashion would be regarded as a lower-class sloven, but rather that he risked presenting himself as a Bohemian or intellectual nonconformist who imagined himself superior to the social conventions (Oscar Wilde certainly comes to mind). Mrs. C. E. Humphry, author of *More Manners for Men* (1907), explains, "It is very bad manners to appear among your friends carelessly or unsuitably dressed. The idea conveyed is that you do not care what they think; that you are utterly indifferent to the opinion they form of you. You may possibly think that you are conveying the impression of being a fine fellow, free from vanity. But there is a very subtle kind of vanity lurking below this sort of thing. It says: 'My intellect and character are above such small considerations as coats and hats, ties and waistcoats. I am a superior person'" (17).[17]

Conformity in moderation to the general decrees of the current mode observed by popular society was a necessary component of nineteenth-century gentlemanly behavior. Dressing oneself according to fashion rather than ahead of or behind it helped maintain social harmony and reinforced norms of middle-class masculinity. Those who ridiculed the rules, etiquette writers warned, ensured that they would be the targets of ridicule. "It is the fashion to laugh at etiquette books," Mrs. Humphry states, "to regard their details as trivial, and to sneer at the number of rules and regulations that are rather suggestive of the difference 'twixt tweedledum and tweedledee.' But, after all, each rule has its use, and the whole of the laws go towards the smooth running of the great social machine. Without etiquette society would be jammed up in a chaotic deadlock" (ii–iii).[18] Here the curtain is pulled away just a bit, and the larger rationale behind the conduct author's argument seems laid bare as a discursive strategy employed to coerce all readers into submitting themselves to the "social machine." This prefigures a kind of Foucauldian theory of fashion: for both the advice writer and the male reader, there is no "outside" the system. Those who resist fashion are nevertheless judged according to its terms, those who refuse to participate in the public display of fashion merely succeed in drawing greater attention to themselves, and those who reject what the system defines as normative are regarded as deviant. For the middle-class gentleman, it is best to fall in line, to surrender to the dictates of "normal" fashion rather than to appear "peculiar" and risk social ostracism.

Clearly, the Great Masculine Renunciation ideology, as well as the conduct literature and social commentators who advocated it, did not demand that the middle-class male, in order to assert sociopolitical legitimacy, renounce his interest in fashionable dress and display. He was, however, encouraged to disavow any publicly detectable concern over his outer man. Etiquette writers regularly conceded that men were as prone to the sin of vanity as women; in *Etiquette of Good Society* (1893), Lady Gertrude Elizabeth Campbell takes great delight in spinning an anecdotal history of masculine dress that spotlights men's tendency to overemphasize personal appearance and indulge in dress as much as women did (85–87).[19] While some conduct writers such as Blenkinsop cautioned men to fight this impulse, urging "never, if you can help it, think of yourself or your dress in company," most insisted that what was most important was to follow fashion without ever *seeming* to be concerned with one's dress or outward appearance (23). The *Habits of Good Society* declares, "Good dressing is . . . to carry your clothes as if you did not give them a thought" (156). For the author of *The English Gentleman* (1849), the concern and effort a man devoted to his dress and appearance was a secret to be left in the toilette and never revealed in public:

> Take care that your things are well made, and that they suit your age and figure. Put them on in the best and most becoming manner that you can. Have nothing slovenly in your appearance. But when you have left your dressing-room, give yourself no further trouble about them. Do not fidget yourself to feel whether your cravat is in its exact place; or whether your hair preserves its destined wave; or whether your waistcoat has a wrinkle too much. . . . And while on this subject, let me beg of you to avoid leaning into every mirror that you may cross; and if you should seat yourself in such a position that your image is reflected in one, do steal as few conscious glances towards it as you can. It is a bad compliment to those you are conversing with; and remember this,—that when your back is turned, it is never passed over.[20] (102–4)

Such advice implicitly acknowledges the deception at the root of masculine appearance. The trick—and it was indeed a kind of trick—was to conceal all the grooming and preening, the minor adjustments and quick checks in the mirror necessary for proper middle-class masculine performance. The gentleman should not care or at least should give the illusion that he does not care about his physical appearance. He should refrain from all discussion of sartorial matters except with his tailor. A man might take as much care in his appearance as a woman, but the work involved in creating his appearance must forever remain hidden from the public.

What should be evident by now is the highly performative nature of the renunciation's sartorial ideals. There was always something disingenuous about a standard of dress and personal appearance that stressed the conscious production of a seamless presentation of naturalness, effortlessness, and a complete lack of concern for one's outer person—a paradox underscored by the conduct book's deliberate, heavy-handed advice. Proponents of the Great Masculine Renunciation presented its aesthetic of simplicity and understatement as if this aesthetic were outside of fashion rather than a fashion in itself, yet the performative nature of identity meant that one could not opt out of dressing for effect. Renouncing ostentation subjugated men to equally detailed, complex rules of dress. To convey naturalness and simplicity was to take on another layer of performance. The careful construction and erasing of the labor necessary to the creation of the illusion of effortlessness required even more management than outright ornamentation did. The performance of middle-class masculinity for which the renunciation called was a self-concealing one, a kind of antidisplay that in fact was more complex in its own way than overt ostentation.

Charles Pooter, the anxious middle-aged hero of George Grossmith's satire on middle-class mores *The Diary of a Nobody* (1892), typifies the ambivalence and performative nature of middle-class masculinity. Seemingly practical minded and penny-pinching, Pooter distances himself from the trendy fashions and unchecked consumption of both his irresponsible dandified son, William (aka "Lupin"), and his easily impressionable wife, Carrie, as he grouses over their overeager bandwagon mentality regarding every latest mode. Pooter confesses to his diary that he disapproves of the checkered suits that Lupin dons on Sundays and of the "fast-coloured clothes and ties" (50) that his son wears to the office, recommending instead "something black or quiet-looking" (117). Pooter is befuddled when Lupin refuses to accompany him on a walk because Pooter is dressed in a straw hat and frock coat (54), and he protests that his son's tastes are "a little too grand" when Lupin expects full evening dress for a small dinner party (160). Likewise, Pooter can only express exasperation when Carrie, upon the instruction of her trendy friend Mrs. James, drapes the drawing room mantelpiece with "little toy spiders, frogs and beetles . . . , as Mrs James says it's quite the fashion" (126).

"I'm a plain man," Pooter explains, "and don't pretend to be in the fashion" (126). Committed to sartorial understatement, he is dismayed to discover that his new suit, which appeared to be a "quiet pepper-and-salt mixture with white stripes down" in the gaslight of the shop, is in actuality "quite a flash-looking suit" with "a lot of green and bright yellow-coloured stripes" (127–28). Yet despite his supposed pragmatism and his disgust over Lupin's and Carrie's affectations, Pooter is by no means immune to concerns for fashionable display. Though his tastes are generally more modest than modish, Pooter is nevertheless highly self-aware of his appearance and clothing. He is conscious of brand names, mentions the stores where he shops, and frequently records his clothing purchases. On August 2, for example, he notes, "Bought a coloured shirt and a pair of tan-coloured boots, which I see many of the swell clerks wearing in the City, and hear are all the 'go'" (49).[21] Pooter is perturbed when his tastes are criticized or when, following frequent humorous mishaps, he finds his clothing damaged, soiled, ill-fitting, or unfashionable. He is humiliated when he forgets to wear a handkerchief or when his tailor cuts his trousers too tight and short. During a dinner party, a dog licks the black off his boots, and Pooter is embarrassed when on the walk home "several fools giggled at the unpolished state of my boots" (133). At another dinner party, Pooter is ruffled by an outspoken guest who decries the middle-class mediocrity of those "with a soft beard, with a soft head, with a made tie that hooks on." "This seemed rather personal," Pooter reflects, "and twice I caught myself looking in the glass of the chiffonier; for I had on a tie that hooked on—and why not?" (138).

Pooter exposes the performativity of the Great Masculine Renunciation by revealing the great deal of time and thought he puts into his clothes and appearance. Much of his diary is devoted to recording tussles with tailors over the cost of repairing his shirtfronts and with laundresses over fading his handkerchiefs. For the same reason, Pooter fails to exhibit the gentlemanly effortlessness and lack of concern for his appearance that he desires. He looks in mirrors, obsesses over insults (real or imagined) to his dress, fusses over stains and lost buttons. He fails to be a proper gentleman because his sputtering makes visible the work that should remain hidden. He vocalizes what should be kept silent by recording the minor inconveniences and frustrations of maintaining middle-class identity through goods.

While nineteenth-century conduct literature consistently promotes a sartorial ideal of plain dress, sartorial understatement, and inconspicuous masculine appearance, we must distinguish between the prescribed ideals of the renunciation and the actual sartorial practice of "real-life" middle-class Englishmen—something I undertake at greater length in chapters 2 and 5—as well as discern the complicated negotiations at the heart of conduct rhetoric regarding "reserved" male appearance and masculine performance. While conduct books may initially seem to support the notion of sartorial reserve, they also suggest strongly that, contrary to the Great Masculine Renunciation's general assumptions, middle-class men did not necessarily remove themselves from the dictates of fashion and adopt a drab, unadorned, and static form of dress immune to change, but rather were urged to conform—to a degree—to the seasonal alterations of fashion. Conduct books ultimately reveal significant ambivalence toward fashion that the broad brushstrokes of renunciation ideology fail to acknowledge or take fully into account.

It should be evident that the notion that the true gentleman abstained from any significant interest or participation in fashion, voiced by conduct writers and other Victorian social commentators, was always merely an artificial construct. And the double bind created by conduct literature's often paradoxical, always ambiguous advice reveals just how contrived and precarious this performance must have been. All the contradictions and fine lines were intended to situate the male reader squarely in the safe, modest tastes of the middle class, but they left him thoroughly confused and unlikely, even unable, to obey the advice offered by etiquette writers. Conduct literature's repeated warnings against ostentatious or "abnormal" dress might indicate that such transgressions were common—or more likely that they were commonly imagined; the repeated stress on subtlety and discretion in dress suggests anxieties that proper men were beginning to display themselves as dandies and women did. The large number of these publications, with their breathless advice and dire warnings, implicitly suggests that they were provoked by the simple fact that a lot of lower- and middle-class men were not renouncing the impulse to flash and flaunt their physical, public selves. Rather, as we shall see in the following chapters, many were interested in high fashion, were adorning themselves with bright colors and stylish cuts, and were not following the oft-repeated rules of "proper" middle-class masculine dress. Certainly many middle-class men—then, as always—did indeed care about cultivating their physical attractions through the use of fashionable grooming and attire. And the rapidly developing consumer industry of the second half of the nineteenth century ensured that more and more men participated in fashion and the consumption it required.

Separate Spheres and the Gender-Commerce Bond

"Separate spheres" ideology, though now under full attack by revisionist historians, nevertheless continues to cast a veil over men's consumer practices, and there is still much to be recovered from underneath its long shadow. Social and economic theorists have recognized for decades that consumer culture and the act of consumption have always been highly gendered (Lunt and Livingstone, 95). The long-standing socioeconomic mechanisms of patriarchal society ensured that when a consumer culture developed during the eighteenth and nineteenth centuries, it would predictably be institutionalized along strictly enforced gender lines. Complementary gender binaries—women consume while men earn, women purchase household and beauty products while men purchase big-ticket items such as cars and stereos—are familiar and vigorously marketed principles of twentieth- and now twenty-first-century gender norms that were certainly employed by nineteenth-century popular and commercial culture as well. Indeed, prevailing notions of Britain's exclusively female consumerism, though inaccurate, are supported by a powerful and popular discursive ideology that sought to remove men entirely from fashionable self-display and the act of consumption.

The familiar historical concept of separate spheres ideology explains that Victorian life was, at least in theory, rigidly segregated between the passive, spiritual, female world of the private home, domestic chores, childrearing, and emotional comfort, and the aggressive, secular male world of the public city street and office, dog-eat-dog business and politics, and financial gain. Such a sexual matrix naturally assigned men the roles of producer and breadwinner and women those of consumer and manager of what men provided.[22] Elizabeth Langland explains that Victorian middle- and upper-middle-class women assumed the important task of creating and managing the cultural currency—as opposed to the economic capital—and representation of middle-class status (25, 7). As the primary consumers and "domestic managers" of the Victorian household, women rather than men controlled class representations, overseeing the buying of provisions and maintaining the performance of middle-class identity through regular, appropriate consumption (6, 8–9). Langland's reading of Victorian separate spheres harmonizes with the Great Masculine Renunciation, for while middle-class men were supposedly distancing themselves from fashionable consumption and display, women were becoming increasingly responsible for performing class status through clothing and other possessions whose representational value was more culturally relevant than their use value (6). As business moved out of the family home, women were marginalized from production, while men were distanced from the direct involvement with the household consumption that they had previously shared with their wives. "Thus," according to historian Erika Diane Rappaport, "the geography of Victorian production and consumption and cultural prescriptions about the gender of shoppers tended to work together to separate men from the day-to-day routines of domestic consumption," leaving women primarily responsible for successful management of the household (*Shopping*, 52). In 1901, *Cornhill Magazine* contributor G. Colmore outlined the husband's dependence on his wife for the overseeing of domestic consumption: "I do not mean to deny to the husband temptations to extravagance, and the virtues of economy and self-denial; but not in his hands is the essential management of the expenditure, and as regards the meeting and overlapping of the two ends of spending and income, his wife can make or mar him" (799).

Langland, Rappaport, and many other feminist historians have employed evidence of this shift in men's and women's relationships to consumption to make larger claims about the transformation of urban centers into feminized public spheres, as women were increasingly leaving the home to make their purchases in the rapidly developing High Street shopping districts (Rappaport, *Shopping*, 52). The act of shopping—increasingly defined as pleasurable browsing for goods among a growing variety of options within a growing number of establishments—"reinforced the separation between two spheres of life, leaving the acquisition of the funds for shopping to man while making the task itself a woman's affair" (Barth, 146).[23] In *Our Miss Gibbs* (1909), a popular musical spoof of Harrods department store, playwrights Adrian Ross and Percy Greenbank play out this gendered consumer relationship, which by then would have been regarded as a humorously familiar norm:

> Customers—
> (Ladies.) Now we will go with all we've got,
>   Some of us paid, and some have not!
>   . . . .
>   Home with our hats and frocks and frills,
>   Husbands will have to pay the bills.
> (All.)   What will they say
>   When they must pay?
>   What will they say? (24–25)

This woman-as-sole-consumer model was further exacerbated by retailers' and advertisers' overt attempts to woo female customers. Lori Anne Loeb contends that Victorian advertisers devoted most of their time and expense to appealing to women, believing they were the most active and influential consumers: "Advertisers perceived middle-class women as the agents of material acquisition" and therefore "accepted the adage that 'the hand that rocks the cradle, is the hand that buys the boots'" (9, 8). Because consumption was socially regarded as a feminine duty, Loeb argues, advertisers rarely catered to the male public (11–12). According to a 1913 article in *Advertising World*, "A full 90% of advertisers have found it or are finding it advisable to leave the man practically out of account altogether when designing their announcements" (208).

Late-Victorian Criticism and Concealment of Male Consumption

Much of the surviving public discourse—and subsequently the character of the contemporary analysis—concerning consumer practices during the decades surrounding the turn of the century gives the impression that shopping was privileged for women but pathologized for men. That men hated shopping, dreading the oppressive tedium, decision making, and intrusive assistance of sales personnel that accompanied this "female" activity, was regarded as a Victorian truism (Rappaport, *Shopping*, 171–72). When the proprietors of Anthony Trollope's fictional drapery shop in his short satirical novel *The Struggles of Brown, Jones, and Robinson* (1861–62) decide to advertise their going-out-of-business sale as a "Solemn Fact" that must be brought to the attention of "every mother of a family in England," deliberation over the wording is short-lived. "Mother of a Family!" exclaims the aggressive young partner George Robinson. "Shall I say, also, of every Father? I should like to include all; but then the fathers never come, and it would sound loaded" (172). Michael Moss and Alison Turton's history of Fraser's department stores and Sean Callery's history of Harrods both assert that Victorian retailers believed men were reluctant to venture much beyond the entrances of the enormous shops and absolutely refused to travel to the upper floors to shop for merchandise (Moss and Turton, 57; Callery, 117).[24] While women shopped for pleasure, taking time to browse leisurely and enjoy the social atmosphere of the large store, men were believed to seek out only what they needed and to spend as little time as possible in the shop.

Whether men genuinely detested shopping as much as Victorian conventional wisdom and advertising copy claim is questionable, as the next chapter demonstrates. But contemporary readings of late-Victorian Britain's almost exclusively female consumption—however misleading they may be—are certainly reinforced by the popular press's regular depiction of those men who did shop as henpecked husbands, effeminate ninnies, or flirting loiterers. Clearly the large majority of middle-class men did indeed shop and purchase goods anyway. But since "the love of shopping serves as a fundamental marker of gender difference," as Rappaport contends, "too close involvement with domestic consumption, and especially with clothes shopping, exposed men to a good deal of ridicule in the nineteenth century" (*Shopping*, 128). Satirical pieces in popular British magazines repeatedly lampooned the figure of the inept male shopper as a "nervous amateur" bewildered by sales personnel, merchandise, and his own wife's shopping savvy (128). Lady Jeune, a contributor to the *Fortnightly Review*, reported derisively in 1895 that a "very amusing letter . . . appeared in an evening paper not long ago, giving an account of a gentleman who went into a shop to buy a pair of gloves, but had no idea what kind of gloves he required, and had to get the question settled for him by the person who served him" (127).[25] Men were also regularly portrayed as undiscerning, gullible consumers. In the 6d novel *We Three and Troddles* (1895), author Robert Andom's naïve lower-middle-class bachelor foursome are easily lured into purchasing unnecessary and inferior goods by London shopkeepers and street vendors, first by an "obliging shopman" who recommends "some twenty or thirty small items . . . which he assured us we couldn't possibly do without" for their disastrous Christmas dinner, and later by a dog-seller who convinces Troddles that the "wretched, muddy-looking dog of the mongrel breed" (55–56) is actually "a thorough-bred retriever, and worth heaps. . . . The man said he is a beautiful water-dog. He once won a prize for swimming" (64).

Victorian critics of men's consumption reserved their harshest criticism for those men who patronized department stores not out of reluctant obligation but because they actually seemed to enjoy shopping and the female world of the department store. In an 1879 article on Whiteley's department store for the *Daily Telegraph*, renowned journalist George Augustus Sala writes, "I found Westbourne Grove crowded principally by ladies and by young gentlemen of that peculiarly bland and amiable type which points them out at once as young gentlemen who have not the slightest objection to going out shopping with their Mamas, their sisters, or their *prétendues*—especially with their *prétendues*" (quoted in Lambert, *Universal*, 105–6). For Sala, such dandies had surrendered their masculinity to the dangerous seductions of the vain and silly feminine world of buttons and bows and storefront promenades. That same year, *Beeton's Manners of Polite Society* pointed to another male aberration, criticizing the strutting dandies who cluttered store counters to flirt with shopgirls:

> Gentlemen, or rather those who choose to take that title unwarrantably, are very often offenders against good taste in their conduct when shop-

ping. Their shopping is not, of course, of a very substantial kind, but, whatever it may be, they are perfectly indifferent to the tradesman's interest, their only thought being to extract enjoyment from, say, half an hour's converse with one or two of the young ladies behind the counter. A pair of gloves or a scarf may be bought in a few minutes, but instead of leaving to make way for other customers, as any sensible man would do, the dandy lingers on, uttering the uppermost nonsense in his brain with as much evident satisfaction as a wit of the first water would utter his jokes. . . . Their talk is all lisped nothings. Their eyes sparkle as they lisp the silliest things; they laugh and make merry, and cause people to turn in wonder that any human being could make himself so thoroughly ridiculous; and they "chaff the girls," to use their own vulgar phraseology, until it has occurred to them that a change of scene would be productive of new delights. Any man of good sense and good taste loses no more time than is necessary in making a purchase, and what he says is to the purpose. (Beeton, 126–27)

Such brazen behavior by these "vain fool[s] in resplendent attire" caused more trouble than merely crowded shop counters (127). For men there was an implicit danger in spending too much time in the shop. Amorous dandies and over-eager male customers upset the strict gender norms that relegated shopping and the leisurely world of the large urban store to the feminine sphere. The shop was a heterosocial—or worse, androgynous—space that blurred the borders between male and female, shopgirl and customer—the very threat that the rigid ideological gendering of shopping was intended to guard against.

Of course, this did not keep men from shopping, patronizing stores, and consuming goods. It did, however, alter how some men made their purchases. Many men employed the cultural gendering of shopping willingly to conceal both their consumption and their consumer desires. Thus, the construction of women as domestic managers bolstered the sexual division of labor, positioning women to serve as ciphers for men's secret, passive consumption of goods. As one of the primary duties involved in women's management of the Victorian household, "consumption became something that women undertook on behalf of men," and retailers and advertisers frequently employed popular notions of gendered consumption in order to design merchandise, display, and sales strategy specifically around female customers' consumption of men's goods (Richards, 206). Many of the larger stores developed entire men's departments around items such as pajamas, underclothing, ties, gloves, and scarves that did not require a custom fit and therefore could be purchased by women "without fear of making a mistake" (Jefferys, 312–13). Other retailers advertised men's goods as loss leaders in order to lure women into the store to buy for their husbands and were confident that these women would continue their shopping in other departments (313). Since early "Gent's Furnishings" departments were frequently relegated to an inconspicuous corner or tucked under a counter of the "Notions" section, having women undertake the purchase of men's items along with the rest of the household goods was often simply easier.

Many women not only shopped and purchased for men but also acted as their husbands' agents with responsibility for the administration of his money. Rappaport explains that until the 1860s the male head of a household was legally liable for most family debt and was expected to be in charge of and aware of all familial consumption. However, nineteenth-century English common law enabled wives (and other family members) to purchase items *for* their husbands, using their husbands' credit for goods regarded as "necessaries." By the 1860s and '70s, purchasing practices had radically shifted; families bought from urban shops and department stores rather than from local merchants who visited the home, and buyers were no longer as likely to be personally acquainted with sellers. These changes prompted legal reforms that made it more difficult for women to purchase items without direct permission from their husbands, but husbands were still held liable for purchases deemed "necessaries" but not luxuries or if plaintiffs could prove they were aware of their wives' purchases (Rappaport, *Shopping*, 51). Consequently, this provided another reason for men to leave consumption in the hands of women: husbands could avoid responsibility for wives' extravagant purchases by arguing that they were not present when the items were purchased.

Thus, the middle-class man could choose to distance himself physically, mentally, and legally from the act of purchase by relying on his wife to mediate his consumption. Moreover, by attributing his consumer lifestyle entirely to his wife, he could conceal his own consumer desires and disavow any personal interest in keeping up appearances. In *Middlemarch* (1872), George Eliot's Tertius Lydgate, an upwardly mobile but debt-laden physician, illustrates how males could employ conventional notions of the gender-commerce bond to displace the responsibility for their social climbing and materialism onto women. A young, energetic physician from a "really well connected" family (67), Lydgate is "better born than other country surgeons" (112); his "clothes hung well upon him" and "even in his ordinary gestures had an air of inbred distinction" (111). He therefore struggles to reconcile his genuine commitment to his humble profession with his vanity and material ambitions: "He did not mean to think of furniture at present; but whenever he did so, it was to be feared that neither biology nor schemes of reform would lift him above the vulgarity of feeling that there would be an incompatibility in his furniture not being of the best" (112). Eliot suggests that Lydgate is never fully conscious of his own expensive tastes. The doctor rents a fine home upon the death of its owner "in an episodic way, very much as he gave orders to his tailor for every requisite of perfect dress, without any notion of being extravagant" (255), and while he "believed himself to be careless about his dress, and he despised a man who calculated the effects of his costume; it seemed to him only a matter of course that he had abundance of fresh garments—such things were naturally ordered in sheaves" (429–30).

When Lydgate marries Rosamond Vincy, the immature and self-absorbed, equally vain and materialistic daughter of one of Middlemarch's most prominent families, he feels additional pressure to maintain appearances and provide a lifestyle in keeping with their mutual tastes. Rosamond dislikes Lydgate's profession, wishing he were something more prominent (335), and feels "disappointment in the conditions of marriage with a medical man even of good birth" (424). To compensate, the physician rapidly accumulates £1,000 in debt from renting and furnishing his fine home:

> How this came about may be easily seen without much arithmetic or knowledge of prices. When a man in setting up a house and preparing for marriage finds that his furniture and other initial expenses come to between four and five hundred pounds more than he has capital to pay for; when at the end of a year it appears that his household expenses, horses and et cæteras, amount to nearly a thousand while the proceeds of the practice reckoned from the old books to be worth eight hundred per annum have sunk like a summer pond and make hardly five hundred chiefly in unpaid entries, the plain inference is that, whether he minds it or not, he is in debt. (429)

When his creditors begin to pressure him for payment, Lydgate grows desperate and overwrought. "He was assailed by the vulgar hateful trials of a man who has bought and used a great many things which might have been done without, and which he is unable to pay for, though the demand for payment has become pressing" (429). Despite his torment, Lydgate finds it difficult to curb his spending and continues to fall deeper into debt, to the detriment of his marriage, and eventually resorts to gambling, before he is finally rescued by the banker Mr. Bulstrode.

The story of Lydgate's financial troubles is perhaps overshadowed in the novel by his growing estrangement from Rosamond, his accidental connection to a complicated corruption plot surrounding Bulstrode, and the countless other characters and story lines in Eliot's rich novel. But what is important to recognize here is Lydgate's primary responsibility for his debt. While Lydgate rationalizes that he must purchase such items and live at such a level to please Rosamond's tastes, the novelist makes it clear that Lydgate is equally desirous of fine goods (including Rosamond herself!). "Rosamond, accustomed from her childhood to an extravagant household," writes Eliot, "thought that good housekeeping consisted simply in ordering the best of everything—nothing else 'answered;' and Lydgate supposed that 'if things were done at all, they must be done properly'—he did not see how they were to live otherwise" (429). Lydgate is reluctant to give up this lifestyle and "could not help looking forward with dread to . . . the necessity for a complete change in their way of living" (437). When Lydgate declares that they must retrench, half-heartedly suggesting that they should live as humbly as his fellow Middlemarch physician Wrench, Rosamond protests, "Oh, if you think of living as the Wrenches do! . . . But I have heard you express your disgust at that way of living," and Lydgate quickly concedes, "Yes, they have bad taste in everything—they make economy look ugly" (475). Lydgate outwardly complains of his wife's extravagant household purchases, but they are luxuries weighted with the upper-class status that he secretly desires. He angrily resents Rosamond's emotional protests against tightening their budget, but only because she vocalizes and exacerbates his distaste for economizing. Rosamond serves as a scapegoat for the physician's consumption, an excuse for why he "must" purchase the fashionable status-conveying goods that he too secretly covets. She mediates the secret consumer desires that Lydgate publicly disavows to maintain a "proper" middle-class masculine performance.

Victorian men may have been initiated into this relationship before marriage, during their university years. In Thomas Hughes's *Tom Brown at Oxford* (1861), the sequel to the enormously popular and influential *Tom Brown's Schooldays* (1857), each male student's consumption is similarly mediated by a "scout," a kind of butler or personal assistant who attends to his young master's purchases. During his first days as a freshman at Oxford, Hughes's hero, Tom, describes the practice in a letter to a friend back home:

> Ah, Geordie, the scout is an institution! Fancy me waited upon and valeted by a stout party in black, of quiet, gentlemanly manners, like the benevolent father in a comedy. He takes the deepest interest in all my possessions and proceedings, and is evidently used to good society, to judge by the amount of crockery and glass, wines, liquors, and grocery, which he thinks indispensable for my due establishment. He has also been good enough to recommend to me many tradesmen who are ready to supply these articles in any quantities; each of whom has been here already a dozen times, cap in hand, and vowing that it is quite immaterial when I pay—which is very kind of them. (7)

What this passage also suggests is that the student was induced by the scout to expand his consumption—to purchase "indispensable" items that he previously never knew he needed. The college years were widely regarded in popular literature as a time when callow young men indulged in extremes in fashion and consumer luxuries, before settling down to the adult duties of marriage and masculine reserve. Hughes consequently portrays Tom's acquaintance and fellow student, the privileged Drysdale, for example, as a "gorgeously attired" dandy in a "loose jacket lined with silk, his velvet cap on his head" (21), whose "whole idea at present was to enjoy himself as much as possible" (20). Drysdale's dormitory quarters are irredeemably cluttered with sporting equipment, tobacco supplies, beer casks, and other evidence of the unserious student's life (21). He and his wealthy and dissipated friends all receive "allowances of £500 a year at least each; and, as they treated their allowances as pocket-money, and were all in their first year, ready money was plenty and credit good, and they might have had potted hippopotamus for breakfast if they had chosen to order it, which they would most likely have done if they had thought of it" (19–20). Scouts therefore provided the valuable service of mediating the young gentlemen's consumption, of acting as a go-between between man and commodity. Scouts served both to facilitate the frequent purchases made by fashion-conscious college men and also to distance them from the actual, feminizing act of purchase. Additionally, scouts served as "practice," introducing young men to the concept of consumer mediation and initiating them to the type of financial relationship they are likely to share with their future wives.

It is significant that while both Lydgate and Tom Brown attempt to distance themselves from their own consumer desires, both fall victim to out-of-control spending. Tom eventually finds himself £100 in debt, and his father sternly advises him in a letter, "You are no longer a boy, and one of the first duties which a man owes to his friends and to society is to live within his income" (276). Despite popular Victorian mores imagining that the male consumer did not even exist, fiction and prose regularly acknowledged that men were not immune to reckless spending habits and that many fell precipitously into severe debt.[26] *Etiquette, Politeness, and Good Breeding* (1870) advises wives on how to deal with husbands who spent too much trying to live up to class aspirations:

> The folly of *"keeping up appearances"* beyond our means is very dangerous. How many of those who are now reaping the bitter fruits of deeds they would once have scorned the idea of, can trace their ruin to this cause! . . . I am sure you will be prepared to agree with me that the influence of a loved and loving wife is almost unbounded; and surely this is a trust which it was never designed should remain unexercised. Use it well, and if you see your husband's ambition carry him too far, kindly, but firmly, remonstrate with him; show him the errors, and warn him of the dangers, of such a course, and I have sufficient confidence in your mutual affection to feel assured you will find this effectual; but, above all, prove to him *practically* that splendour is not necessary to happiness; let him see that, if your home be deficient in some of the luxurious elegancies of your more wealthy neighbours, still, in all the blessings the "household gods" of peace and love can bestow, it can proudly bear comparison with the most favoured of them all. (109)

This passage reaffirms the fact that women were expected to take responsibility for domestic management. But more importantly, it reveals that men were recognized as equally desirous—perhaps more so—of asserting class status through spending and possessions. And as we shall see in the next chapter, the expanding opportunities for male consumption and the siren song of modern commercial culture made it increasingly difficult for men even to feign detachment from consumer goods.

The notions that proper nineteenth-century middle-class men renounced fashionable sartorial display in favor of a stovepipe, hat severity and distanced themselves from the act of consumption by delegating shopping to women—critical premises that have inhibited vigorous, thorough contemporary scholarship on men's fashion and consumption—did indeed exist in popular thought (Breward, *Hidden*, 260). But they were not monolithic dictates or nonnegotiable decrees, nor do they necessarily reflect the real beliefs or behaviors of many middle-class men of the era. While men may not have talked about fashion in public, we should not presume that they made "no study of dress"—indeed, the Great Masculine Renunciation made sure that they thought about it all the time. The paradoxical nature of the advice offered in conduct literature reveals a complicated and ambivalent relationship with ideal standards of male sartorial reserve. The renunciation's prescription of dark, sober dress was encouraged as a way for the Victorian middle class to distinguish its middle-classness and to demonstrate its legitimacy, validity, and superiority. But the "normal" category was broader than we might presume, and not all middle-class men wanted to wear plain/dark dress or to appear middle class. Moreover, the gendering of shopping as female is actually a fairly recent phenomenon that was not as securely in place during the Victorian era as we generally believe. At the same time that historians argue that the sexual segregation of consumption was becoming socially institutionalized through the separation and relocation of the sites of male work and female shopping outside the home, this gender-commerce bond was already beginning to confront powerful economic forces of consumer culture that threatened to dismantle or at the very least redefine it. As we shall see in chapter 2, cultivating the male market by making consumption and the act of shopping attractive for men was one of the main goals of the burgeoning consumer industry.

OUTFITTING THE GENT

The Emergence of the Male Consumer and the Commodification of the Male Body

> Men are properly said to be clothed with Authority, clothed with Beauty, with Curses, and the like. Nay, if you consider it, what is Man himself, and his whole terrestrial Life, but an Emblem; a Clothing or visible Garment for that divine ME of his, cast hither, like a light-particle, down from Heaven? Thus is he said also to be clothed with a Body.
>
> —Thomas Carlyle, *Sartor Resartus*

> That your dress is approved by a man is nothing;—you cannot enjoy the high satisfaction of being perfectly *comme il faut*, until your performance has received the seal of a woman's approbation.
>
> —*Etiquette for Gentlemen* (1838)

*I*N 1890, THE TAILORING TRADE JOURNAL *Gentleman's Magazine of Fashion* positioned reporter T. H. Holding on St. James's Street to take an informal eyewitness survey of what London's men were wearing. Holding reports disappointedly on the sartorial uniformity of Clubland. "There is a remarkable sameness at all times, and perhaps in all centres, between the dress of one of these stylish young gentlemen and another," he writes; "Whatever is the run and the rage, that they all go for; no matter whether it be a black vicuna frock, the double-breasted reefer, or the short waist and long-tailed morning coat of half a generation ago—they must all dress alike" (Holding, "Men's," 7). While the Great Masculine Renunciation may still have been the reigning ideology regarding masculinity and dress, many late-Victorian sources voiced a restlessness with these confining prescriptions of male sartorial reserve and conformity. *Our Miss Gibbs*, Adrian Ross and Percy Greenbank's 1909 musical satire of Harrods, similarly satirizes the mindless submission to "correct" dress practiced by a "Chorus of Dudes":

A fashionable band of brothers

    Are we,

    You see!

Whatever one has done the others

    Must do,

    It, too!

Our clothes and hats are made to match,

    They show it,

We have one bill for all the batch,

    And owe it!

For we're correct

In every respect,

And you note the effect!

In daytime or in night-time,

The right thing at the right time,

We mayn't be great in intellect,

But we are so correct! (15)

The *London Tailor* lamented in 1899, "There never was a time in history when everybody was dressed so alike" (305). In the final decades of the nineteenth century, the cry was heard more and more that the sartorial standards of understatement and reserve that had defined the proper dress of the business-minded middle-class Englishman had rendered male costume bland and predictable. In *The Picture of Dorian Gray* (1891), Oscar Wilde has Lord Henry Wotton complain, "The costume of the nineteenth century is detestable. It is so sombre, so depressing. Sin is the only real colour-element left in modern life" (28).

And indeed, to conservative social critics, sin came in the form of the growing diversions from the reserved dictates of the Great Masculine Renunciation. Anne Hollander contends that fashion changes are meant to create a "disequilibrium"—to upset a sartorial (and social) status quo that has become "too easy to take. Contrary to folklore, most changes are not rebellions against unbearable modes, but against all too bearable ones. Tedium in fashion is much more unbearable than any sort of physical discomfort" (49). The widespread protests against the tedious uniformity of male dress cited above suggest that the Great Masculine Renunciation was not the only sartorial masculine ideal of the late Victorian age and that some men had grown restless under its confines. For many middle-class

Englishmen of the second half of the nineteenth century, fashion became a highly visual means by which to subvert the rigid and confining dictates that defined proper masculine behavior generally, as the growing sartorial options expanded the landscape of acceptable masculinities as well, a phenomenon I explore in the following chapters.

The transformations in retailing and consumer practices during the half century between 1860 and 1914 were nothing less than a revolution. The emergence of the large-scale department store in the 1860s and '70s, the massive expansion of the popular press in the form of inexpensive newspapers, magazines, and books, and the rapid development of increasingly sophisticated advertising techniques brought about an awareness, availability, and affordability of clothing and an ever-growing variety of other goods. Merchants aggressively sought to pleasurably engage male Britons in the world of goods to the same extent as female consumers. They fueled an atmosphere of conspicuous consumption and pleasurable materialism that was made attractive and socially acceptable for large numbers of men in the middle and working classes. With the introduction of the department store and its mass-produced goods came the birth of a large-scale fashion "industry" and an acceleration of mass-marketed fashion trends that expanded the options of acceptable masculinity that mainstream middle-class males could perform.

Yet the burgeoning commodity culture and fashion industry operated against, and alongside, the more conservative discursive ideals of the Great Masculine Renunciation. Male-directed marketing, the department store's expansion into male goods and its cultivation of male-friendly spaces, and the heightened commercial and public attention directed toward male display all suggest that proper middle-class masculinity had become a highly contested area whose rules and parameters were not always as restrictive and reserved as the conventional image of Victorian masculinity conveys. The forces of commodity culture and its young male adherents were engaged in a tug-of-war with the Great Masculine Renunciation over representations of men's bodies. With growing frequency, force, and finesse, marketers actively appealed to men, making their interest in fashion and shopping "safe," without violating existing taboos and norms of masculinity. The growing acceptance of male consumption and display created cracks in those taboos and norms and changed late-Victorian definitions of normative manhood in fundamental ways. Not only were men allowed access into formally exclusively female spaces and activities, but they were also encouraged to have a visual, physical, erotic self to be appraised by the public.

Discerning what many of Britain's middle-class men really wore from the popular rhetoric of periodicals, advertising, and conduct manuals is admittedly problematic at best. At the same time, determining what men consumed or proving that their consumption increased through hard numbers is virtually impossible. Market research on men's consumer habits was nonexistent, and few financial records from the period have survived. What does remain of department store sales records is rarely broken down by department. For these reasons, I have turned my attention to other indicators of increased interest in, discussion of, and promotion of men's consumption of fashionable goods between 1860 and 1914. The promotional strategies and advertising of the men's clothing market and popular and professional literature pertaining to men's consumption and overt sartorial display reveal an overall rise in men's public participation in consumer culture— or at the very least a growing recognition of the male market. To be sure, one must be skeptical of laments by tailoring journals against conformity in men's dress, such as the ones with which I began this chapter, as the trade has an obvious investment in condemning predictable dress and promoting constant sartorial change. Yet even if men's real consumption of clothing and grooming products did not increase at all, the dramatic growth in male-directed advertising, in available male-related items, and in spaces designed specifically for the purchase of those goods by men all point to a dramatic cultivation of the male consumer—one that transformed late-Victorian notions of masculinity and paved the way for the explosive growth in male and youth markets throughout the twentieth century and into the twenty-first.

Creating Male Markets and Appealing to Male Consumers

In November 1893, the *Cutter's Gazette of Fashion*, a prominent trade periodical for tailors, published the comments of a T. Patterson in a paper delivered before the Sheffield Society. In his address, Mr. Patterson celebrated the robust state of London's men's tailoring and extolled the modern advances that had effected its proliferation throughout the provinces and the continent:

> Fashions for gentlemen do not now originate across the channel, but in London, the great centre of the world's life in so many things, she also becomes mistress in what relates to style and fashion in gentlemen's dress. Nor are the provinces lagging behind so much as they used to. It

is no unusual occurrence for a customer to ask for a certain garment or a special shade of color, that has just become the "go" in London. . . . Cheap travelling, and the display of the newest and latest fashions by the purveyors of dress, soon educates the public taste and informs the individual as to what is being worn. (165)

Patterson's comments reveal much about the striking changes both in the popularity of fashionable dress and in English masculinity wrought by the nineteenth-century development of modern consumer culture. No longer was fashion regarded by the middle classes as the domain solely of women, the elite, and the inhabitants of sophisticated capital cities; rather, it was available to and desired by all male Britons. More significantly, Patterson's speech also suggests the eagerness with which the consumer industry pursued and created these growing markets. The tailoring trade was more than happy to expand its customer base by "educating" middle-class men about the consumable tools of the fashionable life of the consumer culture.

To accomplish this, Britain's rapidly emerging consumer culture assisted in middle-class male consumers' reappropriation and transformation of what had previously been considered effeminate or deviant male consumption and self-display through clothing and accessories into publicly acceptable masculine behavior in the later decades of the nineteenth century. Advertisers and merchants worked aggressively to recast shopping and consumption as attractive activities for men, and the first step was to distance their consumer habits from women's. The notion of a man delegating the responsibility of his consumption to his wife, which I discuss in chapter 1, was no longer portrayed as an attractive arrangement by the popular press. Historically, gender distinctions have been an instrumental and ever-present tool for merchants' depiction of goods, and late-Victorian male-directed advertising and product display followed a system of rules and strategies that were consciously distinct from those designed to attract women customers. In shopping, as in everything else, masculinity and femininity were culturally represented in terms of a boundless system of opposites: while men liked the neat and simple display of a few spotlighted items, women preferred tables cluttered with bargains; while men focused on finding and purchasing a specific item as quickly as possible, women enjoyed lingering over options.[1] All this suggests that for consumption to be recast as an appealing and acceptable activity for men, it had to be clearly distinguished from women's consumption. As a means of making shopping attractive, "safe," and masculine, both male consumers and merchants went out of their way to insist that it was not like what women did.

To underscore this distinction, women were regularly portrayed not merely as the primary consumers, but as voracious, compulsive shoppers who overwhelmed and oppressed both shop workers and their husbands with their insatiable desire for goods.[2] "When is a lady not a lady?" went one of the most popular jokes circulating among drapery and department store staff. "Answer: When she attends a sale" (*Draper*, 992). *Our Miss Gibbs* recites another familiar joke by depicting women customers and overzealous shoppers who nonetheless fail to purchase anything: "We'll take a look at all the lot, / All the lot, all the lot, / But we will not / Attempt to buy, / We'll look and try, But never buy!" (5). The reputed female obsession with shopping was pathologized, quite literally, when widely publicized accounts of female shoplifters, many from the privileged classes, popularized kleptomania as a newly recognized medical disorder and elicited growing fears of an "epidemic" rooted in the deviant desires engendered by the department store's seductive spectacle of goods. By the 1890s, the female shoplifter had become a stock character type, endlessly satirized in magazine articles, songs, and plays (Abelson, 8).[3]

If the familiar figure of the female kleptomaniac symbolized the extremes of aggressive female consumption, her foil in the popular imagination was often the figure of the comically passive husband who surrendered complete control over his purchases to his overbearing wife. Magazine articles and cartoons increasingly took great pleasure in depicting men as "the Submerged Sex," led about by domineering women shoppers (Hosgood, 104). In 1897, *Punch* offered tongue-in-cheek advice to a woman seeking an "ideal husband," urging that she choose "a man who likes to go Shopping." "You will find him very useful if managed judiciously," the writer sardonically concluded ("Ideal," 285). Three years later, the trade journal *Master Tailor and Cutter's Gazette* offered what it believed its readership would recognize as a familiar portrait of the maddeningly weak-kneed male customer sent to purchase a suit for himself according to his wife's specifications: "After a particularly fervid demonstration of affability with all the members of the staff, the busy business man explains that he really did not know he wanted a suit, but his wife assured him that he did. This remark gives the game away entirely, and the cutter, who has been hanging on each little utterance, doubles round the corner, says an 'Ave maria,' and resigns himself to his fate" ("Queer," 46). The *Master Tailor's* male customer is entirely emasculated by his wife's control of his consumption. He appears impotent and incapable of developing any opinions of his own regarding style or fit: "When asked whether he requires the coat loose or fairly close fitting he replies, 'Any way; whichever you think best.' Interrogated as to the style of pockets required on the breast, he repeats in an audible whisper, 'Any way, any way.' He seems, indeed, to have reached the acme of resignation." The tailor eventually manages to guide the customer to a selection, but he returns again and again, presumably because his wife is dissatisfied with the tailor's work (46).

Through this system of negative gender-coded stereotypes, men were increasingly urged to take control of their consumption rather than leave it to women. Women were prone to abuse their role as primary consumers, either through compulsive shopping or by bullying their husbands and dictating men's purchases. Female kleptomaniacs and harridan wives were convenient (and clearly misogynistic) devices employed by male commentators to exaggerate all the negative connotations of shopping and relegate them to the female sex. Ridiculing passive, hen-pecked "Molly husbands" and "squaw men" who handed over their consumption to their domineering wives promoted male consumer agency. To foster male consumption, advertisers and marketers attempted to turn the gender-commerce bond on its ear—not so much rejecting or replacing it as redirecting it to encourage men to shop. The old equation of women as consumers/men as producers was shifted to one of women as bad consumers/men as good consumers. Men had to rise out from under the tyranny of their wives' irrational, directionless, and even deviant shopping practices and assert a kind of consumption that was logical, focused, and masculine.

Therefore, merchants of the late nineteenth and early twentieth centuries developed distinctly different advertising approaches considered more compatible with, and attractive to, the male mindset. Convinced that men would not waste time reading the florid descriptions and hyperbolic promises seemingly indispensable to most text-heavy Victorian advertisements, merchants courted male consumers with advertising copy that was clear, brisk, and direct. Advertisers believed that men responded best to a "modern," "strenuous and masculine" "business style" that conveyed an attractive image of manly vigor and productivity (Garvey, 178, 181). They strove to masculinize goods and to make the consumption of those goods appear safe and attractive through direct association with strong, robust male figures whose masculinity was seemingly self-evident. The most masculine— and therefore most popular—male figures were athletes and soldiers, and their

Figure 2.1. Cadbury's Cocoa advertisement (*Illustrated London News,* 19 January 1901, 85)

presence was used to make even ostensibly gender-neutral products masculine and appealing to male buyers. Cadbury's Cocoa, for example, featured illustrations of energetic young sportsmen in their advertisements for decades. An advertisement from 1885 promises *"'STRENGTH AND STAYING POWER.'—To ATHLETES"*, while another from 1901 portrays a rugby player taking a moment during the game to enjoy a cup of cocoa (fig. 2.1). Similarly rugged, eager young men were regularly shown playing tennis, boating, and participating in other forms of vigorous outdoor recreation. The craze for bicycling in the 1880s and '90s made it perhaps the most popular subject of these sporting advertisements

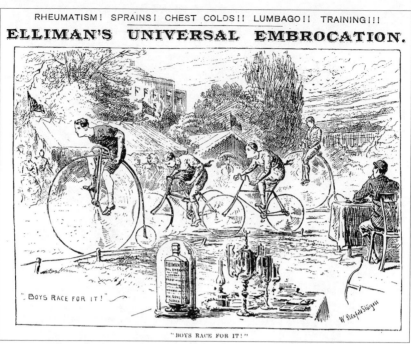

RHEUMATISM! SPRAINS! CHEST COLDS!! LUMBAGO!! TRAINING!!!

ELLIMAN'S UNIVERSAL EMBROCATION.

" BOYS RACE FOR IT!"

"BOYS RACE FOR IT!"

Figure 2.2. Elliman's Universal Embrocation advertisement (*Illustrated London News,* 25 October 1890, 535)

that idealized the "robust masculinity" of the age. An 1890 advertisement for Elliman's Universal Embrocation, an all-purpose patent medicine, depicts a group
of boys racing on bicycles and pennyfarthings and features the slogan "BOYS RACE
FOR IT!" (fig. 2.2). Like Cadbury's Cocoa, Dr. Tibbles' Vi-Cocoa was marketed as
a high-energy sports drink—a turn-of-the-century Gatorade, if you will. Evidence of its efficacy was offered in the form of the written testimonial of "Mr.
J.H. Jefferson, 11 Wincott-street, Kensington, London S.E.," who praised its vital-
izing properties: "Just a line in praise of the excellent Dr. Tibbles' Vi-Cocoa. I
have been a cyclist for the last six or seven years, and I go in for racing a great deal.
I started using Dr. Tibbles Vi-Cocoa some three months ago, and I find a great
difference in my riding. I am now able to stay and endure greater fatigue than I
did before using Dr. Tibbles' Vi-Cocoa. All I can say is, all you claim for it is
quite true. I shall not use any other preparation but yours whilst training this season" (Dr. Tibbles, 8).

An even more decidedly masculine image to the late-nineteenth-century
British male mind, perhaps, was the soldier, who acted out the real life-or-death
struggles on the battlefield that the athlete symbolically played at on the sporting

field. The beef-extract beverage Bovril, for example, adopted the soldier image for an extensive series of military-themed advertisements at the turn of the century. One representative advertisement with the slogan "BOVRIL IS LIQUID LIFE" depicts two soldiers on the front line, one serving his wounded comrade a warm cup of Bovril (fig. 2.3). Advertisers relied heavily on the "conqueror image" in the figures of the soldier and the quasimilitary adventurer because it was a familiar Victorian icon that instantly summoned up powerful jingoistic associations of British imperial might, high adventure in exotic far-off lands, and a bold, rugged, unchallenged masculinity. The images of famous adventurers and explorers of Britain's empire, in particular Henry Morton Stanley, were exploited repeatedly in advertising (Loeb, 80). The middle-class British male, these advertisements implied, could share vicariously in the enterprises of the British empire by shopping for goods related to its exploration. In 1904, for example, Harrods department store took out an enormous front-page advertisement in the *Daily Mail*, explicitly addressed to male readers, claiming that while "Madame may be securing a balldress in one department, . . . you in another can be emulating the example of past customers and be fitting out an Arctic Expedition, just as readily as you can secure a summer holiday tent outfit for but a few of you" ("Harrods Limited," 1).[4] Here the adventurer image is used both to bolster the masculinity of shopping and to distinguish men's shopping from women's, as the man's consumption is deliberately related to high adventure and exotic excursions rather than feminine domestic concerns or the frivolity of female glamour.

At the turn of the century, the widespread patriotic fervor over the highly publicized Boer War (1899–1902) provided the perfect opportunity with which to further the masculinization of shopping for men. Popular enthusiasm for Britain's military engagement inspired clothiers and sellers to use the conflict to connect goods to the war effort and to market civilian versions of war-related merchandise. Window displays in city shops and department stores featured ever more elaborate military and patriotic themes that vied for the male shopper's attention. "National events can generally be appropriately illustrated, and public sentiment expressed, in window dressing designs," declared the trade journal the *Outfitter* in 1900. "The widespread interest taken in the Boer War has been mirrored in the windows of retailers in every part of the country" ("Up-to-Date," 17–18). The *Outfitter* regularly reviewed shop displays throughout the Boer War (fig. 2.4), as if judging a competition. The journal reported, for example, that J. H. Willcox, "outfitter, hatter, hosier, and tailor," of Farnham, Surrey, "had thousands to see

Figure 2.3. Bovril advertisement (*Illustrated London News,* 2 February 1901, 173)

the novelty" of his elaborate window display featuring red, white, and blue bunting, pictures of war heroes and celebrities, mannequins dressed as Red Cross nurses and the war's famous generals and field marshals (including Colonel R. S. Baden-Powell and Lord Roberts), and artifacts brought home from the front ("War," 11). While patriotic zeal affected everyone, men were recognized as the most responsive audience, and many of the more militaristic displays—featuring plaster figurines

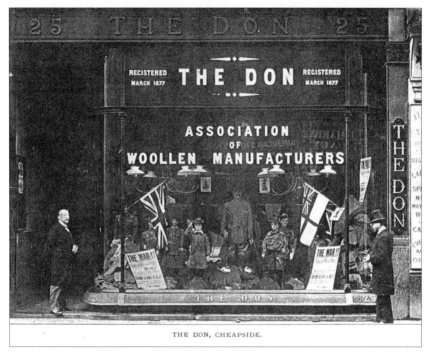

THE DON, CHEAPSIDE.

Figure 2.4. Boer War–decorated display window ("Memo," *Outfitter,* 24 February 1900, 12)

of "12 little khaki-clad Imperials, who carry rifles in their hands, ready to do and dare at duty's call" and signs reading *"Great Slaughter of Prices"* or *"4,000 Boers Captured by these Startling Prices"*—beckoned from tailors' windows ("Up-to-Date," 17–19).

Perhaps the most enduring fashion to come out of the Boer War was the adoption of khaki material and colors in civilian fashions.[5] Inspired by the new rugged material, which evoked both British military might and the exotic locales of its empire, Britain's civilian population rapidly turned khaki into a seemingly inexhaustible commercial phenomenon by 1900. Khaki fabrics and shades found their way onto neckties, handkerchiefs, hats, handbags, and even fine silks. "The 'Gentleman in Khaki' is responsible for a great revolution in man's attire, and khaki bids fair to be the only wear during the coming season," observed the *Outfitter* in February 1900. "Some people think that the thing has been overdone, and that the craze is dying out; but there are, on the contrary, indications that it is increasing in volume and vehemence" ("Memo," 11). Like the empire that inspired it, khaki's dominance in men's attire spanned the globe, and the journal claimed that it had swiftly spread to Belfast, New York, and New Zealand (11). Khaki became especially popular for men's athletic clothing, in particular golf and cycling outfits ("London," 5). The *Master Tailor and Cutters' Gazette* noted that tailors faced difficulties in keeping up with the demands of their male customers for khaki cycling costumes:

> In my last "Notes" I made some reference to khaki for mufti wear. It will be very largely worn this year, but not in the ordinary tweed suit. The "field" it has captured—we speak in military terms now—is the cyclists'. No colour could be better; and the various makes of cloth and the slight patterns—faint red, orange or green (yes, without doubt, green) over checks—which I have seen, and some of which I have had from a leading woollen house, cause me no wonder when I am told that within a few days from submitting their patterns in the West End the first pieces of the entire range were "sold out." ("Early," 92)

Khaki mania seemed custom-made for the male market. The fabric's associations with the spartan, heroic life of the soldier and its marriage to athletic clothing created a virtually inexhaustible variety of highly masculinized goods marketed to an increasingly receptive male consumer base. Military-inspired fashion trends had emerged in Britain before—notably during the Napoleonic era—but what made the khaki craze different was the rise of the technologies of the mass-consumer industry. With the development of large-scale industrial mobilization and modern advertising hype, new consumer trends could be publicized, proliferated, and sold not just to a handful of wealthy, in-the-know elite urbanites but to Britain's male populace as a whole.

The Department Store's Influence on the Growth of Male Consumption

The nineteenth-century development of the large-scale High Street department store,[6] which began in full force in the 1860s and '70s, was particularly instrumental in this (re)construction of males as consumers. Indeed, khaki achieved its widespread success among male consumers in part because of the capabilities of the department store to mass produce[7] and mass market it to the middle classes. However, the department store's integral role in the cultivation of the male market has been historically obscured by Victorian commentators and advertisers, who frequently portrayed the department store as a uniquely feminine space. More-over, as I mention briefly in the previous chapter, men's consumption is further obscured, albeit inadvertently, by the many important recent studies that have emphasized the department store's significant contribution to the feminization of urban centers.[8] Most prominently, Erika Diane Rappaport's invaluable work has traced how the development of London's West End as a revitalized and booming shopping district in the decades surrounding the turn of the century was de-picted by department store entrepreneurs, advertisers, and journalists as an exclu-sively female space for consumption. The crowded, public metropolis, formerly off-limits to the domestic Angel in the House, came to be portrayed as "a sphere for female autonomy, pleasure, and creativity," as the retail revolution converted what was once the all-male domain of bankers, barristers, and businessmen into the center of female fashion, pleasure, and recreation (*Shopping*, 3). With the addi-tion of restrooms, cafés, reading rooms, tea rooms, and libraries, department stores broadened their attractions as comfortable, inviting social rendezvous for women of the middle classes. Women consumers were soon indistinguishably linked to the department store in the public imagination: Emile Zola, for example, named both his novel and the fictional department store that is its subject "the paradise of ladies" (*Au bonheur des dames*, 1883), while Harrods' sixtieth-anniversary souvenir booklet (1909) was entitled *The House That Every Woman Knows.*

Such social rhetoric served to reinforce gender distinctions and institution-alize gender stereotypes regarding women and consumption. However, this re-imagining of the city not solely as a locus of business (not to mention of crime, poverty, and prostitution) but also as a modern commercial and social center—this promotion of shopping as "the core of a new publicly oriented social life"—undoubtedly transformed the cultural lives and consumer habits of turn-of-the-century British men as well (Rappaport, "New," 137). Rappaport acknowledges that Victorian commentators seemed to insist on representing the new urban shopping centers as uniquely female spaces "despite the fact that men often shopped" and "despite a considerable masculine presence on the streets" (148). Since at least the eighteenth century, much of the West End had been—and con-tinued to remain—devoted to hotels, apartments, tailors, and hatters (not to mention prostitutes) patronized by London's fashionable males. Many of the emerging department stores also catered to a mostly male crowd; at John Lewis and Co., for example, three-fourths of the staff and much of the customer base remained male throughout the period (Ferry, 245).

What remains to be acknowledged are the ways in which the department store created a new urban social center for men as well as women and how it actively invited men to participate in Britain's new consumer culture. The department store's widely acknowledged role in generating consumer desires and legitimizing self-gratification for women worked on men as well. The emergence of the department store and the opening of other fashionable public places for the middle classes provided a means through which, a reason for which, and an arena in which men could be interested in consumption, fashion, and self-display. Department stores aggressively strove to whet middle-class men's appetites for consumption and to transform them into active, public consumers by making available and affordable an ever-increasing variety of male-directed goods.

The dramatic growth in men's items offered in Harrods' turn-of-the-century catalogues provides a useful example. In its 1895 catalogue,[9] Harrods' "Gent's Outfitting" comprises twenty-three pages (*Victorian Shopping*, 962–84). The items listed are mostly simple ready-made goods such as collars and articles of clothing that do not require a custom fit, such as pajamas. The few illustrations of the clothing offerings are mainly limited to cuffs, collars, and shirtfronts. Eight years later, Harrods' 1903 catalogue, although smaller overall, devoted nearly twice the space to gentlemen's clothing, offering an impressive array of men's articles: coats, hats, socks, neckties, gloves, collars, pajamas, robes, and "travelling rugs" (*Harrods General Catalogue*, 1903, 907–43). The ready-made items include frock coats, morning coats, dinner suits, dress suits, reefer suits, lounge suits, Norfolk suits, shooting suits, motor clothing, and yacht crew uniforms. There are thirty-three hats (including several varieties of pith helmets), fifty-five kinds of gloves, and three pages devoted to underwear (923–24, 933, 926–28). Collar clips, cufflinks, umbrellas, walking sticks, cigar cutters, and cigarette cases are located elsewhere in the catalogue. Other sections with a decidedly masculine appeal would have been "Bag, Trunk, and Portmanteau Department"; "Motor Department"; "Gun and Ammunition Department"; "Barrack Furniture and Camp Equipment Department," featuring army chests, portable washstands, towel horses, folding bookshelves, folding chairs, lanterns, canteens, and tents; and the "Sports and Games Department," featuring rowboats and canoes, exercise equipment and "developers," boxing gloves, Indian clubs, and supplies for football, cricket, lawn tennis, croquet, archery, and billiards (682–700, 1064–76). Of particular interest in the 1903 catalogue is a special perforated tear-out self-measurement form, with instructions, to be filled out and sent to the store—suggesting another way in which males were invited to take an active role in consumption.

Department store catalogues also reveal the increase in clothing accessories and other personal decorative items adopted by men at the turn of the century. Conduct manuals may have uniformly insisted that the true gentleman renounced jewelry, limiting himself only to a watch placed in a waistcoat pocket, perhaps connected to a gold Albert chain draped across the chest through a chain-hole in the vest. However, the ever-increasing variety of tie pins, cufflinks, rings, gold lockets, umbrellas, and walking sticks offered in Harrods and other catalogues demonstrates the department store's efforts to cultivate and supply a growing market of men eager to decorate their persons with expensive and eye-catching accessories. Further, in September 1898, the men's monthly *Fashion* noted that "pearls are worn by nearly all our smartest men," and it subsequently reported on the wide popularity of tie pins, bracelets, and amber matchboxes and cigarette cases (Brummel, Dress News, September 1898, 21; London Expert, August 1899, 10; Brummel, From Head, May 1900, 18; Brummel, From Head, April 1902, 12). Not only did the variety of clothing options for men grow exponentially, but those clothes required their own accessories for proper care. The popular conduct manual *Clothes and the Man* (1900) recommended purchasing hangers for jackets, straighteners for trousers, and a trouser press to maintain their shape—and spends a total of ten pages detailing the proper use of these appliances (42–43, 91–93, 93–97). The rubberized cotton of the Mackintosh coat was infamous for giving off an unpleasant smell and inspired the creation of several products purporting to eliminate it (Walkley and Foster, 137–38). In 1898, *Fashion* had recommended several varieties of wardrobes "exclusively for men" (fig. 2.5) and reminded readers that "the care of clothes is of more importance than the purchase of them" (Brummel, "Care," 15). Department store stock, advertisements, and advice such as this suggest that for the fashionable middle-class bachelor (who lacked the valets employed by the upper classes), the purchase and care of clothing had become a time-consuming task.

As the variety of available goods increased, department stores found the ready-made clothing market to be an attractive and profitable lure for male shoppers. Ready-made clothing had been available since the eighteenth century but had been worn mainly by the military and the lower classes.[10] Wider acceptance was slow at first, but the advent of the department store, along with the invention of the sewing machine in the 1850s, accelerated both the production and the popularity of ready-mades among the middle classes in the second half of the nineteenth century. An 1860 promotional pamphlet distributed by the prominent Victorian clothier E. Moses and Son made the (probably accurate) claim that 80 percent of

PRICES.

		£	s.	d.
No. 1 — Size 3 ft. 6 ins., Basswood	.. ..	4	4	0
„ 1 — Do. 3 ft. 6 ins., Walnut or Ash	..	6	6	0
„ 2 — Do. 4 ft. ditto.	..	7	16	0
„ 3 — Do. 3 ft. 6 ins. ditto.	..	8	3	6
„ 4 — Do. 3 ft. 6 ins. ditto.	..	10	10	0
„ 5 — Do. 4 ft. 6 ins. ditto.	..	13	10	0

Figure 2.5. Men's wardrobes and dressers featured in December 1898 *Fashion* (Brummel, "Care") (permission British Library)

Britain's population had purchased ready-made clothing. Ready-made clothing items played a vital role in the success of the department stores, being perfectly suited to the large-scale stores' philosophy of moving goods quickly and in large quantities. Department stores began producing and selling their own ready-to-wear items, as well as partially made clothing to be completed at home or by a dressmaker, and "entire battalions of affluent customers deserted to the ready-made camp, calling on a tailor only for dress or fitted wear" (Chenoune, 69). Ready-made suits were widely available beginning in the 1860s, and at the turn of the century, most department stores offered a wide range of ready-to-wear men's and boys' outfitting (Breward, *Culture*, 172–74; Jefferys, 312).

The success of ready-made clothing struck a major blow to the tailoring industry by making affordable and stylish menswear available to a much larger number of British males. A combination of cheap competition from East End sweatshops, advancements in mass production technologies, a decline in conventional tailoring craftsmanship, and a series of labor strikes in the 1890s severely disabled traditional tailoring and provided a wide-open opportunity for the department stores to pick up new business.[11] Many department stores seized an even greater share of the market by opening their own bespoke departments. By 1900, Harrods had opened a tailoring department headed by an "Expert Cutter always on Premises to take Measures," and its catalogue boasted, "Every care taken with detail and a Perfect Fit absolutely guaranteed in every Order" (*Harrods General Catalogue*, 1900, 1313). The 1903 catalogue reports that the "Gentlemen's Tailoring" department had been "extensively enlarged and consists of commodious Show Rooms" to provide military uniforms from regulation patterns and a "new and varied assortment of Coatings, Trouserings, Homespuns, Tweeds, Serges and West of England Suitings to select from, patterns of which, together with self-measurement forms, can be sent by return post when requested" (*Harrods General Catalogue*, 1903, 907).

Not every department store offered tailor-made articles, but by 1900 nearly all had moved into creating environments devoted to cultivating and catering to the male market. While both William Leach and Bill Lancaster claim that "Men's Shops" did not really take off until the 1920s and '30s (Leach, "Transformations," 331) and James Bavington Jefferys contends that "the stores as a whole were not very successful in attracting men shoppers," most menswear departments had been established decades earlier and had—if not flourished—at least expanded in both size and number during the decades surrounding the turn of the century (313). Some department stores, such as Lewis's, sprang from the men's clothing business, and several other major stores, including Whiteley's, Debenham and Freebody's, and Barker's, had expanded into menswear by the 1870s (Adburgham, *Shops*, 153, 145, 163). Harrods did not open its own "Gentleman's Outfitting" department until 1894, with the store's expansion along Hans Crescent, but then pursued the men's market vigorously. By the early 1900s, its ready-made lines and personal tailoring services offered a full range of men's items from military uniforms to motoring topcoats. A 1911 promotional brochure outlined the attractions of "Harrods as a Man's Store": "Harrods have devoted very careful attention to the development of the Men's Departments. They have a high-class Tailoring Department, employing expert cutters and workers; a Ready-made Department which sells ready-made clothing of the best standard, most of which is made in Harrods own workrooms by their regular tailors, and which is stocked in such a great variety of sizes that almost any man can be satisfactorily fitted in a few minutes" (fig. 2.6; *Wonderful*, 11).

Figure 2.6. "Harrods as a Man's Store" (*Wonderful*, 11) (courtesy Company Archive, Harrods Limited, London)

Tailoring shops had always existed as hermetically masculine domains. However, the department store was a decidedly more heterosocial environment and perhaps more immediately associated, to the Victorian male mind, with feminine pursuits. While department stores were well-known sites of female employment and activity and attracted a variety of eager and flirtatious male voyeurs, flaneurs, mashers, and suitors, the belief persisted among merchants that men avoided patronizing the large shops. Department stores therefore worked aggressively to attract middle-class male patrons by affirming their masculinity at every turn. Harrods insisted it was "very popular with gentlemen" and strove to increase that popularity by providing posh smoking and club rooms—spaces that were designed to replicate other familiar masculine environments. Harrods' "Gents' Club Room" was modeled after the exclusive gentlemen's clubs of the West End, "furnished," according to its own publicity, "in the style of the Georgian period carried out in richly carved and moulded mahogany" with a large fireplace and plenty of thick chairs that invited male patrons to linger (fig. 2.7; *Wonderful*, 11; quoted in Adburgham, *Shops*, 273).

Debenhams similarly featured a men's smoking room and gentlemen's cloak room, and its men's department declared, "The distinctive features of our tailor-made costumes are the smart cut and the perfect tailoring given by the men tailors" (Corina, 67, 68). William Whiteley's, the self-proclaimed "Universal Provider," attempted to lure male customers by offering a daily shave with an annual subscription to its hairdressing department, and the *Draper's Record* reported that a department store in Blackpool advertised a private men's room with newspapers and free cigars and coffee (Lambert, *Universal*, 181; Lancaster, 182). Selfridges was perhaps most aggressive of all in targeting the male consumer and devoted much of

Figure 2.7. "The Gentlemen's Club at Harrods" (*Wonderful*, 2) (courtesy Company Archive, Harrods Limited, London)

its advertising to luring the men into the reputedly feminine department store. Much of the advertising rhetoric and promotional techniques employed by department stores to attract male customers nevertheless continued to marginalize and mute their consumption by emphasizing the ease with which men could purchase items and leave the store as soon as possible. Most men's departments tended to be located near side entrances of stores, in the belief that men wished to minimize the duration and public nature of their shopping. Harrods' "Gent's Hosiery," "Gent's Hats," "Tailoring," and "Gent's Boots" departments were clustered in small asymmetrical rooms at Hans Crescent Entrance No. 5 on the ground floor rather than the more public main entrances along Brompton Road (figs. 2.8 and 2.9; *Harrods General Catalogue,* 1909, 4). However, while the store's "Trunks," "Sad-

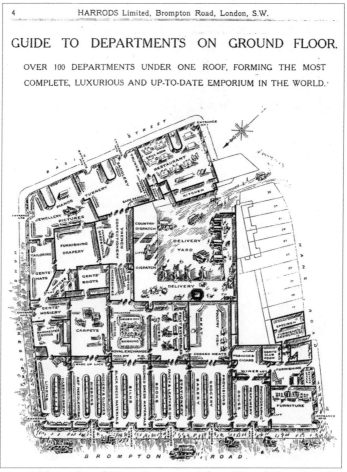

Figure 2.8. Floor plan of Harrods—ground floor (*Harrods General Catalogue,* 1909, 4) (courtesy Company Archive, Harrods Limited, London)

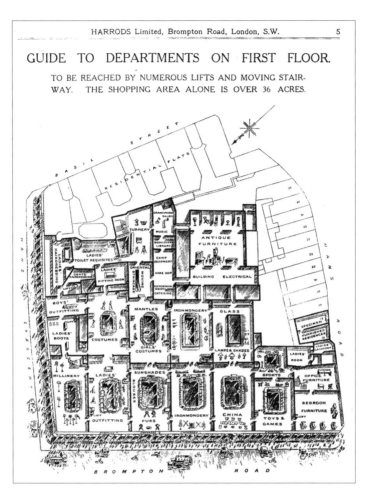

GUIDE TO DEPARTMENTS ON FIRST FLOOR.

TO BE REACHED BY NUMEROUS LIFTS AND MOVING STAIR-
WAY. THE SHOPPING AREA ALONE IS OVER 36 ACRES.

Figure 2.9. Floor plan of Harrods—first floor (*Harrods General Catalogue,*
1909, 5) (courtesy Company Archive, Harrods Limited, London)

dlery," and "Indiarubber Goods" departments—what Harrods' 1911 promotional
brochure *The Wonderful Development of Harrods in Twenty-One Years* calls a "magnificent
centre" for men—were also located near an entrance, they were situated at Entrance No. 2 on Basil Street on the east side (*Wonderful*, 11). The gentlemen's club
was also located on the ground floor, next to the tobacco department, but near
the southwest corner on Hans Road (*Harrods General Catalogue*, 1909, 4). That Harrods' departments and facilities for men were located in three different areas in
completely different corners of the first floor[12] was perhaps the result of the in-
cremental and haphazard evolution of Harrods and many other department
stores that grew in fits and starts by expanding into adjacent buildings. However,

such an arrangement would have required many male customers to pass through the full length of the store to complete their shopping errands. While it can be argued that the separate access doors, along with the rugged and masculine décor of the men's shops, only reinforced the gendered distinctions between men's and women's consumption, the department stores nevertheless succeeded in inviting middle-class men to venture fully into the physical and psychological spaces of modern consumption.

In March 1909—the same month Selfridges opened on Oxford Street—*Punch* printed a cartoon by C. Wallis Mills depicting a dismayed male shopper being greeted at the entrance of a department store by its overeager and officious staff (fig. 2.10). As uniformed doormen take his hat and cane, frock-coated shop assistants bow deferentially, and a shoeshine boy enthusiastically attends to his shoes. One sign posted at the entrance offers "Free breakfast, luncheon, tea, and dinner to all our customers," while another declares, "We are doing this because we love you so." The cartoon's caption reads, "COMFORT IN SHOPPING IS ALL VERY WELL, BUT THIS SORT OF THING IS A BIT EMBARRASSING WHEN ONE HAS ONLY COME TO BUY A COLLAR-STUD." Perhaps Mills's portrait was a slight exaggeration, and it implies a possible backlash against the aggressive enticements employed by department stores to court male customers; after all, the poor shopper seems to express some *dis*comfort at the lavish attention he is receiving. In any case, what is significant is that the men's market was recognized and actively cultivated by department stores. The modern large-scale stores were particularly instrumental in the construction of males as consumers in the way they moved the site of male consumption—for men outside of the upper classes, anyway—from the private and intimate small tailoring shop to the large and very public and heterosocial arena of the middle-class urban department store.

The Marketing of the Male Body and Male Self-Display

Writing of the symbiotic commercial relationship that had emerged between masculinity and goods in Britain during the 1980s and '90s, Frank Mort observes that male sexuality is produced through commodities: "Whether jeans, hair-gel, aftershave or whatever. . . . It was the display of the body *through the product* that was sexy." Modern television and print ads that linger on compartmentalized images of denim hugging thighs, the perfect fit of a finely tailored suit, or the curve of a watch on a French-cuffed wrist evoke "fetishized and narcissistic display—a visual

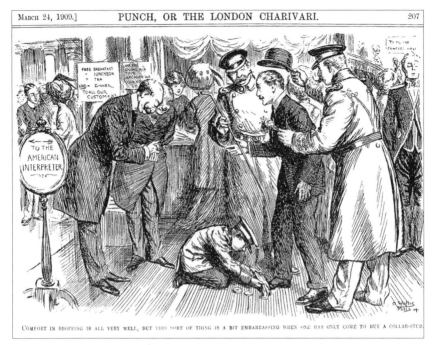

COMFORT IN SHOPPING IS ALL VERY WELL, BUT THIS SORT OF THING IS A BIT EMBARRASSING WHEN ONE HAS ONLY COME TO BUY A COLLAR-STUD.

Figure 2.10. "Comfort in shopping is all very well, but this sort of thing is a bit embarrassing when one has only come to buy a collar-stud" (C. Wallis Mills, *Punch*, 24 March 1909, 207)

erotica. These are bodies to be looked at (by oneself and other men?) through fashion codes and the culture of style" ("Boy's," 201). Jon Stratton argues that until very recently, advertising avoided presentations of the male body as much as possible, keeping it "hidden, invisible," and that the goods most popularly accepted by men—such as cars, tools, cigarettes, and alcohol—have been those associated not with body image but rather with more vaguely defined masculine self-image (185). He contends that the display of the male body in advertising began only in the late 1960s, pointing out that the first male nude used in an advertisement appeared in 1967 (187). Mort, Sean Nixon, and Tim Edwards all cite the famous 1986 Levi's 501 "bath" and "launderette" television ads featuring model Nick Kamen[13] as the symbolic start of the popular commercial sexualization (and fetishization) of men's bodies and their relationship to consumer goods in ways that only women's bodies had been subject to previously.

Yet, as we have seen, fully a century before, advertisers and marketers actively strove to masculinize goods, to create intimate connections between products and male consumers, between goods and male bodies. An 1885 Cadbury advertisement from *Punch* magazine depicts a privileged gentleman in recreational dress (white trousers, short-sleeved shirt, boater hat, sweater cast over his shoulders) enjoying cocoa, while he and his seated female companion watch a boat race taking place just out of the frame (fig. 2.11). The man stands in the foreground, his all-white sporting outfit set against a background of mostly blacks and grays, emphasizing his physical prominence. While his companion reclines languidly, he is all straight lines and right angles. His pose is clearly one of confident, even aggressive, male sexuality: one leg propped up on a chair, prominent buttocks, chest thrust forward, bare muscular arms (which appear tightly flexed even as he holds his cup of cocoa), long sideburns, and a whiskbroom mustache. In ways strikingly familiar to a modern audience raised on advertising, the advertisement conflates consumer and sexual desires—appealing to female viewers who want the man, appealing to male viewers who want to look like the man, and inducing both to want cocoa.

The commercial relationship between "sexuality and goods" operates in two directions: advertisers employ sexual imagery to make products appealing to men, and men use goods to make themselves sexually appealing, as an extension of their sexuality. In other words, bodies make products sexy, and products make bodies sexy. Advertisements such as this one for Cadbury's Cocoa demonstrate how nineteenth-century audiences were invited to gaze upon the spectacle of the male body—to acknowledge the physical, sexual presence of the male form. Late-Victorian advertisers, as well as department stores and the other tools of the consumer industry, served to create a culture increasingly focused on goods and visual display. Between 1860 and 1914, the commercial discourse of merchants sought to expand middle-class men's variety of sartorial choices as well as their interest in self-display in ways not always openly recognized within the strict confines of the Great Masculine Renunciation. Advertisers and social commentators promoted a more open, publicly acceptable relationship between men and goods and particularly between men's bodies and the clothes that covered them. As the period marked a growing public awareness and cultivation of the male body, men were presented as both subjects and objects, as both viewers and displayers of visible, sexual bodies.

The growing variety and affordability of fashion for the middle classes enabled men in greater numbers to use clothing to decorate and call attention to their bodies. While the popular and widespread adoption of the three-piece suit (which I discuss at length in chapter 5) made middle-class men's basic dress more uniform in one way, this is not to say that it made men's clothing necessarily more

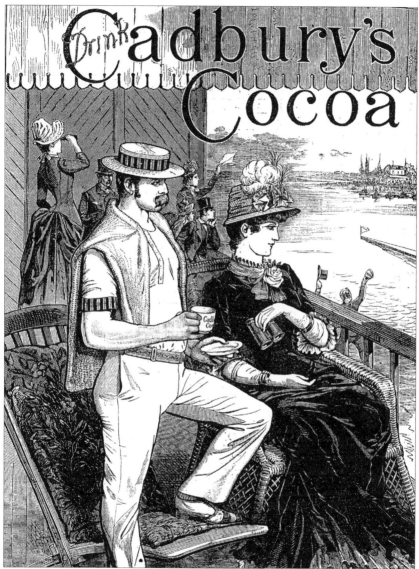

Figure 2.11. Cadbury's Cocoa advertisement (*Punch,* 13 June 1885)

drab or bland, as earlier critics have claimed. In fact, the late Victorian age marked a significant return to ornamentation and fashionable extremes in men's costume. For example, the *Gentleman's Magazine of Fashion* noted in 1888 that embroidery on men's dress suits and waistcoats was becoming fashionable ("Observations," 3). Waistcoats became a particularly popular canvas on which to express one's personal style in the 1890s, and the cut of men's jackets was altered to reveal as much as possible of the waistcoat underneath. "It is the waistcoat in which a man can express his individuality, nowadays, whereas it used to be the tie alone," Mrs. C. E. Humphry writes in *Etiquette for Every Day* (1902). "Some very surprising waistcoats are to be seen, even on well-dressed men" (290). In 1890 the *Tailor's Review* declared that "there is a reactionary return in the direction of the mode of the distant 'Days of the Dandies,' when the waistcoat afforded a field for display of taste and fancy which has since been denied it" ("In Praise of Waistcoats," 88). Above the waistcoat, the thick neckcloths and high upturned collars that had been the height of fashion earlier in the century were echoed in the soaring starched collar at the turn of the century. More form-revealing, body-hugging lines became popular in the last decade of the nineteenth century as well, provoking many fashion writers to hail the return to the "panache" and rococo tastes of the styles of the eighteenth-century aristocracy (Breward, *Hidden*, 36–37).

"Perhaps one of the most difficult things for us to do is to choose a notable and joyous dress for men," Oscar Wilde observed in a lecture during his 1882 American tour. "There would be more joy in life if we were to accustom ourselves to use all the beautiful colours we can in fashioning our own clothes" ("House," 162). Though he was hardly a spokesman for normative Victorian male sartorial display, Wilde's recommendations were nevertheless increasingly adopted in the years that followed. As department stores and clothiers expanded their stock in the decades surrounding the turn of the century, the variety of socially acceptable colors, patterns, and fabrics for men expanded in turn. Large checks were popular for informal suits in the 1890s, and striped flannels were long regarded as stylish on both trousers and lounge suits (Foster, 129; *Clothes*, 191; *Cutter's*, 48). Karen Baclawski notes that "crazy patchwork using scraps of rich fabrics enjoyed a vogue at the end of the nineteenth century" (194), and pale pinks and mauves were the mode in the early years of the twentieth century (Laver, *Dandies*, 14). Along with the eye-catching waistcoats emerged colored shirts in pale blues, yellows, and pinks. "You can get them in almost every colour under the sun," declares *Clothes and the Man* (164); worn with a detachable white collar, they were a perfectly acceptable complement to the modern city lounge suit (Humphry, *Etiquette*, 283). Banded socks were popular during the late nineteenth century, and brightly colored ones were commonly worn from 1900 until the First World War (Baclawski, 195).

What had once been the sole domain of the dandy became permissible, even socially desirable, for the "average" middle-class Englishman at the turn of the century. And the popular literature of the period reflects the growing public attention paid to men's fashionable consumption. *Clothes and the Man* reveals that social attitudes regarding men's public interest in fashion had undergone a dramatic shift. This book's author, the men's fashion editor of the newspaper *To-Day,* known as the "Major," asserts in the introduction, "Some dozens of readers of *To-Day* write to me every week to ask questions about men's clothes" (2). In response, *Clothes and the Man* served as an invaluable guidebook aimed squarely at middle-class men. Its advice is conversational and good-natured and always conscious of cost, offering excruciatingly detailed and methodical instruction on what articles of clothing to buy, how to have them fitted and made, when and where to wear them, and how to care for them. Of its 196 pages, the book devotes 46 pages to coats and another 42 to trousers.[14] The proper purchase and wearing of tie pins merits 8 full pages of discussion. This was quite a change from the markedly vague advice offered by earlier etiquette manuals and their repeated assertions that the true gentleman was never to think of fashion. While, of course, men's interest in clothing and personal display had never really vanished, what was new was the widespread public acknowledgment and social acceptability of masculine fashionable desire. *Clothes and the Man* reveals a new rhetorical arena—the flip side of the Great Masculine Renunciation—in which men's open interest in fashion was affirmed. "It is . . . a mistake to suppose that a well-dressed man is a fop," declares the "Major" (*Clothes,* 16). At the turn of the century, dressing well and cultivating one's appearance could be the prerogative of every respectable man.

Display appealed profoundly to late-Victorian men, the fashion press insisted, and the qualities that had once defined the dandy's problematic class and gender status were becoming more and more acceptable and mainstream to middle-class men. "Men of good form are blossoming forth like butterflies," declares *Fashion.* "The chrysalis has been shed, and the gorgeous creature has emerged" (Brummel, *Dress News,* June 1898, 20). *Fashion's* choice of metaphor is particularly revealing, as it demonstrates how the visual spectacle of dandies, once pejoratively referred to as "butterflies," had been absorbed into mainstream masculinity (Chenoune, 32). These instructive texts imagined a fashionable middle-class man who increasingly fulfilled the essayist Thomas Carlyle's summary of the dandy's sole object: "that you would recognise his existence; would admit him to be a living object; or even failing this, a visual object, or thing that will reflect rays of light. Your silver or your gold . . . he solicits not; simply the glance of your eyes. Understand his mystic significance, or altogether miss and misinterpret it; do but look at him, and he is contented" (198).

In the 1900 novel *Kipps*, H. G. Wells's working-class protagonist exhibits an interest in cultivating and exhibiting publicly his physical appearance. The good-natured albeit simple-minded Arthur Kipps was raised—not insignificantly—in his uncle's general merchandise store and takes a job in a draper's shop. In weighted language that makes explicit the young man's growing awareness of his public physical self, Wells describes his hero's indoctrination into life as an object of display. In Kipps's late teens,

> his costume . . . began to interest him more; he began to realise himself as a visible object, to find an interest in the costume-room mirrors and the eyes of the girl-apprentices.
>
> In this he was helped by counsel and example. Pearce, his immediate senior, was by way of being what was called a Masher, and preached his cult. During slack times grave discussions about collars, ties, the cut of trouser-legs, and the proper shape of a boot-tow, were held in the Manchester department. In due course Kipps went to a tailor, and his short jacket was replaced by a morning coat with tails. Stirred by this, he purchased at his own expense three stand-up collars to replace his former turn-down ones. They were nearly three inches high, higher than those Pearce wore, and they made his neck quite sore and left a red mark under his ears. . . . So equipped, he found himself fit company even for this fashionable apprentice, who had now succeeded Minton in his seniority. (47–48)

Here Wells depicts what might be described as a sartorial "mirror phase," in which the young Kipps experiences a sudden recognition of himself as a "visible object," subject to the scrutiny of the opposite sex and capable of being adorned and made more sexually attractive through fashionable goods. Realizing that his social identity and sexual success will be greatly defined by "the eyes of the girl-apprentices," he immediately seeks to transform himself through fashionable clothes and grooming supplies into a visually appealing image. Further, Kipps illustrates J. C. Flugel's assertion that "it is comparatively easy for the commercial influences to exploit Narcissism in the interests of fashion" (145). According to Robert Bocock, "Consumption built around the human body—its attractiveness to the self as much as to others; its sexual and erotic appeal; its use as a means of expressing a sense of identity—has become a process in which desire is embedded, in which major meanings are located" (102–03). The experiences of growing up—literally—among goods and working in a department store have endowed Kipps with a heightened awareness of appearance and materialism, for they have put him into constant, direct contact with both consumable goods and consumers. While Wells's depiction of Kipps was intended as a critique of the working class, his protagonist represents—in only slightly exaggerated form—the condition of most of England's urban population at the turn of the twentieth century: he has been born and raised within a technologically sophisticated culture of mass consumption and has merged his body with the consumable good, rendering his very body an object to be desired and consumed by others.

In the increasingly visual culture of late-nineteenth-century Britain, men were publicly acknowledged to possess a physical, visible self in ways that had formerly been suppressed. This public visibility often manifested itself in a more open acknowledgment of the sexuality and sexualization of men's clothing and appearance through women's eyes. In 1830 William Cobbett's *Advice to Young Men* had criticized male display, arguing that women "are much too penetrating to draw their conclusions solely from the outside show of a man" and urging men to cultivate their inner qualities, which women would perceive regardless of one's outer façade. "Female eyes are, in such cases, very sharp; they can discover beauty though half hidden by beard, and even by dirt, and surrounded by rags: and, take this as a secret worth half a fortune to you, that women, however personally vain they may be themselves, despise personal vanity in men" (14–15). Cobbett's counsel reflects the conventional sexual dichotomy, implying that women are preoccupied with finery—and can be judged accurately, at least in part, by their attire—while men's desire to be looked at and admired for their physical appearance is vain and immoral and will be punished by women who reject their foppish show. To be sure, such advice was advocated by etiquette literature throughout the Victorian era, and certainly many men had always failed to heed such admonitions, but by the turn of the century, advice in many conduct manuals had radically shifted in tone, offering open acknowledgments of and apologies for men's desire to attract the opposite sex through physical appearance. "It is the female 'appreciation' we men all make for" is the confession in *Best Dressed Man* (1892), "not such as the male unwillingly accords. What reasoning man gives thought to the value, sometimes quite fictitious, put upon him by his own kind? The best of us never gets full value from his fellows. The least worthy not seldom gets more than this from woman. Therefore it is that men of intelligence always play for the better stake" (32). In February 1905, *Fashion* contributor Bessie O'Connor declared,

> Some men are vain enough to imagine that neither men nor woman [*sic*] pay any attention to the clothes of a man. There never was a greater mistake than this. Surely women, who are constantly studying the cut, the lines and the fashions of their own clothes, necessarily observe the cut and the fashions of men's habiliments. . . . Every woman notices whether a man is well dressed or not, and whether he is careful of his personal appearance. . . . I have a critical eye for the garb of the male sex, and I can assure my readers I am not by any means alone in this respect. (5–7)

Turn-of-the-century men cultivated the attentions of the opposite sex through a growing freedom in, and variety of, socially acceptable sartorial choices that accentuated the male body and celebrated masculine sexuality. In particular, men of the later decades of the nineteenth century had moved toward decidedly form-fitting, body-revealing styles. The *Cutters' Gazette of Fashion* announced in 1893 that "the tendency is certainly towards close fitting garments" (48), and *Fashion* noted in 1898 "a decided tendency to shapeliness" ("What," April 1898, 6). Fitted frock coats, fitted jackets, fitted pants, and "neck-brace type collars" were the mode among all classes, and suits emphasized longer and more muscular torsos, padded shoulders, and tight waists (Chenoune, 92). The English-French *Journal des tailleurs* complained in 1879, "The absurd fashion for tight clothes now in vogue has reached the point where you no longer know where to put your wallet and handkerchief" (quoted in Chenoune, 89). The *Tailor's Review* went even further, suggesting that form-fitting men's trousers left little to the (female) imagination:

> Women are beginning to object to and discuss the garments of men. They say it is time there was a reform in men's wearing apparel; that pantaloons form a fashion which should be subjected to immediate consideration; that the spectacle of males attired in a garment so closely approximating the exact shape of the legs is not at all relished by feminines of high moral character; that the wearing of trousers, as now designed, is neither aesthetic in principle nor *en rapport* with the proprieties that should dominate civilized society. . . . If men are shocked by the

sight of a lady in tights, or *au naturel*, is it not to be conjectured that women regard with loathing the current habit of mankind of clothing the legs in an envelope that reveals only too acutely outlines that might be left to the imagination? If it is improper for women to apparel themselves so as to afford a correct idea of the proportions and contours of their nether extremities, is it not in equally bad taste for masculines to indulge in that exposure? (108)

Interestingly, the "Major" suggests similar disapproval of extremes in male display by women who guard old standards of male sartorial reserve when describing the body-slimming illusions performed by the strategically placed rows of buttons on a double-breasted waistcoat:

> Some double-breasted waistcoats are made with the two rows of buttons set wide apart across the chest and gradually getting closer, till they nearly meet at the bottom of the waistcoat. There are advantages to be derived from wearing such a waistcoat. They tend to make your chest appear larger than it really is, and the two rows of buttons meeting at the bottom of the waistcoat make your waist appear a trifle smaller than it really is. If your wife tells you that a man has no business to think about having a waist, you can retort that primitive man had a waist considerably smaller than the waist of primitive woman. She won't like that. (*Clothes*, 64)

This dramatic shift in conduct manual rhetoric suggests that the overarching Victorian societal mores no longer depended on a strict gender dichotomy that distinguished women's vain preoccupation with finery and physical beauty from men's more substantial and cerebral pursuits. Men's and women's vanity in personal appearance is implicitly equated in their mutual desire for a slimmer waistline. Yet both texts represent it as a conflict in which women disapprove of male sexual display. One wonders, however, if the *Tailor's Review* accurately represents women's response to men's tight-fitting trousers. Male legs were widely regarded as "the chief male erogenous zone for nineteenth-century women," and many men paid particular attention to the development and showcasing of their legs (McDowell, 76). In George Meredith's *Egoist* (1879), for example, Mrs. Mountstuart spends a great deal of time relishing Willoughby's legs, concluding, "In spite of men's hateful modern costume, you see he has a leg" (13). The author's lengthy description of the ladies' regard for Willoughby's lower appendages makes palpable the sexual power that a well-shaped pair of male legs could have over a female heart:

> The leg of the born cavalier is before you; and obscure it as you will, dress degenerately, there it is for ladies who have eyes. You *see* it; or, you see *he* has it. . . . Many, with a good show of reason, throw the accent upon *leg*. And the ladies knew for a fact that Willoughby's leg was exquisite; he had a cavalier court-suit in his wardrobe. Mrs. Mountstuart signified that the leg was to be seen because it was a burning leg. There it is, and it *will* shine through. He has the leg of Rochester, Buckingham, Dorset, Suckling; the leg that smiles, that winks, is obsequious to you, yet perforce of beauty self-satisfied; that twinkles to a tender midway between imperiousness and seductiveness, audacity and discretion; between "you shall worship me" and "I am devoted to you"; is your lord, your slave, alternately and in one. It is a leg of ebb and flow and high-tide ripples. Such a leg, when it has done with pretending to retire, will walk straight into the hearts of women. Nothing so fatal to them. (13)

In 1850, Adam Blenkinsop's *Shilling's-Worth of Advice on Manners, Behaviour and Dress* had warned, "Never wear anything tight," because "[b]y tight dressing you reveal the reality" (22). It is doubtful that fashionable youth with a preference for tight-fitting trousers sought to achieve any closer semblance of reality; certainly the man with the narrowing waistcoat buttons did not. Indeed, the decades surrounding the turn of the century also saw an increased use—or at the very least a more publicized use—of cosmetic and body-shaping products by men that served, in Hollander's words, to "fictionalize" the male body (32). If the evidence of tailoring commentators and advertisers is to be believed, these items were no longer solely the affectations of effeminate dandies but had come to be worn by a large number of middle-class professional men. Corsets seem to have been particularly popular. The *Tailor and Cutter* reported in 1884 that "a large number of our fashionable men are going in for stays or corsets" and ten years later that "the corset is worn by thousands of men" (quoted in Cunnington and Cunnington, 284, 344). In 1880, renowned English dressmaker Charles Frederick Worth frequently ran an advertisement in *Punch*, announcing that his company had "added

WORTH et CIE.

WORTH ET CIE. have now added a department for Gentlemen, and every class of Corset, surgical, spinal, for corpulency, and riding, made to measure.

The Ladies' department is still carried on as before.

The Jersey Corset, a speciality of this house, adapted to the Jersey Costume, and also present style of dress.

CORSETS (patented) made for all figures, also for Embonpoint, Deformities, Curvature, and Spinal Complaints.

Instructions for Country Orders and Self Measurement on application to

WORTH ET CIE

4, HANOVER STREET, REGENT STREET, W.

Figure 2.12. Worth et Cie corset advertisement (*Punch*, 31 July 1880)

a department for Gentlemen, and every class of Corset, surgical, spinal, for corpulency, and riding, made to measure" (fig. 2.12). Twenty-five years later, another advertisement for Worth's Corsets was directed to "Officers and Gentlemen" (fig. 2.13). Both advertisements depict an erect, broad-chested, mustachioed man modeling the product—a figure of overt masculinity clearly intended to reassure male customers by dispelling any connotations of effeminacy in the wearing of a corset.

Advertising and department stores also made available and affordable an enormous variety of soaps, colognes, hair dyes, powders, and other articles marketed to men as a means of achieving and maintaining an attractive, youthful gender and class performance. The ever-expanding size of gentlemen's leather dressing cases—depicted in Harrods catalogues filled with a host of combs, brushes, scissors, files, and bottles—suggests that more and more toiletries and other accessories were required (figs. 2.14 and 2.15; *Victorian*, 1061, 1245). In 1859, *Habits of Good Society* had discouraged the use of "violet-powder" after shaving, "now very

"*He that buckles him in my belt cannot live in less.*"—2 Henry IV., v. 2.

Officers

and

Gentlemen

Can command the free attendance of our fitter at their London address when requiring

Corsets

or

Belts

Price List and Measurement Forms Post Free.

WORTH'S CORSETS Ltd., (Dept. B.)
3, HAMSELL STREET, LONDON, E.C.
(Late New Bond Street.)

Figure 2.13. Worth's Corsets advertisement in (*Punch*, 4 January 1905, v)

common among well-dressed men," because "it is almost always visible, and gives an unnatural look to the face" (114).[15] But advertisers worked rigorously to counter associations with femininity through strategically worded advertising copy that appropriated women's beauty concerns and masculinized them. A Williams' Shaving Soap advertisement of 1895, featuring an illustration of a man at a dressing mirror scrutinizing his skin through a magnifying glass, declares,

GENTLEMEN'S FITTED TRAVELLING BAGS, SUIT CASES, &c.

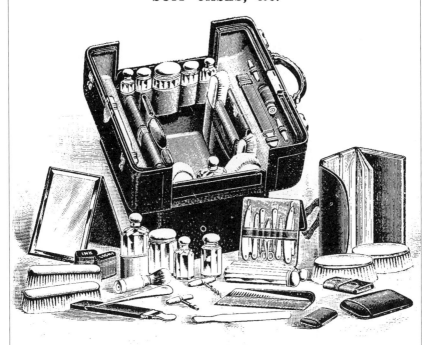

Gentleman's Monitor Dressing Bag.

No. 3390.—Dark green levant morocco, 16 in. with outside pocket, frame with registered lock, patent spring clips, lined maroon roan, fitted with 2 ivory military hair, hat, and cloth brushes, ivory paper knife, strop with ivory handle, ivory turnback Badger shaving brush, metal shoe lift with button-hook, large horn comb in case, 5 bottles with sterling silver dome tops, flask with silver screw tops and electro-plated cup, large folding mirror, board with 2 ivory razors, pair nail scissors, button-hook and nail file, barrel-shaped corkscrew and railway key, blotter with ivory silver-mounted penholder and pencil, oval ink and light boxes, cigar and cigarette cases, housewife, tooth and nail brushes. Price, £16 7s. 6d.

Same as above, but with ebony fittings, £11 10s.

All the above are delivered Carriage Free, subject to the Conditions set forth on page 4.

Figure 2.14. Gent's fitted traveling bag in Harrods Catalogue, 1895 (*Victorian Shopping,* 1061)

GENTS' DRESSING CASES—*continued.*

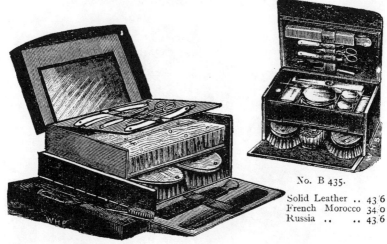

No. B 435.

Solid Leather .. 43/6
French Morocco 34/0
Russia 43/6

No. B 14.

No. B 14   Solid Leather 35/6

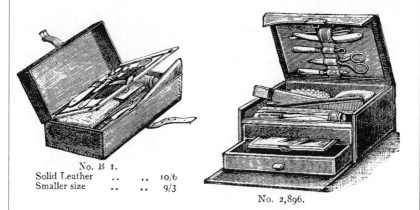

No. B 1.

Solid Leather 10/6
Smaller size 9/3

No. 2,896.

No. 2,896   Covered Dark Red French Morocco, Plated Handle and Lock,
with Cutlery and Brushes, complete as shewn 18/0

**All the above are delivered Carriage Free, subject to the Conditions set
forth on page 4.**

Figure 2.15. Gent's dressing cases from Harrods Catalogue, 1895 (*Victorian Shopping,* 1245)

"Pores—! Do you realize what they are—how *numerous*, how very *hungry* and thirsty? Little mouths of the skin—constantly drinking—drinking—eating—eating—everything within reach" (fig. 2.16). The ad's subject matter and tone seem to depict conventionally female beauty concerns—skin, complexion, the delicate minutiae of pores. But the text turns decidedly masculine and aggressive: "Nothing comes nearer the skin than your SHAVING SOAP—! You apply it with the brush—and, as it were, *force it* into those willing little mouths." While the actual persuasiveness of advertisements such as these is unclear—and precise sales figures do not exist—men's soaps, shaving supplies, and toilet powders had become big business by the turn of the century. At the same time, beards were becoming unfashionable, meaning that more men needed to shave more often, yet this is a chicken-and-egg relationship, and determining whether marketers drove this change or merely responded to it seems impossible. Either way, the purchase and use of all these consumer goods transformed the late-Victorian middle-class man into an object on public display. This was a dramatic and significant reversal of the notions of male sartorial invisibility that had dominated Victorian rhetoric on masculinity only decades before. The commercial cultivation of male display helped bring about the public re-emergence of the male body as aesthetically pleasing and sexually desirable. It also transformed the male body into an object to be modified, enhanced, and decorated through consumer goods.

Figure 2.16. Williams' Shaving Soaps advertisement (*Punch*, 23 February 1895)

Pores—!

Do you realize what they are—how *numerous*, how very *hungry* and thirsty? Little mouths of the skin—constantly drinking—drinking—eating—eating—everything within reach.

Nothing comes nearer the skin than your SHAVING SOAP — ! You apply it with the brush—and, as it were, *force it* into those willing little mouths. Is your Shaving Soap PURE ?

Are you using the famous—

"WILLIAMS'"
SHAVING SOAPS?

It is well to remember that for a good deal over HALF A CENTURY—these soaps have been made by the same firm—in the same place—and with the same scrupulous regard for every detail in manufacture.

It is worth something to know—that in the thousands of Tons of these Soaps—which have been sent all over the world —NOT ONE OUNCE of impure fats or other objectionable — dangerous matter — was ever contained.

Williams' Shaving Sticks—1/—
Williams' Shaving Tablets—6 d.

Sold by Chemists—Hairdressers and Perfumers, or mailed to any address on receipt of price in stamps, by THE J. B. WILLIAMS CO., 64 Great Russell Street, London, W. C.

By the end of the period, the consumer desires that Lydgate attempted to disguise by foisting them onto his wife had come to be presented as much more publicly acceptable, exercised in the public arena of the grand urban department store. The celebratory promotions exhorted by producers, merchants, and advertisers all clearly point to the cultivation of a growing awareness of men's visible, physical, sartorial selves that had emerged in England, becoming more socially accepted, more mainstream, more public, and more middle class by the turn of the century. This acceptance of male consumption and display, fueled by the emerging consumer culture industry, changed late-Victorian definitions of normative manhood in fundamental ways. Whether advertisers continued to insist on the distinctions between male and female purchasing habits or attempted to blur or obliterate those distinctions, the result was that men were beginning to consume to the same extent as women. Men were allowed access into formerly exclusively female spaces and activities, as their consumption moved out of the conventional, old-fashioned, small-scale, homosocial world of the tailor's shop into the modern, large-scale, heterosocial world of the department store. They were permitted to have a visual, physical, erotic self to be appraised by the public. All this marks significant shifts in both socioeconomics and constructions of masculinity. But it also suggests the tremendous cultural influence and reach of the new capitalist consumer machine that underpinned late-Victorian and early-twentieth-century Britain—a force so powerful that it could blur long-held and fiercely defended gender differences. Writing about late-twentieth-century male-directed commercial campaigns that were transforming the traditional macho man into a cosmetics counter–lurking clotheshorse, Antony Shugaar observes, "Sharp gender distinctions have floated away on a wave of cash, and cash trumps gender every time" (70). But such changes had begun well over a century ago, when the foundations of modern commodity culture helped overturn the Great Masculine Renunciation and transformed Britain's middle-class male into an eager consumer and the male body into a object of public display that could be altered, decorated, and even made into spectacle through goods purchased at the department store or tailor's shop.

3

"REALLY THERE IS MUCH MORE TO BE SAID ABOUT MEN'S FASHIONS THAN I HAD IMAGINED"

Fashion *and the Birth of the Men's Lifestyle Periodical*

> It seems to me that what is called in France the ugly sex (*le sexe laid*), has been left out in the cold too long. . . . Now, why should not the ugly sex have a fashion journal, or, if we cannot spare them a fashion journal all to themselves, surely we might allow them a department at least of our periodicals dealing with matters of costume.
>
> —Corisande, "Fashions for Men" (1879)

IN MARCH 1898, A MAGAZINE PREMIERED IN LONDON, HAILING itself as the first popular periodical on men's fashion (fig. 3.1). The new monthly was simply but appropriately titled *Fashion*, and its lively, breezy copy kept its readers abreast of the latest cuts and styles in men's garments, along with regular features on military dress and men's costume in current theatrical productions. In its first issue, *Fashion*'s founding editor, "Beau Brummel, Junr.," declared, "We have the pleasure to inform you that it is our intention to produce shortly a"

MONTHLY JOURNAL
of unique interest and value to the Tailoring and Allied Trades. This journal will not be of an exclusively technical tone, but will be based upon a requirement that has recently become a necessary adjunct to the demands which are now expected from producers of fashionable apparel.

We are aware that there are a number of papers in the field which talk to the manufacturer or producer from the point of view of the trades concerned, but there is none (at present) which advises the tailor, the hatter, the bootmaker, and the hosier from the point of view of the customer who purchases their productions, and who is therefore a much more important person to consider than the technical writer upon things already produced and established. ("Introduction," 1)

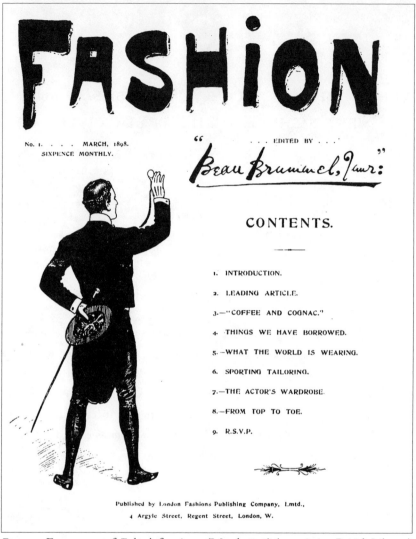

Figure 3.1. Front cover of *Fashion*'s first issue (March 1898) (permission British Library)

The debut of a periodical dedicated to men's fashions received widespread positive notice from its peers in the press, who almost unanimously declared that it was about time. "Man's turn has come at last!" extolled the *Morning Leader.* "No longer is woman to have sole claim to all the fashion papers!" The *Star* declared that *Fashion* rendered "an ancient wrong remedied, and a long-felt want supplied. . . . This is as it should be." And a reviewer for the *Western Press* remarked, "I am only surprised that such a paper has not appeared long before. Men need advice upon the art of dress almost more than women, judging by the mistakes they so frequently make in style, colour, and material" ("In Praise of 'Fashion,'" 15).

Fashion and general-interest magazines for women were plentiful in the Victorian era.[1] But within a highly patriarchal print culture that implicitly assumed a male audience, the notion of a magazine that consciously addressed men *as* men in the same way that women's magazines addressed their readers—that is, as fashion devotees and active consumers—was revolutionary. With a few failed exceptions,[2] previous periodicals devoted to men's fashion were predominantly professional journals for the tailoring trade.[3] Although a small handful of popular-interest periodicals—notably *To-Day* (1893–1905)[4]—offered brief items on men's costume, scholars generally agree that fashion and lifestyle periodicals for a popular male audience did not emerge in Europe and the United States until the 1920s and '30s. For example, Jill Greenfield, Sean O'Connell, and Chris Reid offer a fascinating study of *Men Only,* a British monthly that premiered in 1933. Valerie Steele cites *Adam: La Revue de l'Homme,* an upscale French magazine "devoted to men's sartorial style, with an emphasis on custom tailoring and fine accessories" that was popular from the 1920s through the '50s (Steele, 81). Christopher Breward agrees that fashion magazines for men did not emerge until the 1920s (*Culture,* 171), though in a later work he identifies one earlier example, *The Modern Man,* from the first decade of the twentieth century (*Hidden,* 180–81).

Fashion predates all these examples; its boast that it was "the first example of a permanently successful periodical wholly devoted to male attire, except tailors' technical journals" was widely supported by its contemporaries in the periodical press (Major, 12).[5] From its offices at 4 Argyll Street (near Oxford Circus), *Fashion* was published monthly by the London Fashions Publishing Company and edited by the appropriately pseudonymous "Beau Brummel, Junr."[6] ("Introduction," 1). It sold for 6p a copy, 7/6 for an annual subscription. Proclaiming itself "The West End Gentleman's Magazine and Dress Guide," the magazine offered monthly news on the latest styles of coats, lounge suits, hats, and personal effects, along with opinionated advice on the proper purchase, wear, care, and storage of these items. Its regular features included What the World Is Wearing, a monthly review of popular garments—particularly coats and suits—usually accompanied by small to full-size fashion plates, and From Head to Foot, which offered short items on the latest styles and cuts in garments, moving from hats to shoes. In Uniform and, later, Military Club Notes provided meticulous coverage of modes in British and Continental military attire, providing a fascinating record of a time in which officers' uniforms were still tailor-made and Europe's armies were making the awkward shift from vibrant blues and reds to the camouflage of earth-toned khakis. Often the longest article in the issue, Dress News Collected and Dissected (later retitled "Fashion's" Monthly Review of Men's Dress News) excerpted fashion news from other periodicals and then responded with outspoken relish. While fashion was always *Fashion*'s primary focus, the magazine frequently covered non-sartorial topics as well. Its original lead feature, Coffee and Cognac, often served as a forum for the columnist idiosyncratic pet peeves, criticizing noisy restaurant bands, people who arrive late to theatrical productions, and the difficulty of getting a "decent salad" in the city (Godfrey-Turner, February 1899, 4–6; Godfrey-Turner, May 1899, 3, 6–7; Godfrey-Turner, April 1900, 6). Later, Club Circles would cover popular recreational pursuits, society news, popular fads, and humorous tidbits. *Fashion* also paid some attention to sports, with occasional articles on polo, bicycling, and ping-pong, and in 1901–2 by posting Cricket and Racing Fixtures monthly.

Fashion's debut elicited great excitement within the publishing world, and the magazine expressed its gratitude for "the marvelous kindness of the Press," which had eagerly covered the young monthly's first steps (Godfrey-Turner, October 1899, 4–5). Much space during its first two years was devoted to reprinting (often at great length) complimentary reviews from its periodical peers. A full-page advertisement for *Fashion* featuring celebratory quotations from a lengthy list of other periodicals was repeated for months. Many of these reviews reiterated the *Morning Leader*'s sentiment that the time to recognize publicly men's fashionable display had come. "The newspaper market has always been flooded with journals of fashions for women," observed the *Critic*; "Now we have a serial of the kind for men" ("Critic," 7). The *Gentlewoman* enthused, "Really there is much more to be said about men's fashions than I had imagined, and that sprightly monthly, FASHION, under the editorship of 'Beau Brummel, Junr.,' has such a pleasant way of saying it, that I shall expect to see it in everyone's smoking-room" ("Gentlewoman," 23). Its fellow magazines and newspapers returned the favor, as *Fashion*'s coverage of men's fashions was regularly reprinted and critiqued in other periodicals, including *Punch*, *To-Day*, the *Daily Mail*, and *Lady's Pictorial*. *Fashion* was widely familiar among the American press as well, as its Dress News Collected and Dissected feature often excerpted American articles that make mention of its sartorial news.

By its own admission in its very first article, *Fashion* served in part the interests of the tailoring trade, and some of its advertisements were for publications and equipment valuable solely to tailors. But the magazine more accurately described its role when in 1902 it explained, "FASHION stands between the tailor and his 'client,' and it holds the hand of each" (Brummel, "Some," 5). Its copy was directed mainly to a general audience of male consumers, rather than producers, providing always-opinionated, never-technical news on current styles, ridiculous fads, and the best shops.[7] At the dawn of the twentieth century, *Fashion* laid out as its "New Century resolutions" the tenets that had guided the magazine for its first two years:

> To give its readers the best dress news from only the most reliable sources . . . ; to have its clothes article illustrated, as usual, by fashion figures which do not suggest the tailors' windows in the roads of Edgware, Euston, and Tottenham Court; to go on adding to the evidence in its Letter Book of its determination to refuse to encourage the clothiers who give fancy waistcoats away with ten-and-sixpenny trousers of "West End cut and finish" . . . ; to continue holding the military and sporting interests through monthly articles respectively written by an officer and war correspondent recently returned from South Africa, and a gentleman who hunts, golfs, cycles, and fishes . . . ; in short, to act faithfully up to the character given to it by the *Morning Post* in the words, "FASHION appeals to a special public, and meets its most exacting demands." (Godfrey-Turner, January 1901, 5)

Justifying and Acknowledging a Male Fashion Market

From its premiere issue, *Fashion* actively engaged in—indeed, served as—an ongoing public conversation on the cultural significance of male costume in late-Victorian Britain. As the first men's fashion magazine, *Fashion* initially struggled to justify its raison d'être, combating enduring notions that men took no interest in their costume and that male fashion simply did not exist. A correspondent observed that while "the red-headed girl carefully avoids certain colours which clash with the colour of her locks, and chooses those shades which tone down their vividness," the red-headed man does not, because "he has been taught that it is unmanly to take an interest in one's clothes" ("Our Friend," 23). Responding to an article in the *Lady's Realm* that contended that "a man is never to be seen reading a fashion paper," Beau Brummel, Junr., observed,

I have read the *Gentlewoman* at my club; . . . I have seen men, returning from the City by train, studying with interest—I may say enjoyment—the ladies' papers they have purchased for their wives at Smith's bookstalls; and . . . the windows of the *Lady's Pictorial* in the Strand arrest the substantial attention of almost as many male pedestrians as the windows of *Punch* in Fleet Street. I say also, if I may not be thought too rapacious for self-advertisement, that I have seen countless men (genuine West-Enders) reading FASHION—and have thought all the more of them in consequence! (Brummel, untitled, February 1899, 15)

When "Guinevere," the female fashion columnist for the *Referee*, dismissed male fashion writers by claiming, "The writers do not seem to realise that fashions for men are practically non-existent. So long as a man dresses quietly, and looks like a gentleman, it doesn't matter two pins what he wears," *Fashion* countered in a manner that skewered the paradox at the heart of her argument and of so many male-directed conduct books:

> There is something quite deliciously feminine, because so quaintly illogical, about "Guinevere's" concluding lines, "So long as a man dresses quietly, it doesn't matter two pins what he wears." If it doesn't matter two pins what he wears, why should he be called upon to dress quietly? Again, "so long as a man dresses quietly." Yes—so long as he does! But men who have no taste are apt to dress otherwise; and these men, coming across an article on male fashions, would most likely be reformed by it, and go about for ever after dressed with taste. (Brummel, From Head, April 1902, 12)

At the same time, however, many others among the periodical press expressed the conviction that men's fashion was worthy of notice and called for its own publication. The *Road* opined, "Women have, hitherto, exclusively secured the attention of the fashion publications; but why this should have been we have never been able to find out. Surely men are every bit as particular in their fads, fancies, and fussiness, and are just as worthy of consideration and assistance in the all-important matter of dress?" ("Road," 25). The *Court Journal* applauded *Fashion's* bold leap and declared that "many should be courageous enough to buy it," since "many have to struggle unassisted against their own inherent bad taste. This paper might teach vulgar men to assume a mail of good taste" ("Court," 7). The *Western Press* similarly noted, "Men need advice upon the art of dress almost more than women, judging by the mistakes they so frequently make in style, colour, and material" ("In Praise of 'Fashion,'" 15).

Such sentiments are significant, as they suggest that by the end of the nineteenth century, England's men were widely held to the same sartorial standards as women. In July 1898, *Fashion* reprinted the comments of a writer from the *Leisure Hour* who asked, "Some wise man not long ago spoke of the duty of beauty in dress as a feminine obligation. But is not this duty general?" (Brummel, Dress News, July 1898, 22). *Fashion* responded in kind: "The study of dress is a duty, and a duty from a man's standpoint just as much as a woman's. . . . He should study dress, and he has just as much right to the subject as a woman" ("Our Friend," 23). The January 1900 issue asserted, "To look well is part of the debt one owes to Society, since the seemliness of any assembly is the sum of the efforts of its units. Men as well as women owe something to Society" (Baron, "Personal," 19). *Fashion's* writers often took an almost passive-aggressive approach when urging men to attend to their clothing and appearance, arguing that it might be too much to expect men to concern themselves with fashion to the same degree as women but it would serve them well:

> Colour is carefully studied by ladies in its relation to personal characteristics. It is perhaps asking a man to consider rather too curiously, if one remarks that not every man can advantageously wear, for instance, a pink shirt. Indeed one would not like to be understood as advocating the extreme and rather feminine delicacy implied in a consideration of what in a woman would be called "the complexion" in relation to clothes. Still, a sallow-faced man *might* just refrain from pink; and, at all events, any man can properly refrain from such a relation in the adjacent colours of a coat flower and a cravat as produces what women call . . . "a shriek." Here, and also in regard to neckties and coloured vests, the latter essentially a matter of taste purely, there is no harm in a decent regard to colour harmony. (Baron, "Beau," 10)

Fashion's rhetorical stance is fascinating because it explicitly equates the sartorial concerns of men with those of women. Men and women both have complexions that are affected by clothes; both have an equal social duty to dress well. Greenfield and colleagues' study of the 1930s men's magazine *Men Only* observes that it frequently employed overtly misogynistic discourse to dispel any potential associations with effeminacy (186–90). Yet thirty-five years earlier, *Fashion* exhibited little evidence of similar sexual anxieties or defense mechanisms. Rather than overstating its case—as we might expect—by arguing that there was something "manly" about dressing well, *Fashion* directly connected men's concern for fashion with women's. Rather than emphasizing the differences between men's fashionable consumption and women's, its copy suggests unisex standards that draw the sexes closer together. *Fashion*'s discursive strategy provides dramatic evidence of how the conventional gendering of fashion, consumption, and display had been radically transformed at the close of the Victorian age.

To be sure, *Fashion* regularly portrayed its male readership as just as interested in fashion as women were. Its February 1899 issue hailed the approaching spring as a time "when young men's fancies lightly turn to thoughts of new clothes as well as love" (London Expert, 8). In October 1902, a "Special Notice to Readers" offered "to answer questions privately" by mail for subscribers, "fully realising that no gentleman would care to wait a month for any information on the subject of dress" (8). Time and again, the magazine depicted men as preoccupied with the minutiae of dress to an extent that surpassed even that of the gentler sex. *Fashion* contributor "Lady Province" declared that "the superior sex is as much engrossed with their dress as women, if indeed not more so" (25). Reviewing styles in dress bows, she noted that

> the authority on this important item on gentlemen's attire declares that "rounded ends will no longer be the *chic*, plain square ends being the correct thing." This is all the more bewildering, as the same writer a few weeks previously stated that there was a craze for "rounded corners in every conceivable place," and quotes rounded "lappel-noses" [*sic*], "round-pointed collar wings," and other mysterious things. I do not fancy that a woman would be very much concerned as to whether the ends of any bow she might wear had rounded or square ends, but attention to detail is evidently a characteristic of the lords of creation. (25–26)

Here, however, marks perhaps an instance in which *Fashion* does distinguish men's sartorial concerns from women's, as Lady Province attributed men's preoccupation with the shape of bow corners not to effeminate fussiness but rather to a more masculine desire for scientific precision: "The writer of man's fashions may vie with the chemist in dealing with minute measurements and calculations, and fractions of an inch come in largely in the descriptions" (26).

Fashion *as a "Gentlemen's Club"*

With a confident, chatty tone, *Fashion* directed itself to a sympathetic consumer-conscious reader aware of all the fads and frustrations of male fashion. Its editors and contributors took him into their confidence with an easy intimacy that suggested "you know what we're talking about." The monthly's first issue groused familiarly that the shirt stud "has a way of escaping and going to goodness knows where while you are not looking. The mount disappears in the same mysterious way, but you generally find it in your pants or your socks when you get home" ("Things," 4). *Fashion* later shared its readers' complaints that no decent laundry existed in London and joked that all laundries returned whites and linens either dulled and dingy or torn (Brummel, untitled, February 1899, 12). The magazine depicted a discriminating male reader who perceived and understood the fine details of men's fashion even if women did not. One "young 'fashionable' of the West" wrote in that while praising *Fashion* "to a charming member of the other sex, I was met by the remark, 'I shouldn't have thought there was anything in men's dress to write about.' There is little doubt that the majority of her sex are still in the same depths of ignorance. The feminine eye is quick to perceive the most trivial change in feminine fashions, but seems incapable of recognising any alteration in the costume of 'mere man.' . . . And yet, who can deny the fact that masculine fashions are as much subject to change as feminine?" (Brummel, From Head, July 1898, 13–14). *Fashion* provided a public arena where men's interest in costume and fashionable display was affirmed. Its contents regularly provided its readers with valuable how-to instruction on the wear and care of clothing, such as the January 1899 full-page article on "How to Put on Fox's Patent Puttee" and a December 1901 item offering "Hints on Cleaning Riding Breeches." The regular feature From Head to Foot criticized the noisy salvo that immediately followed the conclusion of theatrical performances as men carelessly "popped" out their top hats (causing only one of the hat's two springs to take the full force), advising instead, "The hats should be let out slowly, not fired off like pop-guns. And the crown, when let out, should be directed inwards, and placed against the chest, to prevent a sudden and uneven release of the springs. The right way takes only three seconds longer than the wrong way" (Brummel, May 1899, 13). In July 1903, the periodical provided readers with a four-column list of "principal requisites that are needed by those about to travel" ("Reminder," 15). Resembling many contemporary women's magazines, *Fashion* served as a forum for the sharing of domestic tips and home remedies regarding the proper storage of clothes, the maintenance of garments, and the removal of stains. The monthly printed a reader's recommendation for getting creases out of waistcoats and passed on the tip from "a friend" who recommended shaving with rainwater (Brummel, Dress News, February 1899, 23; Untitled, August 1902, 7). An excerpt from *The Hunting Diary and Handbook* featured in the December 1898 issue offered instruction on how to clean boot-tops:

> Wash the dirt well off, and remove any stains with a little oxalic acid and a piece of cloth, taking care not to use it too strong. When dry, apply the powder sold by the leading top-boot makers according to directions. Wrap the tops in paper, put the boots on trees, and rub them over with a piece of lemon; use the best blacking obtainable, and plenty of "elbow-grease," and a satisfactory result will be obtained. A good boning improves the surface of the leather. Patent-leather boots should be put on trees and the dirt sponged off; when dry, an application of Meltonian Cream, rubbed in with a piece of flannel and finished off with an old silk handkerchief, will effect a good polish. (Brummel, "How," 24)

Articles such as this reveal the extreme amount of time, energy, and expense required to maintain men's clothing and other items. This was domestic (women's) work that a bachelor had to perform himself—the invisible labor a man must undertake behind closed doors to create a seamless appearance of impeccable sartorial correctness.

Fashion served to justify and normalize men's interest in clothing and appearance by providing within its pages a kind of metaphorical "gentlemen's club" in which the nuances of costume could be safely discussed among men who were interested and educated in fashion. Its copy—featuring a debate over whether the top or straw hat was cooler in summer heat and an entire article devoted to the subject of stud holes—created an environment in which men's interest in fashion and the minutiae of dress was natural, acceptable, and of great significance (Brummel, From Head, August 1900, 16–17; Anglo-French, 21). Items on the latest popular styles and goods along with regular features such as Baggage Fashions promoted a lifestyle of fashionable consumption—not unlike the articles on suits, luggage, stereos, and bourbons that appeared much later in its American descendents *GQ*, *Esquire*, and *Playboy*. Here, among the pages of *Fashion*, men could fuss over ridiculous modes, praise new innovations, complain about bad laundries, and scrutinize the latest styles. Here men's fashion was an important, worthy, masculine topic of discussion.

Fashion's Sartorial Aesthetic

Understandably, *Fashion* placed great emphasis on the social significance of dress as a reflection of the inner man. "Dress is the nearest of man's externals," *Fashion* declared in July 1898. "It is where his influence *begins*. It is the closest and most constant proclaimer of himself" (London Expert, 10). In 1900 the monthly even went so far as to describe dressing as a form of artistic expression. While the bricklayer (and baker and butcher and candlestick maker) "expresses nothing of himself in his work," the "Baron," a regular contributor to *Fashion*, asserts that "the dressed man—whether he be well or ill-dressed—unconsciously reveals himself in his attire; and this unconsciousness (advisedly mentioned) is . . . characteristic of an art" ("Dressing," 13). Yet even when placing great artistic emphasis on dress, *Fashion* nevertheless concurred with contemporaneous conduct books that emphasized understatement and subtlety as the preferred qualities in a gentleman's dress:

> The conspicuously well dressed man is not a well dressed man at all, but merely a block for displaying the best materials and the latest fashions upon. His clothes and all articles of outward attire cry out their quality, and forcibly draw attention to their very newest cut, set, twist, or turn; and you say, "*There's* a dressy man if you like! Everything right up to date, including the walking-stick." The really well dressed man attracts no such remark. Of him you are more likely to say, "That man looks very smart—for some reason or other. Wonder what it is!" You may depend upon it that the man of whom this is said is a man not only of fashion, but of something very important besides—namely, good taste, strong individuality, faithfulness to personal style. ("Sir Robert," 10)

In this respect, *Fashion*'s sartorial aesthetic was relatively conservative. The monthly regarded itself as a defender of "sound and sober style," a promoter of

"Really there is much more to be said about men's fashions than I had imagined"   101

fashion above fad (London Expert, September 1899, 8). While it sought to expand the colors, patterns, and garments available to men and encouraged personal expression through dress, it regularly voiced strong disapproval of anything too colorful, too flamboyant, or too faddish that might make a man's dress call improper attention to itself. Beau Brummel, Junr., tersely condemned extremes of fashion, and *Fashion* stood resistant against changes in costume that revolted too dramatically against tradition, particularly what it regarded as the creeping casualness of dress. Despite oppressive heat waves during the first summers of the twentieth century, *Fashion* insisted that "the man who goes into the presence of women, . . . with sleeves rolled up and otherwise slovenly, proclaims himself a cad and a boor" and that "the coatless man . . . is opposed to all ideas of decency" (Masculine, August 1901, 19–20; Beaunash, July 1904, 19). It blasted the wearing of "a straw hat with a frock coat!" and declared that "the man who crowns a frock-coat with a bowler is socially and civically lost" (Baron, "Full," 21; "Necessity," 20–21). And it voiced its support of the practice by some hotel restaurants (namely, the Carlton) of refusing admittance of men dressed in morning coats for evening meals, advising readers to cease patronizing restaurants that admitted those in improper dress (Godfrey-Turner, September 1899, 4). The magazine was particularly ruffled by ongoing predictions by popular periodicals that the traditional gentleman's silk top hat was "doomed" to obsolescence. "Oh, the 'doom' of that 'topper'!" it sniffed in October 1899; "Really, how awfully sickening it is!" (Brummel, From Head, October 1899, 16). Five years later, in July 1904, *Fashion* still insisted that the top hat would ever endure as "the symbol of wealth, respectability, and the British Constitution" ("Necessity," 20).

Not surprisingly, then, *Fashion* served as a passionate proponent of occasion-specific dress favored by the upper classes. Celebrating the excitement, activity, and variety of modern life as a golden opportunity in which to explore the full range of masculine attire that such elaborate sartorial rules dictated, the magazine cheered that "there was never a time in the history of man's clothing when he felt it necessary to change them so often. There is a peculiar costume for everything. For dinner and after dinner; for shooting and after shooting; for the morning and for the afternoon. There are clothes suitable (to the tailor's eye, not the sportsman's) for every possible human diversion. In fact, there was never a moment when clothes gave a dandy so many opportunities as to-day. He might dress himself seven times a day without risk of being thought eccentric" (Brummel, Dress News, October 1898, 22). The possibilities for activity-appropriate apparel were apparently unlimited, as *Fashion* deliberated in July 1901 over the proper attire for ping-pong (Masculine, 22).[8] The next year, in February 1902, the periodical provided further direction to its readers with the premiere of the "Fashion" Dress Chart (21). The new feature promoted an occasion-specific dress wardrobe made up of several distinctive, specialized costumes through a somewhat complicated table cross-listing occasions and articles of clothing (fig. 3.2). By June 1902, the dress chart had been simplified to feature single-paragraph descriptions of full wardrobes for twelve occasions ranging from time of day to festivities to sports (21).[9]

The dress chart represents only the most obvious example of the unapologetically authoritative tone by which *Fashion* addressed its subject and its readers. Beau Brummel, Junr., clearly regarded his paper as an infallible conduct manual of masculine dress. This was demonstrated most prominently in the regular feature Dress News Collected and Dissected—and, later, "Fashion's" Monthly Review of Men's Dress News—in which fashion news items from other newspapers and magazines were excerpted, scrutinized, and commented on by *Fashion's* opinionated editors. The magazine regularly accused other periodicals of reporting only on

---

1902.]   **THE "FASHION" DRESS CHART.**   **[FEBRUARY.**

DAY DRESS.

OCCASION.	COAT AND OVERCOAT.	WAISTCOAT.	TROUSERS.	HAT.	SHIRT AND CUFFS.	COLLAR.	CRAVAT.	GLOVES.	BOOTS.	JEWELLERY.
DAY WEDDING, AFTERNOON CALLS, RECEPTIONS AND MATINEE.	Frock and Frock Overcoat or Chesterfield.	Double-Breasted, same Material as Coat, or of White Linen Duck.	Striped Worsted of Dark or Grey Tones.	High Silk.	White, with Cuffs Attached.	Military Pattern (Plain Stand-up), or one with Turned-down Points.	Black Ascot or Sailor Knot, with Small Pattern in White or Light Colours.	Grey Suède or Stone-coloured Kids.	Patent Leather, Button Tops.	Gold Links, Pearl Pin.
BUSINESS AND MORNING WEAR.	Lounge or Morning, with Chesterfield.	To Match Coat.	Of same Material if with Lounge. Dark Striped Worsted with Morning.	Bowler with Lounge, or High Silk with Morning.	White Shirt, with Cuffs Attached or Detached.	Double, with Lounge. Stand-up, with Morning.	Sailor Knot, Ascot, or Once-over, in Black or Dark Shades.	Tan or Grey.	Calf.	Gold Links, Gold Watch Guard, Pearl or Plain Pin.
CYCLING, GOLF, AND SPORT GENERALLY.	Norfolk, Single-Breasted or Double-Breasted Lounge.	Of Fancy Plaid, Single-Breasted or Double-Breasted.	Knickers or Flannel Trousers.	Alpine or Golf Cap.	Coloured Flannel.	Hunting Stock or Polo Collar.	Hunting Stock or Ascot.	Heavy Tan or White Chamois.	Calf.	Links and Sporting Pin, Watch Guard.
AFTERNOON TEAS, SHOWS, CHURCH, ETC.	Frock or Morning, Chesterfield or Frock Overcoat.	Double-Breasted, same Material as Coat, or of White Linen Duck.	Striped Worsted in Dark Shade.	High Silk.	White.	High Standing.	Ascot or Sailor Knot.	Tan or Light Grey Suède.	Patent Leather, Button Tops.	Pearl Pin, Gold Studs, Gold Links.

EVENING DRESS.

BALLS, RECEPTIONS, FORMAL DINNERS, AND THEATRE.	Evening Coat, and Chesterfield or Frock Overcoat	White Single-Breasted or Black Double-Breasted.	Same Material as Coat, with Silk Braiding down Legs.	Opera or High Silk with Cloth Band.	White, with Two-Stud Hole in Front.	Stand-up.	Narrow Cambric Bow or Stock Bow.	Pearl or White Glacé.	Buttoned Patent Leather, with Cloth Tops, or Patent Leather Pumps.	Pearl Studs and Plain Gold or Jewelled Links.
INFORMAL DINNER, CLUB, AND AT HOME DINNER.	Evening Jacket, Raglan, Chesterfield or Frock Overcoat.	Single or Double-Breasted, same Material as Coat.	Same Material as Coat, with or without Braiding.	Opera or High Silk.	Plain or Pleated, White.	Stand-up or one with Turned-down Points.	Black Silk.	No Gloves.	Patent Leather, Button Tops.	Gold Studs and Links.

Figure 3.2. First appearance of *Fashion's* dress chart (February 1902, 21) (permission British Library)

short-lived fads and making premature pronouncements regarding large-scale changes in sartorial styles based on only a few dubious examples. On several occasions, *Fashion* condescendingly questioned other periodicals' credentials to report fashion news, accusing their coverage of being erroneous and inept. Coffee and Cognac columnist L. Godfrey-Turner chided, "We must question the right of a paper like the *D.M.* [*Daily Mail*] to pronounce upon matters of fashion or dress" and suggested that "twenty years hence . . . its editor may have learnt that long hair, silk hats, fawn-coloured Newmarket coats, yellow boots, and a pipe, worn all together, do not constitute the wearer an authority on true elegance in dress" (May 1899, 6). The fashion staff of the *Daily Express* were skewered as "first-class humorists if nothing else" for pairing their written descriptions of the latest modes with fashion plates that portrayed contrary cuts and styles (Godfrey-Turner, June 1900, 6). "I verily believe that you have only to tell a certain halfpenny daily paper that the fashionable opera hat is of pink satin with a lace band round it, and it will promptly and seriously inform its unhappy readers that such is the case," *Fashion* remarked with exasperation in December 1898. "The smallest inquiry on the editor's part would elicit the fact that opera-hats were remaining black. Inquiry, however, into the truth of a report too often robs the report of its *raison d'être*—and newspapers must live!" (London Expert, 10).

Fashion, *Advertising, and Growing Men's Markets*

By collecting and responding to fashion news from other sources, *Fashion* positioned itself as the "final word" on men's costume, determining what new fashions were of value, policing men's consumption, and directing men to purchase the right items in the correct manner. While Beau Brummel, Junr., may have regularly warned his readers not to slavishly follow fashion or jump on every new bandwagon, at the same time he provided exhaustive monthly coverage on the latest modes on display in London and on the Continent. Aside from its regular reporting on coats, trousers, and hats, *Fashion*'s content traced the growing popularity of the bandanna, spotlighted fashions in walking sticks, reviewed styles in university hoods, and reported on the revival of snuff use among young men (Brummel, From Head, November 1898, 18; Voyager, 14–15; Academician, 14–16; "Concerning," 20). *Fashion* also provided its readers with faithful illustrations of "A Dozen Collars" (de Winton, 18) and photographs of "The Season's Socks" (Brummel, From Head, May 1900, 19). *Fashion* served as an innovator and advocate of new styles as well. Its October 1898 issue boasted that the periodical "took the 'Raglan' [coat] in hand, and predicted its success" fully six months before (London Expert, 8); and its very own Beau Brummel, Junr., waistcoat was promoted throughout 1898 and '99 (Holland, 16).

Fashion's very existence served as a promoter of men's consumption, and advertising played a large part in this. Beginning with just two commercial sponsors in its premiere issue, the magazine quickly increased advertising space, featuring twelve advertisements one year later in its March 1899 issue. By June 1899, *Fashion* had eliminated its front cover table of contents to make room for prominent advertising space, and the March 1902 issue featured forty-four advertisements within its twenty-eight pages. Its regular advertisers predictably included tailors, hatters, hosiers, and shirt makers—as well as Jaeger "sanitary" woolens and nonshrinking Viyella pajamas—but also the Empire Theatre, Defiance Coach Stables, Niagara Hall "Real Ice Skating" rink, Regent's Park Riding School, Birbeck Bank, Carreras' Celebrated Smoking Mixtures, Cleveland brand bicycles, Slaters Detectives, Kropp razors, and Mr. Leonard Leigh, "turf accountant."[10] Several of *Fashion*'s advertisers were decidedly upscale clothiers bearing royal warrants, including Herbert Johnson, hatter; Stohwasser and Co., military tailors; Henry Heath, Ltd., silk hats; G.W. Kyle and Co., shirt makers; and Alan McAfee, boot makers.[11]

Many advertisers ran the same unchanged advertisement, often in the same location in the magazine, for months or years at a time, and the success of these ads was evidenced by the glowing testimonials *Fashion* proudly reprinted. "You will be interested to know that we have had EXCELLENT RESULTS FROM OUR LAST TWO ADVERTISEMENTS IN FASHION," extolled Jaeger's tailoring manager, W. D. Askew; "Applications for our New Spring Catalogue coming in from the MOST UNEXPECTED QUARTERS: even from staid State Officials in Continental Cities. FASHION, in fact, is MORE UBIQUITOUS THAN WE THOUGHT." G. W. Kyle and Co. exclaimed, "Our advertisements in FASHION have brought MORE RESULTS THAN THOSE WE HAVE INSERTED IN OTHER JOURNALS CHARGING SIX TIMES AS MUCH FOR SPACE" ("Interesting," 17).

Fashion further facilitated the commercial interests of London's merchants while promoting male consumption through informative articles that served as enthusiastic endorsements of particular clothiers. *Fashion*'s editor went out of his way to state explicitly and repeatedly that the products and services advertised in his magazine had met with his discriminating approval and that the appearance of a particular advertisement directly represented a personal endorsement. A notice that ran frequently in the magazine's first year declared, "It is very important that our Readers should know that such is the care we exercise, for their benefit, in the choice of advertisements for admission to this paper, that they may confidently regard our acceptance of the advertisement of any firm as a guarantee that the advertiser deals only in goods characterized by evidence of the best workmanship" ("Notice," June 1898, 16). To underscore this point, Beau Brummel, Junr., asserted that to preserve the reputation of both his periodical and the "high-class trade" promoted therein, he had "declined to publish advertisements relating to rubbish," repeatedly turning away "first-class money as represented by third-class advertisements" for questionable businesses such as "Mlle. Massage, by Monsieur Continental Photographs, by Mr. Mike Moneylender, and by Messrs. Shoddy and Slop, the producers of those 15s. 6d. suits, in the selling of which the articles themselves are not more sold than the purchasers" (Brummel, From Head, November 1898, 18–19; Godfrey-Turner, October 1899, 5).

The debut of a new advertiser was often ushered in with a celebratory article about the merchant or his product. A lengthy item on trouser maker Mr. A. Anderson—"probably the only trouser specialist who, relying upon self-measurement only, and not requiring his customers to be fitted on, can turn out a pair of fashionable trousers that look, and are, in every way a first-class piece of workmanship"—appeared on the same page as his advertisement (London Expert, February 1899, 10). *Fashion* offered multiple recommendations of Mr. A. Grunfeld of 45 Maddox Street "to the notice of those of my readers who may not have 'decided upon' their tailor" ("Good Tailor," 15) and even spotlighted a new waistcoat innovated by the cutter (Brummel, From Head, August 1899, 19). Other articles that served as commercial plugs include "Sporting Garments at Lovegrove's"; "A Good City Hosier," regarding Mr. Ernest C. Hoe on Copthall Avenue; "Boots at McAfee's"; and "Sheffield's Best" razors (Untitled, August 1902, 7). A particular curiosity is a report entitled "My Valet," on businesses that purchased, organized, cleaned, and stored a gentleman's garments for an annual fee, which served as proof, for this report's author, that "men are taking more interest in their personal appearance than formerly, and that this must necessarily lead to an increased demand for first-class clothes" (Brummel, From Head, January 1901, 9).

Certainly *Fashion*'s high-profile advertisements, commercial endorsements, and celebratory articles all demonstrated enormous growth in the men's market at the turn of the twentieth century. The magazine provided regular reporting on a steady stream of new (and occasionally gimmicky) sartorial innovations for men,

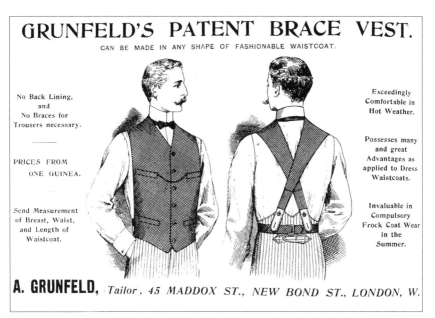

GRUNFELD'S PATENT BRACE VEST.

CAN BE MADE IN ANY SHAPE OF FASHIONABLE WAISTCOAT.

No Back Lining,
and
No Braces for
Trousers necessary.

PRICES FROM
ONE GUINEA.

Send Measurement
of Breast, Waist,
and Length of
Waistcoat.

Exceedingly
Comfortable in
Hot Weather.

Possesses many
and great
Advantages as
applied to Dress
Waistcoats.

Invaluable in
Compulsory
Frock Coat Wear
in the
Summer.

A. GRUNFELD, Tailor, 45 MADDOX ST., NEW BOND ST., LONDON, W.

Figure 3.3. (above) Grunfeld's Patent Brace Vest advertisement (*Fashion*, August 1901, 24)
Figure 3.4. (below) Jaeger's "sporting shirt" illustration (*Fashion*, August 1900, 21)
(both permission British Library)

such as Grunfeld's Patent Brace Vest, a combination waistcoat-suspender garment (fig. 3.3; Brummel, From Head, June 1901, 18), and Jaeger's "sporting shirt," which promised not to bunch up around the waist or come untucked (fig. 3.4). Other peculiar inventions included a "revolving shirt" that "gives a clean front every day for four days, when, presumably, the shirt is considered fit to go to the laundry" (Brummel, Dress News, April 1898, 18) and the "Drimosit," a kind of protective apron to be worn from waist down by motorists (fig. 3.5). I discuss in chapter 2 how producers and merchants in the second half of the nineteenth century expanded men's interest in their clothing

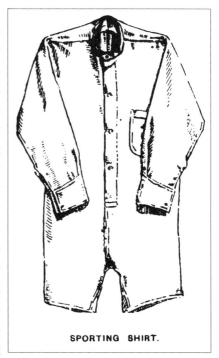

SPORTING SHIRT.

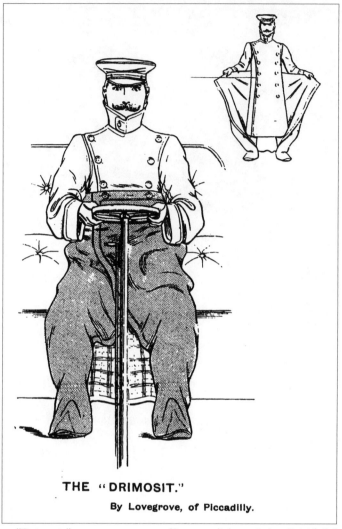

THE "DRIMOSIT."

By Lovegrove, of Piccadilly.

Figure 3.5. "Drimosit" motor apron, 1903 (Brown, 13) (permission British Library)

and appearance by promoting accessories designed for the care and storage of the goods they already had. *Fashion's* content reflected this with regular advertisements and articles highlighting a wide variety of presses, hangers, and wardrobes. The magazine advertised Askew's "Lever" wardrobe (fig. 3.6) and heaped lengthy praises upon Mr. T. M. Lewin's "Lombard" cabinet, which provided a compact series of drawers and shelves for the organization of shirts, collars, ties, handkerchiefs, and gloves (fig. 3.7; From Head, June 1903, 8–9). Moreover, the January 1904

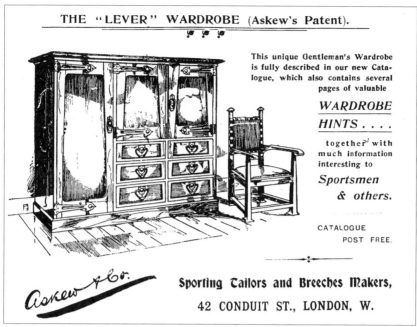

Figure 3.6. (above) Askew's "Lever" wardrobe advertisement (*Fashion,* September 1902, 3); *Figure 3.7. (below)* The "Lombard" wardrobe (From Head to Foot, *Fashion,* June 1903, 8) (both permission British Library)

issue marked the debut of a new regular feature, Baggage Fashion. *Fashion* also promoted Grunfeld's "Coat-Presser & Shape-Preserver" (a special hanger designed to enable users to "Press Your Own Coats and Keep Them Always in Good Shape") and the "Trousanger," which "holds the trousers in such a way as to utilize their own natural weight both in the business of stretching and pressing" and "can be fixed to the wardrobe or the wall in less than a couple of minutes" (fig. 3.8). The periodical regularly reminded its readers that "the well-dressed man who doesn't take care of his clothes must of necessity be

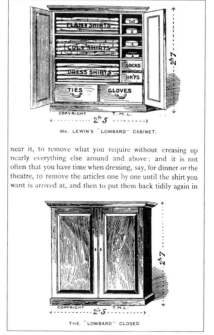

MR. LEWIN'S "LOMBARD" CABINET.

near it, to remove what you require without creasing up nearly everything else around and above : and it is not often that you have time when dressing, say, for dinner or the theatre, to remove the articles one by one until the shirt you want is arrived at, and then to put them back tidily again in

THE "LOMBARD" CLOSED.

Figure 3.8. "Trousanger" advertisement (*Fashion*, July 1901, 18) (permission British Library)

an extravagant man" (Brummel, "Care," 15). By advertising and endorsing such clothing presses and storage cabinets, *Fashion* underscored the growing attention that the fashionable man was expected to pay to the care of his clothing, as well as the increase in the personal responsibility and work necessary to maintain a fashionable masculine appearance. The emergence of such products marked a significant shift from male customers patronizing the services of tailors and launderers to purchasing products that allowed them to do the work of clothing care themselves at home.

Expansion of Male Fashion, Consumption, and Masculine Ideals

Fashion's enthusiastic endorsement of consumer items as well as its many advertisements for clothing, men's clubs, stables, bicycles, tobacco, and skating rinks portrayed a male lifestyle based on the active, regular consumption of a striking variety of goods and services. Indeed, *Fashion's* very existence and success at the end of the nineteenth century demonstrates the enormous social transformations regarding the significance of male consumption and fashionable display that had taken place over the preceding fifty years. Despite predictions from "kind and sympathetic friends" that "Fashion would not survive six months," Beau Brummel, Junr., had founded his magazine with the conviction that men's fashion was sufficiently recognized and that the men's market was such an economic force that a monthly periodical could be sustained (Godfrey-Turner, January 1901, 5). "Although the field [of men's fashion] is limited when compared with that of Fashions in other directions, it is not so barren or tame as some people think," *Fashion* declared. "The world of sport—the region of travel—an intercourse of nationalities—the varieties of pursuits—all so closely touching men on their *natural* side, extend the field immensely" ("What," March 1898, 6). Each issue boldly presented the growing variety of garments, styles, and sartorial license opening to men as well as the growing importance of male dress.

Repudiating "the tyranny of ugliness" observed by dour frock-coated gentlemen living in "a steel-grey age," the magazine's writers insisted, "We must have colour, and we will have it despite over-indulgence and abuse. . . . Colour is but a natural accessory to sartorial excellence" ("Tyranny," 15; Baron, "Colour," 8; Montagu, September 1903, 12). Asserting that "coloured waistcoats should not be discouraged," the magazine devoted much ink to an ever-changing array of hues, patterns, checks, and styles, even promoting a vest with a crocodile-skin pattern (fig. 3.9) in February 1900 (Brummel, Dress News, May 1898, 18; Brummel, From Head, February 1900, 18). During the summer of 1903, *Fashion* declared that "the mode favours brilliancy and variety in patterns and colours" and detailed the emerging selection of striped, patterned, and multicolored shirts (Masculine, August 1903, 14–16). An April 1904 advertisement for Lewin's hosiery shop displayed twenty-six varieties of patterned and colored socks (fig. 3.10).

For *Fashion,* no longer was the question for men "whether the clothes will last it out," but rather "will the style do? Is the cut too old?" (London Expert, September

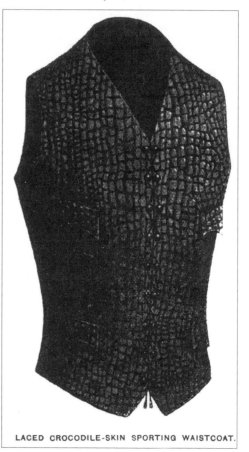

LACED CROCODILE-SKIN SPORTING WAISTCOAT.

Figure 3.9. Crocodile-skin waistcoat (From Head to Foot, *Fashion,* February 1900, 18) (permission British Library)

"Really there is much more to be said about men's fashions than I had imagined"

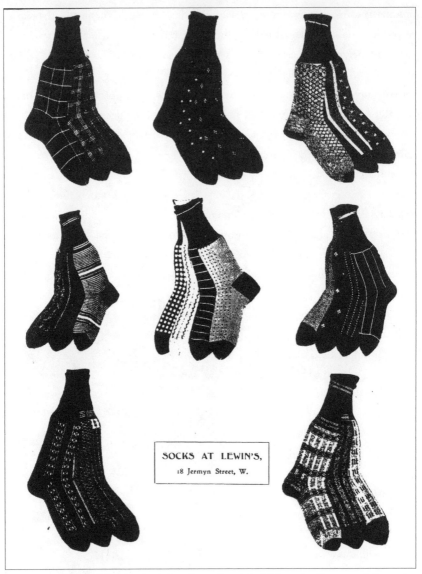

Figure 3.10. Twenty-six varieties of socks at Lewin's (*Fashion*, April 1904, 10) (permission British Library)

1901, 8). Even middle-class professionals had begun to dress with an eye toward the latest mode rather than practicality and sobriety. According to the comments of Mr. C. M. Connolly, "New York's oracle in the matter of masculine attire," reprinted in *Fashion*'s June 1903 issue, "We are devoting more attention to attire— that is, to the correctness of attire—than we ever before bestowed upon it. Our

grandfathers and our fathers boasted of the simplicity of their sartorial requirements. They boasted of meagre wardrobes, and of the bad impression that extravagance in dress made. All this was well enough in their day, but it has ceased
to be forceful and of value where every business calling demands neat and well-
dressed young men" ("Dress as a Matter," 25). For the middle classes, it was no
longer the overt renunciation of fashion that was emphasized, but rather the
proper employment of fashionable attire. But "correctness of attire" did not necessarily mean drab conformity. Even in "that busy district known as 'E.C.' [that
is, the "East Central" postal district that comprises London's business center]. . .
there are infinite gradations," and *Fashion* regularly celebrated personal expression
and visual distinctiveness through variations in costume ("Dress and Character,"
15). "A man can always be perfectly in the mode, and yet be personal in his dressing," advised the Baron in a February 1900 essay. "There is so much room, even
within the strictest bounds of fashion, for the play of taste and idiosyncrasy, that
a man's clothes truly express, and often nearly betray, his character" ("Dressing,"
13). One year previously, the Baron had noted, "The use of Fashion—as distinguished from its abuse—is to enable every man and every woman to make the
most of his and her good looks, by the use of seemly and becoming attire. And
the taste of the individual comes into play precisely here, in the selection among
allowable modes of those best suited to personal idiosyncrasy" ("Beau," 10). This
sort of advice suggests that the rules that governed masculine fashion had loos-
ened and that a much broader variety of dress—as well as personal expression
through dress—was permissible. A later contributor, Bessie O'Connor, offered,
"There is no objection to a certain amount of individuality in dress for a man; so
long as he looks like a gentleman he may even be eccentric" (6).

Fashion, *Masculinity, and Beautifying the Male Body*

Fashion's unchecked celebration of male consumption and sartorial license might
seem surprising considering the supposed rules against flamboyant dress for members of the middle and gentleman classes. Particularly in light of the 1895–96 Oscar
Wilde scandal—which had broken less than three years before *Fashion's* debut and
had supposedly solidified irreversibly the association between homosexuality and
extravagant, dandified dress—the call for "eccentricity" in male attire would
seem potentially reckless to much of its readership. Greenfield and her coauthors
note that because "there was a strong association between the 'homosexual' or

other forms of 'perversion,' and sartorial indulgence" during the years following the Wilde scandal, the editors of *Men Only* in the 1930s "encroached upon potentially dangerous territory in offering in-depth coverage of the latest men's fashions" (186). Presumably the editors of *Fashion* would have been treading far more dangerous waters around the height of the Wilde scandal. And indeed the magazine occasionally stepped carefully, distancing itself from the turn-of-the-century equation of effeminacy, overly refined costume, and homosexuality. Particularly in its early years, *Fashion* belied its own sexual anxieties by defensively insisting on the masculinity of its male readership:

> That FASHION has justified the *St. James's* [*Gazette's*] generous prophesy [that it would appeal to club men], and found what we were determined, after so encouraging a prediction, it should find, is, I venture to think, as much a compliment to our efforts to keep our columns free from the effeminate element, as it is a tribute to the judgment and prophetic powers of our aristocratic contemporary. Club men will not tolerate anything of the namby-pamby sort, and our best answer to those who aver that FASHION can only appeal to infirm young dandies is to point out that one of the chief spheres of our magazine's circulation is the military club. (Godfrey-Turner, January 1901, 5)

In stating its resolution "to show the door, and the street as well if necessary, to the bestial agents of the 'manicurists' of Cleveland Street and the surrounding district" who wished to advertise in the magazine, *Fashion* made not-so-subtle reference to the location of the infamous 1889 London scandal that implicated several members of Parliament and even the royal family with a gay brothel (Godfrey-Turner, January 1901, 5).[12] But in doing so, the editor suggested that the magazine had to struggle against the assumption that a men's fashion magazine would mainly cater to homosexuals. To combat such assumptions, *Fashion's* articles sometimes emphasized the decidedly "manly" sartorial aesthetic it promoted by condemning the outlandish modes of the Wildean invert. Responding to reports by the "clubman" reporter for *Ladies' Field* regarding the popularity of outlandish four-inch-high collars among fashionable men, Beau Brummel, Junr., wrote, "If the 'clubman' of the 'Ladies' Field' is not a woman, he's a—well, he doesn't know much about his subject" (Brummel, Dress News, June 1898, 24). While bold colors and daring stripes were acceptable for shirts, *Fashion's* contributor "Montagu" asserted, "I cannot see any place in men's dress for weak yellows, effeminate pinks, and baby blues. They savour too much of the boudoir and the afternoon tea. A man needs be manly in all things to-day" (July 1902, 15).

In its early years, *Fashion* took particular aim at the male corset, as the corseted dandy served symbolically as the very figure of the fashionable male in the popular imagination that this periodical sought to overcome. One of its first issues featured a small untitled satirical cartoon of a monocled gentleman trying on a very feminine-looking corset in front of a full-length mirror (fig. 3.11; Brummel, *Dress News*, May 1898, 22). Yet four years later, in January 1902, *Fashion* revealed that it was still struggling with an image problem: "The conclusion has been jumped to in certain quarters that because FASHION deals with men's modes

Figure 3.11. Cartoon of gentleman trying on corset, from *Fashion,* May 1898 (Brummel, Dress News, 22) (permission British Library)

"Really there is much more to be said about men's fashions than I had imagined"

it must necessarily be an effeminate publication, designed to appeal specifically to young (and old) gentlemen who wear corsets and spend the morning in Bond Street getting their hair curled. If this were true, FASHION would be crowded with unpleasant advertisements, and the proprietor would be a wealthy man" (Brummel, "Some," 5). As he had a year earlier, Beau Brummel, Junr., boasted that he regularly rejected "nasty" advertisements for effeminate products, this time targeting specifically men's corsets:

> An advertising agent called at FASHION office a few weeks ago, and asked the price of the back page, with the view, he said, of placing with us a series of advertisements having reference to gentlemen's belts. These "gentlemen's belts," however, turned out to be something very different, and the illustrations which the agent desired should embellish the advertisement depicted a row of pretty young men in ladies' corsets, with their fingers daintily placed on their bulging hips, after the fashion of the female figures in the advertisement pages of the *Gentlewoman,* the *Queen,* the *Lady's Pictorial,* etc. The agent left FASHION office quicker than he entered it. (Brummel, "Some," 5)

Exactly one year later, however, in January 1903, the first advertisement for Worth's corsets appeared in the pages of *Fashion* (fig. 3.12).[13] Waging an aggressive image-reversal campaign, the magazine accompanied the ad with three articles extolling the value of corset use by men. One piece approached the subject by first acknowledging *Fashion*'s own apprehensions. "Corsets for men!" began the writer:

> There is such a lack of virility in the sound that I can imagine robuster readers of FASHION in all parts of the world giving vent to their feelings in sufficiently pungent Anglo-Saxon. The feminine man, from his boyhood upwards, has never enjoyed a position of much kudos among English-speaking people. He has been regarded as a sort of neuter gender among human animalia, a kind of hybrid creature who could claim none of the respect that was apportioned to either definite division of the sexes. The mere fop, who considers his part in life as begun and ended with his sartorial embellishments, merits inclusion in this emasculate genus which inclines rather to the feminine way than to the male side of our species. ("Belts," 8)

WORTH ET Cᴵᴱ.,

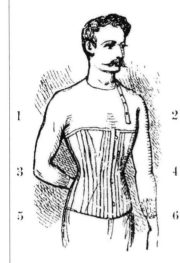

Makers of

Ladies' and

Gentlemen's

CORSETS, BELTS,

SURGICAL CORSETS,

AND FINE

UNDERCLOTHING.

Measurements to be taken over Vest and under Shirt.

1 -2. Circumference of Chest (inches) ...

3 --4. „ „ Waist „ ...

5- 6. „ „ Hips „ ...

Height ... ... (feet) ...

PRICES { Ready-Made .. .. from **1 guinea.**
{ Made to Measure.. ,, **2½ guineas.**

489a Oxford Street.

(Late 134 New Bond Street.)

Figure 3.12. Worth et Cie corset advertisement (*Fashion*, January 1903, 21) (permission British Library)

After this confession of initial skepticism, however, *Fashion*'s contributors launched a prolonged offensive to dislodge the powerful association of corsets with extreme dandyism and effeminacy among its male readership. In an effort to masculinize corset use, the magazine embraced the euphemistic term *belt* that it had mocked only a year before. It downplayed conventional associations with femininity by emphasizing the corset's benefits for the active, physical male lifestyle. "By what one reads occasionally in the papers about corsets for men," observed celebrated dressmaker Charles Frederick Worth in an interview with *Fashion*, "it is evident that the popular idea with regard to these things is that they are worn principally by dandies. But my business has shown me that in reality, they are chiefly sought after by the most athletic and soldierly of men, who are desirous of keeping their figures in order, so that they may continue in the pursuit of their various sports without looking clumsy or unfit" ("Corsets and Their Worth," 16).

To demonstrate this claim, *Fashion* noted that "broad-boned belts or corsets were almost as common among Army officers as their very braces" and reprinted an item from the *Sun* reporting that "more than 18,000 corsets were made yearly for Frenchmen, and 3000 were shipped to England, principally for Army officers" ("Corsets and Their Worth," 16; "Corsets in the Army," 8). Another January 1903 article asserted that "there are numbers of men, soldiers and good sportsmen, names well known on the polo ground and as hard and straight riders across country, who do not disdain the adventitious comfort and support of a good belt." According to the writer, the corset "acts like a gymnasium belt" to provide support during "the rough-and-tumble of the Rugby game" ("Belts," 8). The magazine also emphasized the health benefits of "surgical corsets" that enabled the wearer "to follow sport or occupation without feeling the discomforts and disadvantages of his affliction." Worth explained that one customer "who had been strictly forbidden by his doctor to hunt this season, was daily disobeying orders, because, in a Worth corset, he felt no ill effects from the exercise. In this, no doubt, we have the explanation of the popularity of surgical and other corsets among a class of men who hunt and play polo" ("Corsets and Their Worth," 16).[14]

Significantly, throughout this breathless promotional blitz, *Fashion* never once suggested that the corset might be worn to improve one's figure. Rather, the magazine sold the corset to its male readers through strategically weighted language that played upon late-nineteenth-century concerns regarding physical activity, manly stamina, and sexual virility. Contributors advised that "when hunting in some of the wilder parts of the world, where the going was of the roughest, a good flexible supporting belt was of wonderful assistance in the preservation of one's staying powers" ("Belts," 8). The wearing of a corset aided in "increasing the output of individual exertion," warding off fatigue and "prevent[ing] this retreat, as it were, of the bodily forces to a position of inferior strength and resistance" (9, 8). "Consequently a man is enabled to endow his action within a given time with much greater potency." *Fashion* concluded. "Even a Sampson, aided in this way, would find his powers productive of vastly greater results" (9).

The periodical even suggested that wearing a corset was almost a patriotic duty, as it helped maintain English masculinity: "Whether hunting at home, or living a life of hardship and adventure abroad, there is scarcely a part of the world where Englishmen are not called upon to put forth their best powers, either in their own interests or in those of the state. The addition to their abilities and usefulness gained by a duplication of their power of endurance is self evident and needs no demonstration" (9).

Despite its initial campaign, *Fashion* must have understood that the air of effeminacy surrounding the corset lingered, as the magazine continued attempts to dispel such notions in the subsequent months. While the debut of the Worth advertisement and the magazine's accompanying endorsements generated a great deal of attention from several periodicals that reprinted the articles in full, *Fashion* aggressively downplayed the suggestion that it had "set the daily papers talking about 'The Male Waist'" and dismissed as erroneous reports that it had inspired a rage among "smart men of the West" for "lacing themselves in to 22 in. waists" (From Head, April 1903, 12–13; "Fashion's" Monthly, April 1903, 20–22). One contributor (who declared that no one had "advocated manliness and good taste in men's dress more stoutly and unremittingly than I have") criticized the "causeless prejudice" against the garment, insisting, "Men do not wear corsets or waistbands, as they are correctly known, from dandified and effeminate motives, but simply because the pressure against the stomach prevents or retards *embonpoint*." For this reason, he argued, the corset wearer should "no more think it a subject for jeer and jest than if he should use glasses to aid his sight" (Beaunash, March 1904, 10). *Fashion* reader R. L. P. of Kensington boasted, "I have three or four friends about my own age (twenty-four) who wear them, and no one could accuse any of us of being effeminate—at least they would regret it if they did!" ("Fashion's" Monthly, May 1903, 22). A few disapproving readers agreed with the incensed letter-writer who protested, "We have heard a great deal about the new woman. Is the corseted popinjay with the twenty-six inch waist to be the new man?" But *Fashion* reported that "quite 75 per cent. of the letters addressed to the Editor on the subject" were from male readers enthusiastically expressing approval, and many of them confessed that they had already been wearing corsets for years ("Fashion's" Monthly, April 1903, 22; "Fashion's" Monthly, May 1903, 22).

It is impossible to determine whether men were wearing corsets in greater numbers than before, or merely admitting that they wore corsets in greater numbers than before. Perhaps the letters from zealous readers were fabrications. In any case, *Fashion*'s dramatic reversal on the corset and the mostly positive reaction it elicited from both the periodical press and its readers is a significant example of how fashions and consumer behaviors once regarded as effeminate or transgressive were transformed by nineteenth-century consumer culture into acceptable, desirable, even manly acts. The accelerating forces of British consumer capitalism could overcome even powerful social anxieties regarding homosexuality and change once-deviant items into mainstream masculine goods. However, it was not only through the corset that popular notions of acceptable male display were expanded. While *Fashion* had criticized the use of hair dyes and other age-defying cosmetics in 1898,[15] in 1904 it announced, "Beauty has so long been considered the prerogative of the fair sex that it is time the mere man should look to himself, and consider in what way he can best improve his appearance." The magazine consequently recommended the services of Mrs. Ada S. Ballin,[16] a cosmetic surgeon "who in the course of the past twelve years has treated many thousands of cases of both sexes and of all ages for defects of the appearance" and who "has now let it be known that she devotes special attention to male patients who go to her, of course only for troubles of the face, head and hands." The article highlighted Ballin's success with treating embarrassing or malignant facial disfigurements such as "a port wine stain birthmark, a large mole on the end of [the] nose or some wart-like growth on the face which might, if neglected, have generated into a cancer," yet it also mentioned her successful treatment of a brewer's assistant who "asked her to improve the shape of his eyebrows as he was shortly going to Dublin and hoped to find a wife there."[17] The article concluded, "It may easily be seen, therefore, that it is not only vanity which prompts men as well as women to pay a visit to the sympathetic little beauty doctor. Many of both sexes employed in business to whom old age is a terrible bogey, go to her for the treatment of incipient baldness or to have their fading hair restored to its original colour" ("Improving," June 1904, 13). Significantly, *Fashion* deflected the notion that a man's desire to stave off the inevitable signs of aging could be rooted in such a feminine anxiety as vanity, choosing instead to imply the potential threat to his professional career. An article for a "hair restorer," which the writer insisted was "not a dye," similarly argued that "there are thousands of men, and among them [writers, doctors, solicitors], who find it pays them to keep with them as long as possible the signs of youth, and who look upon the approach of the grey head with anything but feelings of joy" (Brummel, "Valuable," 22).

Fashion *and Class*

From its front-cover "mascot"—a gentleman in evening dress holding up a monocle—that graced every issue,[18] *Fashion* directed itself toward an elite, privileged male readership—one that patronized West End tailors, wore occasion-specific clothing and evening dress, and purchased new garments every year to keep up with the latest modes. Through articles and news items on theatergoing, ocean-liner travel, automobiles, horses, hunting, sports, and urban amusements, along with its advertisements for expensive tailors, riding clubs, and luxury items, the magazine celebrated a male lifestyle of wealth, leisure, and fashionable consumption. "'FASHION' is subscribed to by gentlemen in the highest society," the magazine pronounced in July 1899 ("How to Dress," 3), and one year later, Beau Brummel, Junr., affirmed that "FASHION is a Magazine for the clubs in the West End, [and] for the best hotels in all parts of the world" (Brummel, untitled, June 1900, 5). "Smoke!" was a heavily promoted Hal Ludlow illustration from December 1898 (fig. 3.13) depicting a clearly upper-class champagne-toasting gentleman in evening dress whose fantasies of a dancing girl materialized in the smoke from his cigarette; it conveyed the kind of masculine image celebrated in *Fashion*—that of the well-heeled, fashionable, laddish bachelor on the town, not unlike the *Playboy* man envisioned by Hugh Hefner fifty years later.

Whether this upscale image accurately reflected *Fashion*'s actual readership is unknown. The magazine did occasionally acknowledge a middle-class audience as well. "We cannot all be equally rich," conceded the Baron in September 1899, "and FASHION, I hope, is useful to a good many thousands of men who wish to dress with taste and seemliness, but cannot afford to be extravagant in the process" ("Shams," 7). A review by the *Westminster Gazette* asserted that *Fashion* "always contains much useful information, not only for the smart man about town, but also for the less aspiring who must perforce keep down their tailor's bill" (Untitled, January 1899, 16). In May 1903, the magazine reprinted at length an

"SMOKE!"

"FASHION," CHRISTMAS 1898.

Figure 3.13. Hal Ludlow's "Smoke!" (*Fashion,* December 1898, 3) (permission British Library)

article that had originally appeared in *To-Day* regarding how much a man should spend annually on various articles of clothing to keep expenses low ("Fashion's" Monthly, 19–20). Significantly, *Fashion* repeatedly promoted the decidedly middle-class notion (often extolled in conduct books) that attention to neatness and posture helped the man with a modest income make the most of outdated or worn garments: "With prim, well-braced shoulders, an erect carriage, an athletic habit, even the worst clothes may be made to look almost comely" (Baron, "How," 17). The monthly addressed middle-class concerns for economy by acknowledging that the practical purchase and meticulous care of a few conservatively cut sartorial basics was far preferable to spending a fortune on the latest fashions and then treating them poorly. The October 1898 installment of From Head to Foot asserted, "It is not so much the man who spends large sums at his tailor's that always looks smart and well-dressed, as the man who buys a moderate amount of clothes and treats them properly" (Brummel, 15). Moreover, *Fashion*'s frequent how-to articles on the cleaning and maintenance of clothing and accessories describe labor that would presumably have been undertaken by servants in an upper-class home, providing additional evidence that the magazine's readership was far from elite. Particularly confounding to the question of class regarding *Fashion*'s target audience is the inclusion of the monthly dress chart—for if the magazine imagined its average reader as an upper-class gentleman possessing an innate understanding of proper dress for all occasions, then to whom is the rather pedantic dress chart directed? Were the rules that governed occasion-specific attire not obvious after all? Or was the magazine actually geared more toward facilitating the aspirations of a social-climbing middle-class and nouveau riche audience?

Whatever the explanation, if *Fashion* had any middle-class readers, they were confronted with a single, decidedly upper-class sartorial aesthetic—one based on rapidly changing, tailor-made, occasion-specific, frock-coat-and-topper-centered dress—that contrasted many of the emerging distinctive fashions and consumer practices of the bourgeoisie that I outline in chapter 5. Privileging the fashion of the elite, the magazine overtly assumed the primacy of what has become known as social emulation theory[19] and presumed that all "people who are not sufficiently accustomed to what is ordinarily called society" possess the "very proper wish to adapt themselves to the manners of the class they desire to enter" (Major, 14) and consequently "ape the dress of the order immediately above them in the social hierarchy" (Baron, "Shams," 7). While it conceded that "modes exist, and are rightly considered as modes, in every rank of society," and that these modes exhibit "an organic life of their own," *Fashion* held little admiration for the costume of the middle class (Mantalini, "Other-Class Fashion," 18). Criticizing the dour uniformity of traditional middle-class garb, the "Baron" sniffed, "A horrific somberness, associated with the very negation of smartness in cut, has always been the best dream of the *bourgeois* class, who are shocking dressers, and find nothing so 'genteel' as a close approximation to the professional apparel of the undertaker" (Baron, "Colour," 9). The costume of the upper-middle class and the nouveau riche was even less forgivable: "The successful Englishman of the self-made class . . . is seldom a smart man in the sartorial as well as the commercial sense. He is desperately partial to broad-cloth frock coats, narrow black silk bows, and stove-pipe 'toppers'; and he dearly loves badly-fitting gloves, and elastic-spring boots with flat little buttons down the fronts, whose object is solely one of decoration, and whose appearance is wholly clumsy and unstylish" ("Some," 8). For the editors, the self-made middle-class "gentleman" distinguished himself from the lower-class "bounder" only by the addition of flashy jewelry and baubles. Both, however, were guilty of patronizing "the 'cheap imitation' industry" of ready-made clothing, which *Fashion* warned its readers against relentlessly (London Expert, January 1900, 10). "There is nothing in the way of clothes that betrays its origin quicker and more thoroughly than a ready-made waistcoat of the fancy order," the magazine exhorted, advising its readers to steer clear of the ready-made dealers and cheap tailors of "Oxford Street and other thoroughfares of Philistia" (London Expert, January 1900, 11; Mantalini, "Concerning," 15).

Fashion revealed common Victorian social anxieties—explored in chapter 4—by underscoring the sometimes-obvious, sometimes-imperceptible (or imagined?) sartorial differences between the classes. It attempted to draw a clear distinction between its own sartorial philosophy and that of overdressed fops and mashers, between those who follow fashion and those who follow it slavishly or clumsily. In a lengthy article entitled "On Overdoing It," the Baron outlined the boundaries between foppery and gentlemanly dress:

> A fop is one whose attiring betrays the too close attention of an ill-balanced or an empty mind. He is dressed with expenditure and wasteful cost; but without intelligence, without taste, without reserve. . . . He is known at a glance, for that his clothes attract that glance, and suffer you to forget (what you notice first in a well-drest man) the personality of the wearer. . . .
>
> The over-drest man, be he fop or mere bounder, is never comfortable, and lacks always the repose of a man really well-attired. . . . The bounder, who is no gentleman, is so pitifully self-conscious and egocentric that he must needs be for ever worrying lest his tie be acrook, or lest someone be observing him with critical disfavour. The true repose of

gentlemanhood, solicitous only for the comfort of others, bars out all self-conscious fidgetting. The cad thinks only of himself, and just as he "does himself" too well at dinner, so he dresses himself too showily at all hours.

The Baron explained that fops of all classes are inevitably guilty of overconscious exaggeration and excess. "Just as a gentleman is unmistakeable, even in rags, so the fop will continue to be overdressed, even in sackcloth or in the costume of the coster." Perhaps surprisingly, the Baron did not attack dandyism itself; indeed, he asserted that "the really fine dresser" exhibited a "legitimate dandihood" immediately discernible from the overdress of the fop or bounder. The "honest gentleman" quickly forgot his attire and any personal defects, appearing natural and self-possessed. The Baron implied that the gentleman and the fop invested the same amount of painstaking labor into their attire. But for the gentleman, all the "work" of proper dress was behind him; it took place in the privacy of the tailoring shop and his bedroom:

> He has spent moments of judicious thought on the commanding of his suit. The patterning of trousers best suited to the bulk or the exiguity of his limbs, has had sound selection, and the mode of the moment has been artistically interpreted to make the cut of his coat at once fashionable and becoming. The collar he chooses consorts well alike with the nature and occasion of his dress, and with the length and girth of his proper neck; his cravat is a work of art; his tie-pin has reticence in its beauty, and in it[s] richness, modesty. He wears his clothes well: it is the man of taste within them who attracts the delighted eye of the critical. On his dressing-table lies the publication it were orgulous to name, but which he peruses with judgment, while the fop ignores it or reads it awrong. ("On Overdoing," 20–21)

As I discuss in chapter 1, the gentlemanly masculine ideal—celebrated endlessly in conduct books—of appearing as if one took no notice of his dress was a carefully constructed fiction achieved by the meticulous concealing of the labor necessary for a polished public exterior. *Fashion* too suggested that gentlemanhood was rooted in how one carried himself and the ability to appear unself-conscious of his outer person. In doing so, the magazine—perhaps unconsciously—facilitated the blurring of class distinctions by possibly assisting some working- and middle-class gentlemen who were clever enough to take its lessons to heart and "pass" as members of a superior class. Telling its middle-class readers that all they needed was a few carefully selected clothing staples, erect posture, and a confident attitude, *Fashion* served as a guidebook to the aspiring nonelite, promising the secrets for how to appear like a gentleman.

Despite its short life of seventy-nine issues, *Fashion* appeared to have enjoyed respectable commercial success—as well as great celebrity within the periodical world. While no circulation or financial records survive, *Polo Magazine* reported in 1899 that *Fashion* had nearly tripled its circulation in its first nine months. By February 1900 it had expanded to three editions (English, American, and Indian), and a Buenos Aires edition was added the following July ("Notice," February 1900; "Special Notice to Advertisers"). According to its promotional copy, the magazine circulated "largely in New York, San Francisco, Chicago, Calcutta, Paris, Vienna, Berlin, Cairo, Buenos Aires,"[20] and a third of its subscribers were Americans (Untitled, March 1901, 18; From Head, January 1902, 25). *Fashion* frequently commented on responses from its readership, at one time declaring, "The Editor says that he could comfortably retire for quite a fortnight . . . on as many pounds as inquiries he has received" regarding a blue serge sacque suit depicted in the February 1899 issue (London Expert, March 1899, 11). However, one of *Fashion*'s columnists revealingly acknowledged—if only once—that the magazine had struggled to find a regular audience. Upon the publication of its twentieth issue, Coffee and Cognac columnist L. Godfrey-Turner reflected that "despite the fact that FASHION entered the great field of journalism armed with the distinction of being the first paper for men, we, its proprietors, have for these twenty months had a hard and anxious fight, . . . for, to tell truth, we discovered in the opening months of our little magazine's career that, as regards numbers, the people who make it a rule to purchase a thing because of its novelty represent a somewhat insignificant section of human creation." Godfrey-Turner claimed that the editors regarded their magazine's meager readership philosophically, resolving to strive harder to justify its existence beyond mere novelty and to "make the paper acceptable to club men, and useful to club men's tailors." By the twentieth issue, he was able to boast, "The knot was got over—the river crossed—the corner turned. Tailors of all parts of the world wrote us letters of thanks; their customers wrote us letters of congratulation," though he offered no specifics regarding how this was achieved or in what manner the magazine was improved (Godfrey-Turner, October 1899, 4).

From the legions of effusive reviews that were reprinted ad nauseam within its own pages, *Fashion* clearly received a great deal of favorable attention within the world of the periodical press. The magazine's leadership paved the way for its peers, and the *Pelican* observed in 1899 that "many of our leading contemporaries have taken to discussing men's modes since 'Beau Brummel, Junr.,' made a success with his 'West End Gentleman's Magazine and Dress Guide,' FASHION" ("Pelican," 10). A lot of the fashion news being discussed, however, was directly from or about *Fashion,* as the magazine noted in October of that same year that the September issue had been "quoted and reviewed" by twenty popular periodicals (Untitled, October 1899, 24). Perhaps *Fashion's* role, then—as evidenced by its presumably small readership and the regularity with which it was cited in English and American periodicals—evolved into that of a valuable reference tool regarding fashion news for fellow papers, rather than as a widely read magazine for a popular audience. Perhaps its fellow periodicals made regular references to it because it was an anomaly and because they could not obtain men's fashion news from any other source. In this way, however, *Fashion's* ultimate influence was perhaps quite significant, since its clothing news, sartorial prescriptions, and fashion aesthetic were disseminated—if indirectly and frequently uncredited[21]—to a larger, more widespread, more diverse male audience than the magazine could have ever achieved itself.

In September 1904, *Fashion* printed a joint August–September issue, explaining that no August issue had been released, because "the Editor decid[ed] that operations in the men's wear trade were far too insignificant to chronicle" (Brummel, "Notice," 5). After this, the magazine disappeared for four months, returning for a final issue in February 1905. It offered no explanation for its hiatus, nor were there any indications in its copy that this would be its final appearance. Obviously, however, *Fashion's* demise did not mark the end of men's fashion publications, as they emerged in force in the 1920s and '30s, continued through *Playboy* in the '50s, and have experienced a recent surge beginning in the '90s with new titles such as *Maxim, Stuff,* and *FHM,* reaching large male audiences on both sides of the Atlantic. Perhaps turn-of-the-century England was not quite ready for a men's magazine, yet the very appearance of *Fashion* suggests that there was a significant interest in, and a market for, this kind of publication and the consumer-oriented masculinity it represented. *Fashion's* very existence—however brief—demonstrates that men's fashion and men's interest in fashion had become widely recognized and that men as a consumer force had become impossible to ignore.

FROM DANDY TO MASHER TO CONSUMER

Competing Masculinities and Class Aspirations

Dandyism is, after all, one of the decorative arts.

——Max Beerbohm, "Dandies and Dandies"

The old saying to the contrary withstanding, external appearances do not always afford the least satisfactory evidences of a man's character. As for the "cad." You have him in an instant. He betrays himself offhand. He tries to affect the gentleman, but in externals only. You have him on the hip directly he opens his mouth.

——*Best Dressed Man* (1892)

The gent possessed three important attributes: flamboyant and self-conscious dress, rakishness, and counterfeit status.

——Judith R. Walkowitz, *City of Dreadful Delight*

$\mathcal{D}$ESPITE RADICAL CHANGES IN MEN'S CONSUMER HABITS AND A new mainstream openness regarding sartorial display between 1860 and 1914, many voices within British popular discourse continued to criticize and condemn men who participated in shopping, fashion, and the public exhibition of purchased goods as "bad," even potentially dangerous, consumers. On those occasions when male dress was explicitly acknowledged, discussed, or described at length, the popular press (conduct literature, novels, magazine commentary) was still far more prone to address incorrect forms of men's costume. Overt, visible male consumption was typically caricatured—and demonized—among the middle classes through the figure of the dandy, and the majority of the contemporary historical and critical literature on men's fashions has concentrated on this type.[1] Since at least the eighteenth century, middle-class writers had most frequently depicted the dandy as a dangerous and unattractive upper-class gentleman: vain, ostentatious, idle, and sexually predatory. The dandy was a prominent inhabitant of British society and fiction throughout the first half of the nineteenth century and distinguished himself from normative forms of masculinity by his emphasis on outer appearance and conspicuous consumption.

As the satirical symbols of improper, transgressive masculinity, dandies became contested figures, markers of class tensions whose function as class critique was wrestled over by the bourgeoisie and the elite. The dandy was important to the Victorians as a symbol on which to pin increasingly contested notions of both class and gender. However, he was never a static figure with a single, fixed identity. Beginning around midcentury, the negative qualities attributed to the upper-class dandy—particularly his preoccupation with clothing and his conscious self-display—were gradually shifted to the middle (and working) classes, where they were partly appropriated and transformed into acceptable, mainstream masculine consumer behaviors. Certainly, the growing popularity of more fitted, body-hugging, ornamented men's clothing as well as the (covert) use of cosmetics and body-shaping clothing by men, which I discuss in chapter 2, suggest a middle-class mainstreaming of dandyism's affectations. As the working and middle classes caught up with upper-class consumption and status markers were blurred, many among the elite (as well as conservative members of the middle classes) attacked the growing fashionable consumption and public display of the nonelite through the figure of the fast, flashy, and crudely flamboyant "masher." Through the masher, the dandy was co-opted and transformed in some popular discourses from an upper-class to a middle-class caricature as a means of discrediting the middle-class male's expanding socioeconomic power. Further, the masher's costume evoked new class anxieties as it came to represent blurrings of sartorial and social borders. Many among the working and middle classes developed sartorial and consumer tastes that mimicked those of the elite, thereby causing class confusion and conflict.

The Nineteenth-Century Dandy

Thomas Carlyle famously defined the early-nineteenth-century dandy[2] as "a Clothes-wearing Man, a Man whose trade, office and existence consists in the wearing of Clothes. Every faculty of his soul, spirit, purse, and person is heroically consecrated to the wearing of Clothes wisely and well: so that as others dress to live, he lives to dress" (197). While often lacking claims to high birth, the English dandy nevertheless enjoyed—oftentimes on borrowed money—the upper class's education, aristocratic privileges, and social circle. He led the life of a gentleman of leisure, consumed by a slavish devotion to impeccable correctness in all matters of dress, gestures, taste, and wit. To be sure, dandies had been around for millennia—Aristotle (384–322 BC) and the Athenian statesman and general Alcibiades (ca. 450–404 BC) were two oft-referenced ancient examples—but the dandy of the nineteenth century was notably different from his predecessors for a number of reasons. By the early decades of the century, he had moved out of the intimate, elite sphere of the royal court and into the public, crowded fishbowl of the modern city. While ostensibly the successors to the prancing "fops" of the eighteenth-century court and aristocracy, early-nineteenth-century dandies actually represented a "*repudiation* of fine feathers," exhibiting a sartorial aesthetic completely antithetical to the lace-cuffed, wigged, powdered, perfumed performance of their predecessors (Laver, *Dandies*, 10). George Bryan "Beau" Brummell (1778–1850), the paragon of Regency-era dandyism (fig. 4.1), renounced ornamentation, excess, and large sartorial expressions in favor of simplicity, understatement, and the reduction of dress to a few carefully selected essentials. The dandy's immaculate shirtfront, perfectly knotted neckcloth, and flawless manners were meant to represent his monklike discipline, his refinement and restraint, and what fin-de-siècle essayist and fellow dandy Max Beerbohm later called his "exquisite ordering" (22). Brummell neatly summarized the dandy's ascetic sartorial standard in his oft-quoted dictum, "No perfumes, but very fine linen, plenty of it, and country washing" (quoted in Amies, 11). In the dandy's strict rejection of ostentation in favor of understatement, he initially appears to have been allied with the middle-class ideals of the Great Masculine Renunciation. Yet he overtly rejected the bourgeois pillars of utility, thrift, and hard work at the same time that the middle-class male was embracing them. With no occupation and no obvious source of income, the dandy consciously set himself in direct opposition to the "new bourgeois domination of society" and strove to maintain "an aristocratic lifestyle in a bourgeois world" (Auslander, 91). His crisp white linen, confining stays, and wasp-waisted jackets distinguished the dandy from the middle-class male with his drab frock coat, thick boots and sensible pocket watch of the middle-class male, and also expressed an overt contempt for bourgeois Protestant capitalist values.

The dandy was therefore upsetting to early Victorian middle-class norms of masculinity. Brummell's maxim that "if John Bull turns round to look after you, you are not well dressed: but either too stiff, too tight or too fashionable" may have mirrored the renunciation's emphasis on a natural, artless male performance

Figure 4.1. Richard Dighton's 1805 portrait of Beau Brummell (reprinted in Amies, plate 8)

that rendered one's physical self invisible (quoted in Amies, 11). But for the middle classes, the upper-class dandy was in practice all show and silly flamboyance. The dandy's raison d'être was always self-conscious display. Of course, middle-class dress served as a kind of class-specific self-display too, but conveying sobriety, hard work, and serious-mindedness seemed somehow more legitimate than conveying elitism, idleness, and overrefinement. Distinguished from normative nineteenth-century forms of masculinity, the dandy eschewed the traditional middle-class men's roles of producer and breadwinner, preferring instead a passive life of lounging about private drawing rooms and the city streets, avoiding legitimate work, awaiting an inheritance or a wealthy bride. Dandies were "terrifying in their nonreproductivity" (Auslander, 92); upsetting conventional gender norms, they were "educated for consumption rather than production" (Curtin, 95). In this way, the dandy aligned himself with women's preoccupation with outer appearance and conspicuous consumption. A dangerous figure of transgressive masculinity for the middle classes, the dandy seemed to "parody bourgeois feminine roles" with the decoration of both himself and the home, which he transformed from a domestic and familial space into a homosocial bachelor pad (Auslander, 90–91). Baudelaire declared that dandyism was "a kind of self-worship, . . . the love of astonishing others and the delight of being astonished oneself," and indeed the dandy cultivated every aspect of his body, gestures, and physical presentation for consumption by an admiring public (420). The middle-class conduct book *Habits of Good Society* (1859) directly contradicted Brummell's dictums, decrying, "A dandy . . . is the clothes on a man, not a man in clothes, a living lay-figure who displays much dress, and is quite satisfied if you praise it without taking heed of him" (157).

The Transformation of the Elitist Dandy into the Middle-Class Male Consumer

The representations and meanings of dandyism underwent a radical transformation from Brummell at the beginning of the nineteenth century to Oscar Wilde and the Aesthetes at its close. The Regency-era dandy's emphasis on meticulous understatement and gentlemanly reserve gradually shifted into an embrace of the brash, the ostentatious, and the conspicuous. While well-known dandies of the 1820s, '30s, and '40s—including Benjamin Disraeli, Count D'Orsay, and Edward Bulwer Lytton[3]—regarded themselves as disciples of Brummell's ideal, they were "clearly anxious to appear conspicuous, the antithesis of Brummell's intentions," favoring sartorial and social flamboyance over subtlety (Lambert, "Dandy," 62). As the dandy's world of the elite court circle was disappearing, his new audience was a popular one, and his distinctive traits shifted from intangible, interior qualities such as his wit and manners to more visual, exterior—and consequently commodifiable—qualities, in particular his clothing (Williams, 121–22). And as the importance of the dandy's clothing increased, it tended to grow in ridiculously exaggerated directions. By the middle decades of the nineteenth century, the dandy had become a familiar stereotype, endlessly lampooned in prose and cartoons for his enormous bow ties, preposterously stiff and high neckcloths, and body-hugging jackets and trousers so tight that they restricted all movement (figs. 4.2 and 4.3). His unabashed love of attention and big sartorial statements connected him more and more closely with the "gents," "swells," and "fast men" of the middle and working classes from which he had once sought to distinguish himself.

The more traditional dandy never completely disappeared; indeed, he made a popular revival in the 1880s and '90s with the likes of Wilde, Beerbohm, and the

Figure 4.2. "What a miwackulous tye, Fwank" (*Punch* 25 [1853]: 18)

X. 42. "Did you call the Police, Sir?"

Swell (who would perish rather than disturb his shirt-collar). "Ya—as, a—I've had the misfortune to dwop my Umbrellaw, and there isn't a boy within a mile to pick it up—a—Will you have the Goodness!"

Figure 4.3. X. 42. "Did you call the Police, Sir?" (*Punch* 24 [1853]: 58)

young Winston Churchill (Laver, *Dandies*, 94–100). Yet as the century progressed, many of the upper-class qualities of dandyism gradually crept down the social scale to appeal to working- and middle-class males, assisted by a commodity culture that democratized the dandy's preoccupation with consumption into normative consumer practices. The rejection of upper-class excess and dissolute living that may have defined middle-class ideals earlier in the century was at least partially obliterated by the seductive forces of late-Victorian commerce, which glamorized consumption and display. As I argue in earlier chapters, the emerging consumer industry helped make shopping "safe" and masculine for the middle-class male. The dandy's sexually transgressive threat as "a man who commodified himself as an object for the consumption of others" had become mainstream and was absorbed by middle-class consumer culture; the once-elite flamboyance of the dandy was transformed into the conspicuous consumption of the bourgeoisie (Auslander, 91). Late-nineteenth-century would-be dandies from the middle classes—mashers—fixated on the more physical, visible aspects of dandyism (furniture, personal effects, and clothing), and these were the aspects most easily reconfigured into purchasable commodities. While the average man could never attain the wit, polish, and pedigree of the upper-class gentleman, he could acquire the exterior semblance of his lifestyle. The genuine dandy had all his clothing and personal goods custom-made, but his tastes could be replicated and mass-produced—albeit in cruder versions—for an aspiring middle class often hungry for items believed to exude an aura of elegance, panache, and individualistic flair.

Thus, Baudelaire's lament that "the dandy as a self-created spectacle" was disappearing under the homogenizing and mediocritizing forces of modern democracy was premature (422). Dandyism never disappeared—Wilde and Beerbohm made sure of that. What is more, it was picked up—perhaps in a more diluted, commercial form—by mainstream middle-class popular culture. Display and spectacle appealed profoundly to men of all classes, and for many, ostentation was transformed into a "domestic duty rather than a public vice" (Breward, *Hidden*, 61). In the late-Victorian and Edwardian era, fashion demanded that possessions be well displayed in the home; the body was no different as a venue of display. While jewelry had once been taboo for men, the *Warehouseman and Drapers' Trade Journal* reported in 1879 that "the custom of wearing inexpensive jewellery gains ground every day" ("Fashionable," 165). Middle-class men were eager to adopt the form-fitting jackets, checkered suits, and colored vests sold by the department stores, and while too-tight trousers may have been regarded as "utterly mashy" (quoted in Cunnington and Cunnington, 299) by the *Gentleman's Magazine of Fashion* during the 1880s, this did not stop men from wearing them. Although it may have begun in part as a revolt against the uniformity and mediocrity of the encroaching bourgeois culture, dandyism ultimately merged with the bourgeoisie, transformed into a commodifiable style available at Swan and Edgar's. Yet the men of the middle classes frequently denied their movement toward dandification and attempted to distinguish themselves from the dandy through euphemism.

The men's monthly *Fashion* declared, "We have something better than the dandy now: we have the 'smart man.' He is a far better ornament for the public eye, and as he exists in very large numbers—which the dandy never did—he is a far more profitable institution to the tailors" (Brummel, Dress News, October 1898, 22). Revealingly, the differences between the dandy and the "smart man" are unclear, for here the qualities that once made the dandy suspect—the transformation of his body into spectacle and commodity—remain intact. However, reinventing the dandy as the "smart man" made him safe, attractive, and masculine for the middle classes.

Authentic dandies of both the Beau Brummell and Oscar Wilde varieties might have abhorred the bourgeoisie, but what they shared with it was the emphasis on self-expression through consumption and the transformation of the self into a consumable good. As dandyism was diluted into consumption, both the late-nineteenth-century dandy and the mainstream middle-class male sought individual distinction and personal expression through possessions, decorating, and the collecting and displaying of things. Walter Pater's famous Aesthetic tenet to "burn always" with a "hard gem-like flame" could be translated into insatiable, nonstop consumption—not unlike Dorian Gray's voracious attempts to collect and study jewels, perfumes, and other expensive decorative and sensual arts (188–89). Indeed, Rachel Bowlby contends that "in its forceful promotion of the momentary personal pleasures promised" by objects of beauty (or consumer goods), Pater's conclusion to *The Renaissance* (1877/1893) "could be said to mark the beginning of modern consumer culture"; his pronouncement that "Art comes to you proposing frankly to give nothing but the highest quality to your moments as they pass" (190) can be alternately read as "a textbook example of advertising copy rather than an original aesthetic statement" (Bowlby, 24). Marketers' aggressive attempts to entice Britons with goods, to encourage them to give in to their consumer desires, and to urge them to seek instant (if only temporary) gratification through the purchase of goods mirrored Lord Henry's call for a "new Hedonism," to "be always searching for new sensations" (Wilde, *Dorian Gray*, 23). While critics have long striven to pin down the ambiguous vice(s) committed by Dorian Gray—having read them as homosexuality, sadomasochism, and masturbation—the decadence that saturates Wilde's novel might very well also lie in the deviant sexual inversion implicit in the figure of a man infected by the out-of-control, insatiable consumer habits believed to be unique to the female sex (Sinfield, 101–3). Wilde and the Aesthetic dandies continued to insist on a wide gulf separating them from the bourgeoisie, but the differences were sometimes superficial ones, lying only in what and how they consumed. The once-transgressive dandy—or at least one manifestation of him—became transformed into the mainstream male, proficient in public consumption and self-display. The dandy's self-display became all about consumption as the middle-class male's consumption became all about self-display—the two trajectories intersected in the late nineteenth century, motivated by the powerful institutions of modern commodity culture.

From Dandy to Masher

Not everyone was comfortable with this commercial conflation of elitist and populist ideals. As the middle classes began to assume some of the traits and goods of the elite, the upper classes sought to redefine the social borders. Thus, at the same time that the dandy's formerly deviant traits were democratized and commodified into middle-class masculinity, conservative upper- and middle-class commentators attempted to revitalize and redirect the transgressive semiotic power within the negative figure of the dandy by equating him with the clumsy, showy, flashy displays of bourgeois manhood. At the same time that the middle classes dismissed the occasion-specific tailor-made dress of the upper classes as overdone, uncomfortable, and self-conscious, the upper classes regarded the costume of the aspiring middle-class masher in the very same light. It was widely asserted that Britain's "common" gentlemen who purchased their ready-made suits and baubles in London's department stores and bazaars could achieve only what fashion historian Farid Chenoune terms a "patchy elegance." Middle- and lower-middle-class males, such as "the worker in his Sunday best, the shop assistant all decked out, the middle-class civil servant whose wife hoped to make a 'gentleman' of him, the hairdresser who approached outlandishness, the traveling salesman who took on big-city airs, the *nouveau riche* who was a bit too flashy," became the perennial butts of journalists and cartoonists for their awkward, misguided attempts at upper-class sophistication (figs. 4.4 and 4.5; Chenoune, 131). The stress that Beerbohm and other traditional dandies repeatedly placed on "true" dandyism's simplicity and subtlety were intended as an indictment of the lower and middle classes' clumsily garish attempts at a déclassé dandyism.[4] Antagonism grew—in the words of a popular song from a musical comedy of the era—among "the famous and the rich" against "those who tried to pose as sich" (Willis, 151).

STANDING NO NONSENSE.

'Arry. "Phew !"—(*the weather was warm, and they had walked over from 'Ammersmith*)—
"bring us a Bottle o' Champagne, Waiter."

Waiter. Yessir—Dry, Sir ?"

'Arry (*'aughtily, to put a stop to this familiarity at once*). "Never you mind whether
we 're Dry or whether we ain't !—bring the Wine !"

Figure 4.4. "Standing No Nonsense" (*Punch*, 8 May 1880, 215)

'Arriet. "I WILL SAY THIS FOR BILL, 'E DO LOOK THE GENTLEMAN!"

Figure 4.5. "I will say this for Bill, 'e *do* look the Gentleman!" (*Punch*, 15 March 1905, 190)

These parvenus and pretentious upstarts were satirized endlessly through the new stereotype of the "masher" in the second half of the nineteenth century. The dandy and the masher were both caricatures of improperly flamboyant male display; the dandy was a negative stereotype of the upper-class man, while the masher was a negative stereotype of the middle- (and working-) class man. If the middle classes had depicted the early-nineteenth-century dandy as the extravagant and frivolous aristocrat, the elite classescame to depict the masher as the gaudy nouveau riche poseur—one who tried too hard to affect upper-class status through clothing and other forms of overt self-display but succeeded only in underscoring his lowly and unsophisticated origins. Having most likely originated in the United States, the term *masher* was quite common in Britain by 1882,[5] though the type was known by many other monikers, including "chappie" and "Piccadilly Johnnie" (*Oxford English Dictionary*, vol. 9, 424). By any name, the masher was a dandy for a postindustrial, mass-production, middle-class world. He was distinguished by his exaggerated ready-made fashions, ridiculously affected speech or "fast" slang, and a jaunty streetwise masculinity. H. G. Wells, in his 1900 novel *Kipps*, recorded the youthful masher uniform of the 1890s in a description of his shop-clerk protagonist's dress: "His costume is just as tremendous a 'mash' as lies within his means. His collar is so high that it scars his inaggressive jaw-bone, and his hat has a curly brim, his tie shows taste, his trousers are modestly brilliant, and his boots have light cloth uppers and button at the side. He jabs at the gravel before him with a cheap cane and glances sideways at Flo Bates, the young lady from the cash desk" (50–51). But Wells's description also conveys the social criticism inherent in the masher stereotype: the false "modesty" belied by Kipps's "brilliant" costume and the weak, "inaggressive" body that compromises his attempts at confident display.

Mashers were observed in all social strata. An 1888 *Punch* cartoon entitled "The Height of Masherdom" depicts a clearly upper-class gentleman decked in evening clothes conversing with an acquaintance at a dinner party (fig. 4.6). The most up-

THE HEIGHT OF MASHERDOM.

' WELL, TA-TA OLD MAN! MY PEOPLE ARE WAITING UP FOR ME, YOU KNOW!" "WHY, DON'T YOU CARRY A LATCH-KEY!" "CARRY A *LATCH-KEY!* NOT I! A LATCH-KEY 'D SPOIL ANY FELLER'S FIGURE!"

Figure 4.6. "The Height of Masherdom" (*Punch,* 4 February 1888, 57)

scale version of the masher, often referred to as a "cad," regarded himself as a direct descendent of the Brummell-era dandies and was recognized by "his overcoat almost down to his ankles, his top hat with its brim extravagantly curled up at the sides, his excessively high stiff collar, his monocle, and, above all, his gleaming white spats" (fig. 4.7; McDowell, 84). Lower-middle-class mashers—known as "swells" or "gents"—originated mainly from the clerks, apprentices, and tailors[6] who made up the lower fringes of the respectable classes. The swell was depicted

"The 'Cad' acts on the offensive."

Figure 4.7. "The 'Cad' acts on the offensive" (*Best Dressed Man,* 44)

Figure 4.8. The 1870s masher; illustration by Alfred Concanen (Green and Lee, 1) (permission British Library H.1561.[11])

by newspaper cartoonists and music hall comedians as a slick-haired mustachioed urban dandy in a tight-fitting jacket and sporting a walking stick (figs. 4.8 and 4.9). In *Twice Round the Clock* (1858), George Augustus Sala described the "long surtout, double-breasted waistcoat, accurately-folded scarf, peg-top trousers, eyeglass, umbrella, and drooping moustache" of the quintessential midcentury swell

Has an idea that the first impression is everything, and is got up accordingly.

Figure 4.9. The 1870s masher among "A Lot of Lovers" (Ross, 45)

(195). Even further down the social scale were working-class swells in checkered suits and bowler caps, popularized most famously in the figure of *Punch's* gleefully vulgar Cockney rake "'Arry" (featured in fig. 4.4).[7] Long before he adopted his upper-class Aesthetic persona, Oscar Wilde was photographed in just such a costume while at Oxford in the mid-1870s (fig. 4.10).

The distinctive markers and titles that identified the masher continued to evolve and splinter well into the twentieth century; for example, a suburban version of the masher, called the "knut" and known mainly for his brightly colored socks, enjoyed his heyday immediately before the First World War (Laver, *Dandies*, 109).[8] Further, the meaning, qualities, and identity of the masher, swell, or cad depended on who was portraying him and to what end. These stereotypes were employed within competing fictions of class identity and relationships that served to reveal the subjectivity of class. The upper classes regarded mashers as middle-class poseurs, while the middle classes regarded mashers as working-class poseurs. The swell, meanwhile, was a critical image of the working classes imposed upon them by the middle classes (Walkowitz, 44). In all his incarnations, the masher served as a derogatory stereotype intended to discredit the presumptions of one class's aping the lifestyle of a higher class. The fact that today mashers are mainly remembered as working-class may point to the middle class's ultimate success in deflecting the masher image away from itself and onto a less privileged group.

For conservative members of the middle classes, the masher represented additional dangers. Aspiring to look and live like the upper classes led to reckless spending and abandonment of the middle-class values of hard work and thrift. The masher suggested a more threatening form of the English bachelor, whose idle, lounging lifestyle was tolerated only because it was understood to be temporary, terminated in good time by marriage. He was a caricature of deviant masculinity, a man in arrested development avoiding his adult responsibilities. He conveyed a lifestyle of uninterrupted leisure, sleeping during the day and carousing at night. Moreover, the masher's dangerous sexual nature was always clearly understood through his popular reputation as a "lady-killer,"[9] an urban nocturnal prowler, "daintily picking [his] way in white spats through the sordid alleyways" to do some fashionable "slumming" in the East End or haunting music halls and stage doors of the West End (Adburgham, *Punch*, 145). The sartorial theatricality and strutting, even aggressive masculinity of the masher symbolized the threat of improper, misused bourgeois manhood—a man who had failed to shed the dandified dress grudgingly permitted during his youth or college years and

Figure 4.10. Oscar Wilde in checkered lounger while a student at Magdalen College, Oxford, in the mid-1870s (courtesy Getty Images, photographer unknown)

had eschewed the prescribed path of heterosexual monogamy, suburban domesticity, and middle-class industry, preferring instead a dissolute life of fashion, leisure, sexual promiscuity, and urban worldliness.

Masherdom and Anxieties Regarding Sartorial Class Mimicry

It is perhaps impossible to determine how many men truly assumed the costume and lifestyle of the masher, if only for a brief while, but the masher was deeply unsettling because his sartorial style and social habits blurred Victorian Britain's clearly delineated class borders. Nineteenth-century advice manuals and essays from the popular press repeatedly offered passionate warnings against crude attempts by would-be mashers to dress above their class. "In general, it may be said that there is vulgarity in dressing like those of a class above us," remarked *Habits of Good Society* in 1859, "since it must be taken as a proof of pretension" (135). In 1900, *Clothes and the Man* recounted the cautionary tale of a foolish man who buys a fur coat, is therefore assumed by everyone to be a wealthy gentleman, and falls into financial ruin in his attempts to maintain the charade (184–86). What is not as widely acknowledged is that conduct manuals also frequently warned against the temptations of dressing beneath one's class. "If you carry a stick, eschew the monstrosities in which 'Arry and Bob delight," *The Glass of Fashion* advised in 1881, "but on the other hand avoid the pitiful abortion of a school which distinguishes itself by aping simultaneously dandyism and decrepitude" (176–77). Social commentators were deeply unsettled by those who were imagined to dress beneath their station because they were fascinated by the shady lifestyle of the lower classes. *Fashion* reprinted the lengthy comments of one reader distressed over "the coster-like character of certain of the clothes of the 'well-dressed man,'" including country morning coats cut "on the lines of the coster's Bank Holiday coat" and the use of velvet trimming "so beloved of the coster" ("On Velvet," 10–11).[10] *The English Gentleman* cautiously articulated a warning against the fast dress of London's East End gents:

> There is another . . . mode of dress . . . which, especially amongst young men, is often dignified with the name of fashion. . . . I mean a rakish, roué sort of dress,—imitative at one time of stage coachmen; at another of prize-fighters; at another of some equally reputable class; but all taken from low life, and adapted with singular infelicity to persons who, if

their rank of gentility means any thing, are supposed to be men of refinement. If their ambition is to command envy from the imitated, and to show how well they can beat them at their own weapons, no doubt they may very easily succeed; but if they gain any respect from persons of their *own* class, it is only because the world is more thoughtless or more lenient than they deserve. Whatever forms it may take as you grow older, I earnestly hope, that, at the least, it will be thought no object for your emulation. (104–5)

This warning bears a striking resemblance to Eliza Lynn Linton's famous polemic "The Girl of the Period" (1868) against the imitation by fashionable young Englishwomen of the racy costume and scandalous lifestyle of the Parisian demimonde. Anxieties regarding respectable middle- (and upper-) class men emulating the dress and habits of disreputable classes, professions, and character types were rooted in larger Victorian fears—outlined brilliantly by Peter Stallybrass and Allon White—of a diseased and degenerate urban riffraff and the potentially hypnotic power of lower-class deviancy over decent men. The masher was criticized because he represented simultaneously dressing above and below one's class. The masher's danger to middle-class propriety was his conflation of upper- and lower-class performance—a *mashing* of class identities and social roles. For many among the conservative bourgeoisie, the masher created the link between the upper and lower classes' predilection for dissolute sexuality, idleness, and irresponsible consumption. He frequently blended his aristocratic aspirations with a kind of crude, decadent flash that suggested to the moralistic middle-class mind the aesthetic of the music hall, the boxing ring, the racetrack, the public street, and the brothel. He was iconic of mass consumer culture's mixing and blurring of social categories through public spaces such as the urban department store and the goods and styles it made available to nearly everyone.

The ongoing English debate over the question of what defined the true gentleman intensified during the Victorian era, as the decline of the traditional aristocracy and the continued growth of the middle classes rendered conventional social categories increasingly unstable. Certainly, the title of gentleman no longer applied exclusively to the nobility, as middle-class commentators insisted that true gentility lay not in high birth but in morals and manners that could potentially be achieved by anyone. The new availability and affordability of upper-class membership only complicated matters further, and conservative Victorians feared that the role of the gentleman might become merely a status marker divested of all moral qualities and attainable by any ambitious social climber (Adams, 53, 152).

Clothing rendered visible the divisions that maintained social roles and defined class belonging. The quickening pace and increasingly visual nature of late-Victorian London both emphasized the need for visual codes that enabled people to read one another quickly and exacerbated their reliance on a mobile form of social status display—namely, clothing. Previously, class identity had been defined by one's birth, residence, education, speech, and vocation (or whether a man worked at all). In late-Victorian times, class had to be discernible on the body in the form of one's clothing, and Victorian commentators repeatedly declared that the gentleman's clothing—its quality, fit, care, fashionableness, and suitability to the occasion—distinguished him from other men. Such distinctions were not always clear, as mass production and department stores placed inexpensive knockoffs in the hands of the nonelite. Yet the insistence on discernible social distinctions in dress—even when perhaps none existed—remained a popular rhetorical stance necessary to the maintenance of the Victorian belief that one's status, profession, and character—the very "text of one's existence"—was visibly written on the body (Chenoune, 36). "Costume," wrote Max Beerbohm in 1896, "enables us to classify any 'professional man' at a glance, be he lawyer, leech or what not" (24–25). A man's profession and class were read by his jacket, his hat, what he rode in, and how he carried himself. "Perhaps there is a tendency among Englishmen to judge a man too much by the shape of his hat or the kind of collar he wears," conduct author John Wanamaker confessed; "But one must remember that in England if you *wear* the wrong thing, you will probably *do* the wrong thing, and generally *be* the wrong thing" (1).[11]

Such assertions were predicated on the powerful Victorian conviction that outward appearance reflected inner qualities. Conduct manuals proliferated this view by asserting that fashion was "the criterion by which a stranger forms his first judgment of our taste and habits" (*Etiquette of Modern Society*, 11), "a fair index of the mind of the wearer" (*Manual*, 126), and "one of the forms in which we naturally give expression to our taste, our constructive faculties, our reason, our feelings, our habits—in a word, to our character, as a whole" (*How to Behave*, 31). They repeatedly emphasized that dress should be appropriate to one's age, profession, and social station. In 1881 *The Glass of Fashion* acknowledged that while mass production had homogenized men's dress to an extent, class divisions could—and must—still be observed:

There is a certain uniformity in all dress nowadays, it is true. . . . Duke and costermonger wear coats of the same "cut;" the lady of rank and the seamstress's apprentice alike figure generally of the same form, if, indeed, it happens that the material of them varies. Yet a difference *does* still obtain, and we are continually meeting with persons of whom we say, "They are dressed above their station," and consequently above their means. No man with a limited income should aspire to a fashionable appearance. Let him be "point-device in his accoutrements," let neatness stand impersonated in him, let his clothes be of good texture and admirable cut, but let him keep within that class-limit which is easily recognised though not easily defined. (175)

The world of fiction also contributed to the promotion of class-specific costume. In his novel *Endymion* (1880), Benjamin Disraeli's famous tailor Mr. Vigo advises his clients to dress "according to your age, your pursuits, your object in life, . . . your set" (145), and Dickens and Thackeray poke great fun at their characters, particularly older women, who choose to dress in a manner ill suited to their age or social position.[12] The repeated stress placed on self-imposed sumptuary codes was meant as an attempt to recharge the notion of the gentleman as a position that could not be purchased or mimicked by those not born to it. Obviously, the emphasis on class-appropriate dress was aimed not at the upper classes but rather at the middle and lower classes, as the guardians of social borders feared that fashion would be used as a kind of disguise, a kind of mystifying armor used to deceive, to conceal the truth about oneself. People needed to be read quickly in the accelerated pace of city life, and clothing therefore needed to be an accurate, reliable identifier.

One curious manifestation of this fear was the recurrent complaint by gentlemen that conventional evening dress rendered them indistinguishable from servants. "Instances are on record," noted the *Warehouseman and Drapers' Trade Journal* in 1879, "of gentlemen at balls being under delusions and calling upon their host's most cherished guest and bigwig to bring them some lobster salad at suppertime, or to fetch them their hat and coat in the hall; but the only wonder is, considering the marvellous similarity of the costumes worn by gentlemen and waiters on those occasions, that such mistakes do not occur a great deal oftener" (Corisande, 386–87). Such stories—perhaps apocryphal and often in the form of jokes—were the regular fodder of the popular press and the gossip of tailors. The

author of *Best Dressed Man* recounted a typical incident during which he was cha-
grined to find himself mistaken for a waiter by a banquet of "snobs":

> Every man is willing to be appraised at a higher value than the public
> generally puts upon him. I recollect at a very splendid banquet of direc-
> tors, men not quite of the front rank, socially, but of money and influ-
> ence (a little of both, we know, is useful), having occasion to give the
> chairman a point for his after-dinner speech. Making my way to his
> place at head of the table, I was twice insolently checked by collateral
> snobs. "Waiter, bring the cigars!" said one; "Waiter, why the devil don't
> you bring that coffee; and attend to this table?" expostulated the other. I
> am bound to think my conventional white choker and glossy dress-coat
> were mainly answerable for the accidents. (59–60)

A George du Maurier cartoon that appeared in *Punch* depicts a similar incident, in which two identically attired gentlemen at a formal dinner party both
confuse the other for a waiter (fig. 4.11). By the 1880s, the criticism against standard evening dress had grown so familiar that the *Gazette of Fashion and Cutting Room
Companion* could refer to it simply as the "waiter argument," and many called for
a radical redesign of formal evening wear ("Thoughts," 71).[13] Yet several fashion
authorities and journalists dismissed such objections. "It is not necessary to have
a distinguishing dress for a waiter," *Clothes and the Man* (1900) concluded; "If a
gentleman is a gentleman, no one is likely to mistake him for a waiter, and if he
is not a gentleman, what does it matter if the mistake is made?" (67–68). In a
sense, the concern over the "waiter argument" played out the larger Victorian
concern over sartorial class distinctions in miniature, revealing both the anxiety
regarding class blurrings and the confident assertion that social divisions are always perceivable.

The continued dissemination of this "physiognomy" of dress was vital to the
upper class's maintenance of traditional socioeconomic distinctions between itself and the rising middle class's conspicuous consumers. As the bourgeoisie began
to acquire the goods representative of upper-class status, the elite insisted more
and more on the belief that differences and distinctions continued to exist, that
class was still readable, that, despite their best efforts, lower- and middle-class en-
croachers always maintained and readily revealed their true social status. When
Sala described in 1858 how the flashy clothes worn by lower-class mashers intend-

INCONVENIENCE OF MODERN MALE ATTIRE

First Stranger. " Here—hi! I want a knife and fork, please!"
Second Stranger. " Con-found you—so do I ? "

Figure 4.11. "Inconvenience of Modern Male Attire" by George du Maurier (*Punch,* 21 February 1891, 95)

ing to impress were nevertheless covered in grime, the lesson was obvious: true class identity was always visible (*Twice,* 85–87). Forty years later—when ready-made factories and department stores had enabled the lower and middle classes to dress identically to the upper—Sala insisted nothing had changed: "If you will be kind enough . . . to draw up in a line in the Mall of St. James's Park, say, a hundred individuals, impartially selected from divers sorts and conditions of men, and clad in suits of dittoes [lounge suits with all three pieces cut from the same material], I venture to think that I am physiognomist enough to be able to pick out from the array, so many stablemen, and so many hunters and whippers-in" (*London*, 248). *Best Dressed Man* echoed that the "real Simon Pure passes current everywhere," while "the imitation may usually be detected by some flaw, however slight, in the general make-up: it may be in the matter of rings, or scarf-pins, or watch-chains, or neck-ties" (102). Indeed, in Arnold Bennett's novel *The Old Wives' Tale* (1908), Sophia Baines's caddish and ne'er-do-well husband Gerald Scales inevitably reveals a chink in his sartorial disguise while living the high life in Paris: "He was dressed with some distinction; good clothes, when put to the test, survive a change of fortune, as a Roman arch survives the luxury of departed empire. Only his collar, large V-shaped front, and wristbands, which bore the ineffaceable signs of cheap laundering, reflected the shadow of impending disaster" (345). In May 1898, *Fashion* ran a cartoon entitled "Three Men in a Cap . . . Illustrating the Power of Fashion" (fig. 4.12). The cartoon purportedly demonstrates how the same cap could appear radically different on a gentleman, a masher, and a working-class man, suggesting that something inherent about one's class was always apparent beneath the clothes. However, the cartoon does not illustrate "the power of fashion" at all; rather, it illustrates the power of *class* to render three men completely distinguishable despite identical caps. A man gave away his class not simply by what he wore but also by how he wore it.

The pretender's counterfeit costume was always depicted in direct opposition to the aesthetic of naturalness, understatement, and plainness characteristic of the true gentleman, as outlined in chapter 1. His upper-class performance was invariably overdone: he was overdressed, overperfumed, and guilty of preposterous affectations of gestures and speech. False gentlemen could always be identified by their flashy dress, as vulgar and unsophisticated types were inevitably drawn to showiness and cheap ostentation. "Gentlemen seldom indulge in gaudy or light colours," *Blunders in Behavior Corrected* (1855) observed, "but quasi-gentlemen do blaze a little in this way, and carry their character with them accordingly" (20). Ready-made manufacturing and department stores were partly responsible for the look of the masher, as retailers often exaggerated current trends and sartorial details to attract the lower-class customer (Chenoune, 69–70). Mass production placed in the hands of the middle and lower classes inexpensive, often poorly rendered versions of formerly elitist goods.

Wells's shop-clerk hero Kipps provides a familiarly critical (if fictional) Victorian depiction of the lower class's crude endeavors to emulate upper-classness.

Figure 4.12. "Three Men in a Cap . . ." (*Fashion*, May 1898, 22) (permission British Library)

Having come into a substantial inheritance, Kipps attempts to assume the well-heeled lifestyle for which he is ill suited and unprepared. His efforts to perform his new social status are awkward, and he exhibits a primitive, lower-class interpretation of upper-class tastes and behaviors. His first new purchase of clothes reveals his nouveau riche taste for flash: "Kipps had been rich a week or more, and the change in his circumstances was visible upon his person. He was wearing a new suit of drab flannels, a Panama hat, and a red tie for the first time, and he carried a silver-mounted stick with a tortoiseshell handle. He felt extraordinarily different, perhaps more different than he really was, from the meek Improver of a week ago. He felt as he felt Dukes must feel" (123–24). Later, when Kipps and his new wife, Ann (a provincial haberdasher's daughter), decide to build a home, their design reflects their awkward and wrong-headed mimicry of aristocratic aesthetics. With the assistance of a pushy architect and Kipps's uncle (who asserts that they will need a billiard room, landscaping, and a gardener to live up to their position), Kipps and Ann decide to build an impractical eleven-bedroom mini-mansion (290). The newlyweds decorate their new estate in a "style of mediocre elegance" (295), and Kipps insists that the household be managed by multiple servants: "We got to keep up our position, any'ow. . . . It stands to reason, Ann, we got a position. Very well! I can't 'ave you scrubbin' floors. You got to 'ave a servant, and you got to manage a 'ouse. You wouldn't 'ave me ashamed—" (292). Despite all the expensive trappings of their new respectable lifestyle, Kipps and Ann grow paranoid, believing themselves constantly subjected to the condescending stares and sneers of the middle and upper classes and terrified of making the slightest social error. Kipps's paralyzing fear of behaving incorrectly prevents him from entering restaurant after restaurant while walking the London streets (219); likewise, Ann sends friendly callers away, too embarrassed to tell them she is the lady of the house (304). Wells's condescending portrait of the Kippses' experience reflects the common belief that the lower (and middle) classes were ill equipped to handle the rigors of upscale life, even when supplied with the means to ape its physical appearance.

Dandies, Mashers, and Homosexuality

As mentioned earlier, because his idle status, fastidious attention to the minutiae of dress, and flamboyant mannerisms mirrored the conventional characteristics of female performance, the dandy was increasingly equated with effeminacy. Certainly, antagonism toward effeminate behavior accelerated during an age in which rugged masculinity and athleticism were enthusiastically celebrated by popular culture. Conduct books consistently equated interest in dress with effeminacy,[14] and any man who seemed to care too much about his appearance risked accusations that he was weak and womanish. Popular literature usually portrayed the dandy in a cartoonishly sissified manner as a highly emotional, perfumed, lisping individual who wore extravagant and romantic clothing and worshipped style and appearance above substance. Effeminacy was widely regarded with ridicule and suspicion, and upper-class dandies, mincing shop clerks, and rouged exquisites were familiar caricatures in popular culture. In *Vanity Fair* (1848), for example, William Thackeray lampoons Joseph Sedley as a foolish, idle, bloated Regency dandy who, "vain as a girl," lives "like a gay young bachelor" and takes "the hugest pains to adorn his big person" (28, 27).[15] Count Fosco, the mysterious foreign villain of Wilkie Collins's novel *The Woman in White* (1860), exhibits a taste for brightly colored waistcoats that the heroine Marian Halcombe lists among the "incomprehensible oddities" of this mysterious foreigner (244). "He is fond of fine clothes as the veriest fool in existence," she observes, "and has appeared in four magnificent waistcoats already—all of light garish colours" during his first two days at Blackwater Park (244). Count Fosco's curiously effeminate touches—his sartorial frippery, his fawning attention toward his pet mouse—are meant to underscore his sinister nature, "as if there was some hidden connection between his showiest finery and his deepest feeling" (308).

The notoriety of the Aesthetic movement only heightened the anxious association between dandyism and effeminacy. Nineteenth-century discourse portrayed Aesthetes as "men who, by turning their lives into art, abdicated their class and their gender and normative heterosexuality" (Auslander, 93). Dandies such as Beerbohm and cartoonist-novelist du Maurier feared that their own male heterosexual status was endangered by the Aesthete's transgressive blurring of men's and women's spheres. Talia Schaffer contends that, in a self-conscious move to distance themselves from Wilde's effeminizing decadence, Beerbohm and du Maurier retreated into a more traditional Brummell-style dandyism based in a "semimilitary, or semi-monastic" sartorial simplicity,[16] while successfully disseminating a savage caricature of the Wildean Aesthete as a long-haired, velveted, swooning ninny clutching a lily. This image had been familiar for at least a decade prior, as W. S. Gilbert and Arthur Sullivan's 1881 operetta *Patience, or Bunthorne's Bride* represents the quintessential late-nineteenth-century satire of the English dandy (fig. 4.13).[17] It was an unfairly reductive stereotype of the entire Aesthetic movement—

" YOU HOLD YOURSELF LIKE THIS."

Figure 4.13. "You Hold Yourself Like This." Colonel Calverley, Major Murgatroyd, and the Lt. the Duke of Dunstable dressed as Aesthetes; scene from the souvenir program for Gilbert and Sullivan's *Patience*, 1881. Illustration by J. E. Kelly. (Courtesy David Stone Collection)

undoubtedly inspired in part by the custom-made "Little Lord Fauntleroy" costume[18] that Wilde wore on his 1882 American lecture tour (fig. 4.14)—that has nevertheless endured to this day (Schaffer, 39).

Many cultural histories of nineteenth-century masculinity mistakenly suggest that men struggled unceasingly to combat what was regarded as the ever-present threat of effeminacy and, by extension, homosexuality. Popular trends in both male athleticism and medical science were premised on the belief that men were not inherently "manly," thereby placing enormous weight on the successful achievement of a "proper" masculine performance. These historians have argued that medical science's categorization of sexual "perversities"—particularly homosexuality—led to a "general tightening of definitions and norms of masculinity during the Victorian period" (Nixon, "Exhibiting," 297).[19] This emerging awareness of homosexuality, these historians argue, alongside concerns that commodity culture's spectacle transformed men into feminized fashion plates and promoted a male-male gaze,[20] served to pathologize dress and behavior labeled effeminate. Jon Stratton even goes so far as to suggest that effeminacy was associated with male-male desire as early as 1780 and that the Great Masculine Renunciation was partly motivated by an impulse to eradicate the potential of a homoerotic gaze by rendering men's appearance invisible (120–21, 182).

Other scholars, however, have more convincingly argued that Victorian anxieties over "homosexuality" did not arise until very late in the nineteenth century. Indeed, the very term *homosexual*, and the concept it embodied, entered the language only in 1892.[21] What Tim Edwards terms in the twentieth century "the constant slithering of the 'not masculine' into the 'effeminate' and therefore the 'homosexual'" was not necessarily an obvious or logical leap for most nineteenth-century Britons (4). Randolph Trumbach urges historians to acknowledge shifts in cultural models of homosexuality and not to read the past retroactively with contemporary understandings of homosexual behavior. Before the final decade of the nineteenth century, same-sex sex had been historically perceived as an act—something one did—and not as the revelation of a personality type or psychosexual identity. This change occurred later, with the institutionalization of a "normative" sexuality first outlined by Michel Foucault (Sinfield, 12). According to Jeffrey Weeks, nineteenth-century concepts of homosexuality were "extremely undeveloped" among the public at large, and "neither the police nor the court were familiar with the patterns of male homosexuality" (101). We must therefore be careful not to equate Victorian dis-ease over effeminacy with homophobic anxi-

Figure 4.14. Oscar Wilde's custom-made "Little Lord Fauntleroy" suit for his American tour, January 1882. Photo by Napoléon Sarony. (Courtesy George Eastman House)

eties, as direct associations between effeminacy and homosexuality did not emerge until the Wilde trials of 1895–96. Certainly the effeminacy exhibited by Wilde and his fellow Aesthetes invited ridicule prior to the trials, but it was considered reflective of their overrefined sensibilities;[22] likewise, upper-class gentlemen were permitted a wide range of feminized dress and behaviors.

Unquestionably, the conflation of effeminacy and homosexuality was sealed by Wilde's 1895 "gross indecency" conviction.[23] The highly publicized trials irrevocably outed underground Victorian homosexuality, linked Aestheticism to deviant male sexuality, and rendered any evidence of effeminate dandyism and sartorial excess immediately suspicious. After the trials, Joe Lucchesi maintains, "the image of the elegantly attired gentleman became indelibly associated with decadent male homosexuality, to the extent that simply calling someone an 'Oscar Wilde type' was sufficient to invoke the damaging link" (163). When, noting that the men's journal *To-Day* had offered advice to a reader's inquiry on how best to dye men's underwear pink, its rival *Fashion* pointedly responded, "There is something indescribably more than luxurious about coral pink or pale blue pants of silk. They seem somehow—perhaps I am wrong—to claim companionship with green carnations and dyed hair,"[24] the implicit reference to Wilde and warning against homosexual affectations were clear (Brummel, "Dress," *Fashion*, October 1898, 20).

However, the heightened public anxiety regarding "deviant" male sexuality did not have the far-reaching effects on mainstream male behavior suggested by Weeks, Stratton, and others. While the emergence of the homosexual as both an identifiable pathological type and a comical stereotype served to define and regulate normative masculinity, it did not cause middle-class men in large numbers to abandon behaviors that had supposedly come to be openly coded as "queer." There is little or no evidence to suggest a marked reduction in men's public consumption of goods and fashionable self-display in the years following the trials. The creation of men's shops in department stores and the proliferation of male-directed advertising discussed in chapter 2, as well as the growing variety and versatility of menswear and the widespread popularity of casual wear and sportswear (explored in chapter 5), strongly suggest that men's open interest in fashion and shopping did not decrease, much less retreat back into the closet, after the public "outing" of homosexuality in Britain.

The reason, simply put, is that "dandies," "decadents," and "Aesthetes" were all understood by the middle classes as upper-class male transgressors of gender (and by extension consumer) norms, while "mashers," "swells," and "dudes" were working- and middle-class male transgressors of class. There was always something implicitly effeminate—and therefore implicitly non-(re)productive—about the upper-class dandy. But the objections to the masher were never directed toward his masculinity; indeed, he was often perceived as too heterosexually predatory. Rather, he was criticized because he aped the upper-class sophisticate, often in very clumsy and crude ways. Masherdom—a distinctly urban, aggressively heterosexual, working- and middle-class form of dandyism—existed alongside the overly precious dandyism of the Wildean "invert" and could have never been mistaken for it. Indeed, today the term *dandy*—though admittedly archaic—is equated with effeminate mannerisms and a womanly preoccupation with clothing, while *masher* and *cad* endure in our language predominantly as sexual monikers, suggesting wolfish sexuality. The middle- and working-class masher therefore survived intact after the Wilde trials. Mainstream middle-class masculinity—and the consumption that had become an inseparable part of how it was defined—emerged relatively untouched by the Wilde scandal and continued to move with the consumer industry that fueled it.

The way in which we dress stabilizes our identity, and for Britons of the late nineteenth and early twentieth centuries, fashion was widely acknowledged as a vital form of visual classification—both self-imposed and imposed by others' readings (Wilson, 12). What clothes "mean" is not determined solely by what the wearer wants to convey but also by what others read into them, which in some cases can be the opposite of the wearer's intentions. Conduct authors and the other guardians of the existing class system warned that the class interloper, aspiring to gain entry into the elite through flash and color, succeeded only in underscoring his weakness of character and his lowly social position. Yet even when the counterfeit nature of the pretender's dress was immediately and visibly apparent, the costume of the dandy and the masher was dangerous because it revealed the performative nature of both dress and class. Conduct books and conventional Victorian wisdom spoke against extravagant clothing, clothing that called attention to itself, clothing that misrepresented one's station or means—that is, clothing that exposed the artifice and performativity of dress by overdoing or transgressing culturally accepted sartorial conventions. As I discuss in chapter 1, a gentleman was expected to dress so that others were unaware of the performance and accepted it unconsciously. The wearing of ostentatious or class-contrary costume by dandies and mashers threatened the status quo for all by revealing the artificiality of class distinctions. Hence, Victorian social commentators devoted most of their energies to describing incorrect dress; in a Foucauldian sense, normative, proper dress was implicitly defined through the identification and setting apart of transgressive dress.

As we shall see in the next chapter, the gradual commercial transformation of one form of the dandy into the masher was only one strategy employed by the

English middle classes to negotiate class relations during the second half of the nineteenth century. Rather than emulating and commodifying upper-class costume, many middle-class men rejected it outright, choosing instead to embrace the liberating possibilities of modern mass production to develop their own distinctive class-specific uniform. If the upper classes were going to insist that the middle-class male was always discernible in his upper-class disguise, then many middle-class men were happy to adopt—proudly and unapologetically—a bold and energetic costume that identified their bourgeois status so there would be no mistake in the matter.

READY TO WEAR

Class Performance and the Triumph of Middle-Class Sartorial Taste

The clothes of the gentility do not say "I am a man—and how!" but "I am a gentleman, and I hope to attract women not by asserting my masculinity but by demonstrating my membership of a social class."

    —James Laver, *Dandies*

There is a wide and deep philosophy of clothes, as Teufelsdröckh has shown us; and we may even go so far as to say that the habits and disposition of *a nation* are shown in its style of dress. Look at our English costumes of the present day. Are they not those of an active, majestic, vigorous people, who delight in bodily exercises, and travel wide and far?

    —*The Glass of Fashion* (1881)

There is now no single fashion, nor has there ever really been.

    —Anne Hollander, *Sex and Suits*

*H*AD YOU STROLLED ALONG A LONDON STREET—PERHAPS ONE of the fashionable rows of the West End or one of the bustling corridors of the City district—during the waning decades of the nineteenth century, you would have borne witness to a striking transformation of the male costume that had characterized the earlier Victorian era. Disappearing were the traditional long frock coats, top hats, tailcoats, and the rigid observance of the sartorial rules of London's wealthy West End and sober City business, replaced by shorter loose-fitting coats, lighter fabrics, an expanding variety of hats, and a general embrace of informality and robust sportiness. The streets were peppered with men wearing the increasingly ubiquitous lounge suits—popularly called "dittoes" because jacket, trousers, and waistcoat were of the same material. A reporter observing what the men of the St. James's Street clubs were wearing in 1890 was "bound to confess to having noticed more men walking about town in suits of dittoes than I have ever beheld during the many years I have known London" (Holding, "Men's," 7).

Seven years later, another observer, having stationed himself near Charing Cross, reported, "There were nearly two Lounges to one Morning Coat, and quite three Lounges to one Frock Coat, the proportions per thousand working out as follows: Lounges 530, Morning Coats 320, and Frock Coats 150" (*Tailor and Cutter*, 20 May 1897). By the 1890s, some men had also abandoned traditional formal evening dress for lounge suits and sports jackets. The lounge suit was becoming so socially accepted at the dawn of the twentieth century that even infamously conservative conduct book authors had to concede its dominance. In 1902 Mrs. C. E. Humphry's *Etiquette for Every Day* recommended "a lounge suit, all three garments made of the same material" for business and morning wear (283). And in 1910, John Wanamaker, author of *The Etiquette of an Englishman's Dress*, declared, "Nowadays more business is done in the city in lounge suits than in tail coats. Heads of firms think nothing of turning up at their offices in short jackets" (6). While many aristocrats and older men clung to the traditional uniform of the regal top hat and dignified frock coat well into the 1920s and '30s, the younger, professional, middle-class set eagerly took up the new taste for practical, sporty, less formal, fashionable male attire.

As the one commodity always on display by the consumer, clothing serves as the most immediate and most visible cultural marker of one's social status. Fashion has therefore historically been rooted in the formation and maintenance of class and social distinctions. Cultural theorists, historians, and economists have most often apprehended fashion in terms of a "trickle-down" model of class and consumer hierarchies, in which the lower classes invariably strive to imitate the clothing of the upper classes. This notion of "social emulation" was first posited in 1899 by American economist Thorstein Veblen, who argued that all material wants are motivated by a desire to emulate the consumer behaviors of others. Consumption is never simply a matter of satisfying basic needs, but rather a means of improving social status. Veblen's socioeconomic framework assumes that those at the bottom or middle invariably seek to improve their status by mimicking the consumption of those at the top of the social hierarchy. Five years later, in 1904, German sociologist Georg Simmel delineated Veblen's theories specifically in terms of clothing, arguing that members of inferior classes mimic members of superior classes, who in turn adopt new sartorial markers in an ongoing large-scale social cycle of chasing and sidestepping. Veblen's and Simmel's articulation of "social emulation" theory emerged as one of the primary theoretical apparatuses for twentieth-century historians of commodity culture. It became the central, guiding tenet of fashion theory when it was taken up in 1930 by J. C. Flugel, who argued in his highly influential sartorial treatise *The Psychology of Clothes* that "fashion spreads inevitably downwards" (140). Flugel explained that fashion is created and perpetuated when subordinates aspire to the position of superordinates, thereby threatening the "distinctive outward signs and symbols" of class identity (140, 138). Unwilling to abandon the signs of their superiority, the higher social classes retain their sartorial distinctiveness through the adoption of a new form of dress that reestablishes the desired distinction (138).

Subsequent fashion theorists and historians, from James Laver in the 1940s to Neil McKendrick in the 1980s,[1] were quick to adopt Flugel's framework, but in doing so they have replicated the original limitations of Veblen's and Simmel's premises—that the cultural meaning of consumption is always limited solely to status-striving. Only recently has this approach been challenged by consumer historians and theorists, including Ann Bermingham, Amanda Vickery, Colin Campbell, and Christopher Breward. While "social emulation" is a useful starting point for tracing some consumer behaviors among the classes, it lacks adequate explanatory power to account fully for the variety of radical transformations in men's fashion in Britain at the turn of the twentieth century. These include the phenomenal success of sportswear, the growing informality of men's clothing styles and fabrics, the emergence of the three-piece lounge (or business) suit, and the popular reemergence of the dandy in various forms, not to mention the influence of counterculture fashions from the Aesthetic and Bohemian movements.

Clothing and other consumable goods do not merely reflect differences and make them visible, as Mary Douglas and Baron Isherwood contend.[2] Rather, cultural consumption is one of the means by which these differences are produced and maintained. The late Victorian era was a time of rising class tensions and the blurring of clear-cut borders of social identity. This was reflected in overt renegotiations of male costume and consumer practices. The sartorial image of the turn-of-the-century British male became a contested site for the struggle of competing class identities, masculinities, and social lifestyles. Multiple trajectories of men's fashion occurred simultaneously. Englishmen of the middle classes emulated the sartorial ideals of the upper-class gentleman at the same time that they were developing their separate fashion aesthetic to distinguish their own emerging class.

The turn of the century marked a significant turning point in men's fashion history, in that middle-class costume evolved—at least in part—independently of upper-class sartorial aesthetics. Many among the middle classes did indeed seek to imitate some upper-class consumer practices, and certainly the emergence of department stores and mass production provided the means through which the middle classes could afford the goods that had previously characterized upper-class membership. However, they also used the department store and its goods to assert their own distinctive middle-classness. Thus, around the turn of the century, the trajectory of British men's fashion was bifurcated: in a reactionary move, the traditional upper classes, believing themselves encroached upon by the nouveau riche and middle-class imitators (including the "mashers" discussed in chapter 4), relied increasingly on occasion-specific clothing and complicated fashion rules to maintain their elite social status; the middle (and, to a certain extent, working) classes enjoyed the growing ability to purchase a greater variety of clothing, to personalize their clothing choices, and to develop their own sartorial ideals. Between 1860 and 1914, many among Britain's middle-class males sought class identity and social power through neither a Great Masculine Renunciation of fashionable display nor social emulation of the elite, but rather through the development of a distinctive and versatile sartorial style that allowed for both the practicality of the business suit and the informality of sportswear. Middle-class fashion—practical but not dour, casual yet relevant to the modern professional world—emerged as the dominant popular image of the twentieth-century British male.

Victorian Social Emulation

While fashion had historically been the pursuit of a privileged few among the court and aristocracy, the modern machinery of consumer capitalism and mass production helped democratize fashionable consumption and make it more accessible to vastly more people. Entry into London "Society" had always been cautiously guarded, yet by the late nineteenth century, purchasing one's way into the upper social circles had become easier. The social emphasis on conspicuous consumption increased dramatically by the 1880s, as the new order of the prosperous middle class eclipsed the old elite (Breward, *Hidden*, 60). Breward observes that "the margins within which it was possible to achieve an aristocratic appearance were very wide" (*Hidden*, 60); by 1900, many could appear wealthy and indulge in the good life even with only £1,000 a year—an income near the upper cap for what was still regarded as the middle class (Camplin, 90).[3] The newfound availability and affordability of once-exclusive upper-class goods meant the blurring or, in some cases, complete obliteration of age-old class markers. Lady Agnes Geraldine Grove, author of *The Social Fetich* (1907), remarked "how superficial the distinction is between the two uppermost classes [namely, the upper and middle], which are becoming so merged as to be scarcely distinguishable," and she noted with dismay that male and female counter employees at shops and department stores were customarily referred to as "ladies" and "gentlemen" despite the misnomer (17, 116–17).[4] An individual's social status became highly ambiguous, as the old visual hallmarks (from clothing and carriages to posture and gestures) grew less distinct. In Arnold Bennett's 1908 novel *The Old Wives' Tale*, a London cabman incorrectly assumes, from the clothing and demeanor of Matthew Peel-Swynnerton and Cyril Povey, two young men from the Potteries, that they are wealthy aristocrats: "The appearance and manner of his fare, the quality of the kit-bag, and the opening gestures of the interview between the two young dukes, had put the cabman in an optimistic mood. He had no apprehensions of miserly and ungentlemanly conduct by his fare upon the arrival at Euston. He knew the language of the tilt of the straw hat" (461). Yet clearly this was a language in which it was no longer possible to be fluent, as the rising wealth of the middle classes and the availability and affordability of clothing and other consumable goods meant that theoretically any young middle-class man (if not the working-class cabman) could look like an upper-class gentleman.

Long before Veblen and Simmel articulated their theories of social emulation, the notion that the lower classes invariably imitated upper-class costume was popularly accepted by Victorian Britons. "Imitation is the great principle which governs Fashion," declared social reformer Ada Ballin in 1885, "and Reason in these matters plays but a very minor part" (258). In their illustrated *London, A Pilgrimage*, celebrated artist Gustave Doré and author Blanchard Jerrold depicted the city's lower classes decked out in crude reflections of upper-class fashions:

> An English crowd is almost the ugliest in the world: because the poorer classes are but copyists in costume, of the rich. . . . The workman approximates his nearest to the cut of the [famous London tailor Henry] Poole. The English carpenter wears a black tail coat—like the waiter, the undertaker, and the duke. Poor English women are ghastly in their patches trimmed in outlandish imitation of the fashion. *Le Follet's* plans penetrate to Shoreditch: and the hoop, the chignon, and the bonnet no larger than

a d'Oyley, are to be seen in Drury Lane, and behind apple stalls. In these base and shabby copyings of the rich, the poverty of the wearers has a startling, abject air. It is, as I heard a stranger remark, "misery advertised."

. . . In England all classes, except the agricultural, dress alike—with a difference. Observe this lemonade-vendor. His dress is that of a prosperous middle-class man—gone to shreds and patches. (25–26)

The upper classes objected to these vulgar imitations; many complained openly that servants dressed—or aspired to dress—above their station (McKendrick, 95–96). And Victorian journalist Douglas Jerrold documented linen-draper assistants' well-known reputation for aping the finery of aristocratic gentlemen: "It has been stated to us that, at this moment, there is a conspiracy among the shopmen in a certain West-end house, to outdress an illustrious Count; and, sinking the shirt-studs, it is thought that one Assistant has already achieved the undertaking!" (241).

Unquestionably, consumer culture provided the prosperous middle classes access to the clothing, furnishings, and other consumable goods once exclusive to the privileged elite, and many were eager to take up the visible hallmarks of upper-class belonging during the late nineteenth and early twentieth centuries. Widespread economic prosperity, in tandem with dramatic shifts in English social dynamics, made the lifestyle of the gentleman (or a reasonable facsimile, at least) seem more attainable than ever before for an increasing number among Britain's nonelite males. To that end, many middle- (and working-) class males sought the instruction of conduct manuals.[5] Nancy Armstrong and Elizabeth Langland have both emphasized conduct literature's significant contribution to the formation of women's domestic roles in the seventeenth through nineteenth centuries. Armstrong argues that conduct books' cultivation of the domestic woman (as the ideal companion to the emerging middle-class male, to whom she surrendered her economic power in favor of moral authority) was the formative event of nineteenth-century social (and literary) history (59–95), while Langland contends that conduct books facilitated middle-class women's management of class representations, defining the terms by which social distinctions were maintained (21–32). But this "women as cultural arbiters" argument makes perhaps too sharp a distinction between the sexes. Men were also expected to perform and display status during the Victorian age. While the largest audience for conduct books may have been women, conduct literature (as I describe in chapter 1) also placed great emphasis on man's costume as an outward, visible sign of his social station.

Such manuals were highly instrumental in giving license to social-climbing aspirations by purporting to offer advice on upper-class manners and aesthetics. Entrusted to provide the gateway into upper-classness, they were therefore published in huge numbers.[6] Victorian conduct books professed to offer detailed and foolproof instructions on the amorphous and ever-changing rules of gentlemanly conduct. While the etiquette genre was produced for middle-class readers by anonymous middle-class writers, conduct manuals often advertised the credibility of their advice by claiming aristocratic authorship by "a gentleman" or "a peer of the realm" or "the Countess of ********" (Curtin, 47–49). When Arthur Kipps, the working-class protagonist of H. G. Wells's novel *Kipps* (1900), is made wealthy by an unexpected inheritance, he feels "be'ind" and "out of it" and longs for the proper manners and carriage to match his newfound fortune (131). His house agent friend Chester Coote naturally offers him several conduct manuals to study, including "a precious little volume called *Don't* . . .—a book of invaluable hints, a summary of British deportment"; "*Manners and Rules of Good Society*, by a Member of the Aristocracy"; "that admirable classic, *The Art of Conversing*"; and Ruskin's *Sesame and Lilies* (143, 149, 203).[7]

What was most important was the semblance of upper-class membership; as a result, conduct manuals placed great stress on the creation and maintenance of a proper appearance. G. R. M. Devereaux's *Etiquette for Men* (1902) urged readers to dress for social and professional success: "It is impossible to ignore the fact that a man's personal appearance plays no unimportant part in his success in business and in his social position. No business man cares to have about him a slovenly, ill-dressed individual, whose every inch conveys the impression that he is underpaid. To get on you must be a credit to your employer, to yourself, and to your tailor. In whatever profession you engage, if desirous of preserving your self-respect and the respect of others, it is incumbent on you to be careful of your personal appearance" (17). With this in mind, conduct books advised the purchase of high-quality items, particularly clothing. *The Glass of Fashion* (1881) warned, "Do not wear shirts at 42s. per dozen unless you are obliged; let your collars, handkerchiefs, socks, under-garments, all be of good make and shape" (176). In 1900, *Clothes and the Man* urged "every man to pay a good price in the first instance" for his clothes: "It pays to dress well in the sense that it pays to keep up appearances— your appearances. You assist in preserving your self-respect when you put on good clothes. If you are engaged in any business or profession, you are much more likely to succeed if you are well dressed than if you are badly dressed" (15). Conduct manuals repeatedly rationalized that expensive, well-made clothes were the most economical in the long run, and the importance of well-made, smart-fitting clothes led etiquette writers to recommend that their readers patronize a good tailor. Lady Colin's *Everybody's Book of Correct Conduct* (1893) advised, "However subdued your dressing may be, be sure and have coat or gown made by the best tailor or dressmaker that you can possibly afford" (78), and *Best Dressed Man* (1892) urged, "Give good heed, we say, to the Style, Fashion, and Fit of your Clothes. Go to a good Tailor. Place yourself in his hands. Let him point out the *Mode,* and do you adopt it" (142). However, the number of men from the middle classes who chose— or could have afforded—to patronize the fashionable and expensive tailors of the West End is unclear, and this question urgently calls for further research.

Upper-Class Responses to Middle-Class Upward Mobility

As the middle classes began to appropriate the goods, services, and venues of upper-class consumption, the age-old aristocratic elite faced an uphill battle to maintain the traditional markers of upper-class membership. For centuries, Britain's privileged elite had derived its wealth—and thus its social, cultural, and political power—from land. Yet the nineteenth century witnessed a notable decline in land-based titled wealth, as the leading source of large incomes shifted to commerce and finance—that is, to the new fortunes of the industrialists, bankers, factory owners, and railway magnates, as well as to the more modest prosperity of the expanding middle class. With the formerly solid assets of land, birth, and family wealth destabilized and their economic and political power on the wane, members of the upper classes sought to reassert their status by relying increasingly on more overt, visible symbols—particularly clothing—to justify the stratification of society and to distinguish themselves from their social inferiors. Thus, the variety of costume worn by aristocratic gentlemen, as well as rules regarding its wear, grew exponentially in the last decades of the nineteenth century.

Most prominent was the heavy social emphasis placed on occasion-specific rules governing when and where clothing should be worn. Distinctions between city wear and country wear and between morning and evening dress had always existed among the elite, but during the late Victorian years, the temporal and functional nature of dress was compartmentalized for nearly every hour and occasion, with specific costumes prescribed for morning social calls, afternoon business meetings, evening dinner parties, nights at the opera, visits to the Ascot races, outdoor picnics, and an expanding array of sporting events. To cite just one example, according to *The Etiquette of an Englishman's Dress* (1910), proper boating costume "for punting and so on" consisted of

> white flannel trousers *without* a belt or cummerbund but pulled in with a
> small strap at the back. The trousers are turned up to show white cash-
> mere or silk socks with a silk cloth, or plain coloured sock of bright
> colouring, the favourites being salmon pink or mauve.
>   A thin flannel, cotton, or silk Oxford shirt of a plain or striped ma-
> terial with soft double cuffs and a box pleat down the front is worn with
> these trousers, and as the coat is generally in the bottom of the boat, the
> cut and design of the shirt is vastly important. (Wanamaker, 11–12)

"The law of fitness," reported *How to Behave* in 1883, "imperatively demands that you should have one dress for the kitchen, the field, or the workshop, and another, and quite a different one, for the parlour; one for the street and another for the carriage, one for a ride on horseback and another for a ramble in the country" (34). Wealthy gentlemen advertised their class through the wearing of clothing consecutively, rather than simultaneously as they had in the eighteenth century. The trade weekly *Tailor and Cutter* seems to suggest that the fashionable man spent most of his day changing in and out of clothes: "A tweed suit is his morning wear; in the afternoon he dons a Frock coat, a smarter waistcoat and a bigger tie. In the evening he dresses for dinner. Perhaps his dinner clothes will be exchanged for a smoking suit later" (*Tailor and Cutter*, 1890). Indeed, the gentleman was widely acknowledged to change his complete attire three times a day and sometimes even more often.

Clearly, this expensive sartorial game of cat and mouse represented an attempt by the elite to deter social climbers, making it socially and financially difficult for middle-class aspirants to keep up with the ever-increasing number of costumes and rules governing dress. When ready-made look-alikes began to appear in department stores, the bar was raised higher still, as the elite emphasized subtle distinctions in cut, color, fabric, and style and ridiculed the vulgar "ill-fitting" and "off-the-rack" copies worn by the inferior classes. Impeccable fastidiousness was the rule, and no detail was too small to be overlooked. For example, *Routledge's Etiquette for Gentlemen* was insistent on the proper wearing of gloves: "Never be seen in the street without gloves; and never let your gloves be of any material that is not kid or calf. Worsted or cotton gloves are unutterably vulgar. Your gloves should be fitted to the last degree—of perfection" (44).

Hence, the emphasis fell on increasingly minor, almost imperceptible distinctions of dress. As mass production techniques improved, putting quality clothing in the hands of more and more of the nonelite, enduring differences between tailor-made and ready-made clothing were heavily underscored by the wealthy and by conduct authors to maintain a difference in the minds of the middle and upper classes. The tailoring industry, which had been struggling for some time against the tide of ready-made clothing, also had an obvious investment in promoting subtle details and the virtues of a professional cut. Reflecting in 1960, former West End hatter Frederick Willis recalled that in turn-of-the-century London, "No man of discrimination would dream of buying his hat at a big store"; instead he patronized smart hatters "accommodated in small, old-fashioned shops which the ordinary citizen passed unnoticed" (152).[8] Proper gentlemanly fashion during the nineteenth century had always emphasized plainness, understatement, and subtlety, but later it began to emphasize qualities that were virtually invisible except to the trained eye. In 1893, conduct author Lady Colin declared, "It is a test of your style being really very good that only the fashionable should be fully able to appreciate it. If it attracts notice from common persons in the street, you may be sure there is something wrong, or that you have gone too far" (78). *The Glass of Fashion* similarly cast true fashion as something unattainable by the vulgar, uneducated masses: "It is often asserted that nowadays all classes dress alike; the clerk like the peer, the wife of a London tradesman like the wife of a blue-blooded patrician. Is it so? The various articles of which their attire is made up—its component parts, so to speak,—may be the same, but they differ in that undefinable something which is the impress made on a person's dress by a person's character. You can tell the gentleman from the snob, however they may be dressed; they *wear* their clothes differently" (167). The revealingly defensive rhetoric of the elite— besieged by poseurs in the department store–bought ready-made wardrobes— regularly represented fashion as a hermetic, esoteric quality that could be perceived and appreciated only by the upper classes.

I Shop, Therefore I Am Middle Class

While Veblen's and Simmel's social emulation theory provides a partial explanation for imitative consumer behaviors practiced by many men of the middle classes, ultimately it proves inadequate to delineate the increasingly complicated sartorial matrix of Britain between 1860 and 1914. Consumer theorist Colin Campbell maintains that "behaviour which is imitative is not necessarily also emulative": the fact that a middle-class shopkeeper could afford items formerly available only to the upper classes did not necessarily denote that he was attempting to imitate the lifestyle of the upper classes. Goods such as coffee, tea, chocolate, and sugar have an "immediate and obvious" appeal and therefore "are likely to be desired for their own sake rather than for any prestige which may be attached to them" (40). Moreover, consumption can also be motivated by hedonism, escapism, and the desire for novelty. The work of Ann Bermingham, Amanda Vickery, and Lori Anne Loeb has offered similar challenges to Veblen and Simmel and has paved the way for more rigorous scholarship of the complexities of turn-of-the-century costume and consumption.[9]

Middle-class fashionable consumption was not entirely driven by imitation of the aristocratic elite. Rather, overtures toward social emulation existed alongside increasingly independent assertions of a uniquely middle-class sartorial and consumer aesthetic. Contrary to popular assumptions, the elite did not necessarily dictate fashion for everyone else, nor did the lower and middle classes always aspire to imitate the dress of the elite; instead they often invented their own styles and forms that more closely reflected their tastes and lifestyles (Breward, *Hidden*, 57–58). As the nineteenth century made way for the twentieth, fashion originated not solely from above but also from below—from the worlds of the working class, the country, the playing field, the stage, and Bohemian countercultures. Thus, middle-class clothing emerged in large part as a separate—and often oppositional—development not dependent on upper-class sartorial innovations and trends.

Expanding consumer buying power, in tandem with the humming machinery of modern commodity culture, enabled the middle classes for the first time to drive the evolution of fashionable consumption. Middle-class affluence surged in Britain during the economically prosperous years of the late nineteenth and early twentieth centuries. At the same time that mass production led to decreased prices for former luxury goods, living standards among the middle class rose. Membership in the middle class increased sharply because of the growth of white-collar employment. The number of Britons earning an annual income of £140 or more increased by about 170 percent, from around 307,000 in 1860–61 to about 833,000 in 1894–95 (Loeb, 3–8; Gourvish, 15). Even though expenditures on rent, food, and clothing increased, the actual money surplus remaining in the average family budget rose steadily between 1850 and 1914 (Fraser, 66). According to David Reed, "Between the periods 1865–1874 and 1895–1904 there was a 22% growth in earnings in Britain. As price changes have been allowed for, this indicates a substantial rise in overall surplus disposable income" (93). As incomes climbed, so did expectations and standards for the quality of life befitting the social status of the middle class. Many items that had once been produced in the home were available for sale at department stores and smaller shops during the final decades of the century. Shopping had transcended utilitarianism; as a result, the consumption of consumer goods, services, and pursuits—clothing, furniture, carriages, servants, dining, travel, theatergoing—accelerated dramatically among the middle class.[10] More and more, middle-classness was defined by the acquisition and use of material goods. Wells's hero Kipps, a new arrival to this world of comfort, prosperity, and conspicuous consumption, is offered instruction in proper consumer behavior by his investor friend Walshingham: "This rising man of affairs showed Kipps how to buy the more theatrical weeklies for consumption in the train, how to buy and what to buy in the way of cigarettes with gold tips and shilling cigars, and how to order hock for lunch and sparkling Moselle for dinner, how to calculate the fare of a hansom cab—penny a minute while he goes— how to look intelligently at an hotel tape, and how to sit still in a train like a thoughtful man instead of talking like a fool and giving yourself away" (189). Earlier nineteenth-century rhetoric regarding the virtues of gentility and propriety, hard work and domesticity, and sobriety and reserve that had once supposedly characterized the middle class was subordinated as middle-class membership was increasingly expressed in consumer terms. In the increasingly visual and spectacularized culture of late-Victorian Britain, status and identity were conveyed and read via visible, commodifiable signs. And as "a new and insecure elite," members of the middle class were eager to reinforce their status—and to distinguish it from those above and below[11]—through class-specific consumption (Steele, 79).

Providing the stage for all this was the department store. The Victorian department store was largely a middle-class phenomenon. While Harrods is now associated with a decidedly tony London crowd, throughout the nineteenth century it catered mainly to a middle-class clientele; its turn-of-the-century advertising slogans included "The Cheapest Stores in London for Everything" (1897) and "Everything for Everybody" (1902).[12] Social emulation did play a factor in the large urban stores' success, to be sure. The lower and middle classes began to have available to them what Cissie Fairchilds calls "populuxe" items—"inexpensive versions of aristocratic luxuries like fans, snuff boxes and umbrellas"—believed to offer the means by which they could fulfill their upwardly mobile aspirations (230). And department store advertising made generous use of the word *gentleman*, hoping to attract the working- and middle-class consumer who wanted to imagine himself as a gentleman and to purchase a gentleman's clothing and accoutrements. But increasingly, department store consumption came to be associated as much with middle-class belonging as with yearnings for upward mobility.

The department store helped make more visible and overt the performativity of class by connecting class identity more directly to consumable goods. Once the large stores had, in Émile Zola's words, "democratized luxury," these newly available goods were rapidly absorbed into middle-class identity. Michael B. Miller's intriguing history of Paris's Bon Marché illustrates how enmeshed the middle class was with the department store: the grand bazaars of the modern metropolis were "a world where middle-class culture itself was on display," and through them consumption became a bourgeois act (3). The department store played a significant role in educating the middle classes on how to be middle class by leading them to think of class identity and lifestyle in terms of commodities. It presented shopping as a legitimate, respectable pleasure, and it retrained the middle classes to spend the surplus income they had been accustomed to saving. The act of consuming material goods in the department store conferred upon its customers membership in the bourgeoisie. "The very definition of bourgeois," writes Miller, "was no longer sharing a certain lifestyle, but rather buying certain goods in order to live that way of life. . . . Identity was to be found in the things one possessed. Consumption itself became a substitute for being bourgeois" (185). The ability to consume (both properly and frequently) reflected the quality of one's character and legitimized one's entitlement to middle-class (and even upper-class) belonging.

A significant part of this consumption was clothing, and the department store was instrumental in popularizing the concept of fashionableness for mainstream, middle-class consumers. While for most outside of the elite, clothing had always been regarded as a basic necessity—to be made at home or purchased secondhand—department stores introduced the revolutionary concept that clothing might be replaced merely because it was out-of-date, rather than worn out (Corina, 69). The four seasons were marketed as distinctive divisions in a fashion cycle, within which each required its own costume (Barth, 142). The visual tools of the department store—advertisements, fashion plates, catalogues, window displays—instilled in the middle-class audience a profound interest in personal appearance. The department store's leadership in the popularization of ready-to-wear clothing was undoubtedly its most far-reaching contribution to fashion, as mass-produced ready-mades offered the middle classes both fashion and variety at an affordable price. Signs of the tailoring trade's decline around the turn of the century indicate that customers were changing their buying habits in preference for ready-made department store clothing and were less interested in upper-class notions of tailored fashion.[13] Ready-made clothing made upper-class fashions attainable to the middle classes, but at the same time it shifted middle-class sartorial aesthetics and consumption away from the snobbish venues and fastidious custom fit that characterized upper-class dress. Through the department store, the tide of mainstream fashion was steadily finding a more middle-class source, as bourgeois styles diverged more and more from what was regarded as à la mode by the elite. Clearly the department store had much to gain by "educating" the growing middle classes to consume its inexhaustible supply of goods. Yet the department store was also a liberating social force in allowing the middle classes to practice their own form of consumption in their own arena and to develop their own aesthetic and lifestyle—one that was increasingly distinct from that of the upper classes. The department store enabled the middle classes to explore, cultivate, and exert their own middle class-ness, albeit through material goods.

The Emergence of the Middle-Class Uniform: The Lounge Suit

The department store's popularity among the middle classes proved indispensable to the overwhelming success of what became the most important nineteenth-century evolution in male fashion: the emergence of the three-piece suit as the basic uniform of the professional middle-class man. The modern business suit originated in the late 1850s and '60s from the lounge (or "sack") coat as an alternative to the distinguished but confining frock coat, which contoured at the waist before skirting away from the body, sometimes reaching below the knee (fig. 5.1; Martin and Koda, 151). The shorter, looser, and boxier lounge jacket provided more comfort and was quickly adopted as informal wear for the country, recreation, and casual pursuits (fig. 5.2; Byrde, 154). The early lounger's tweed, cheviot,

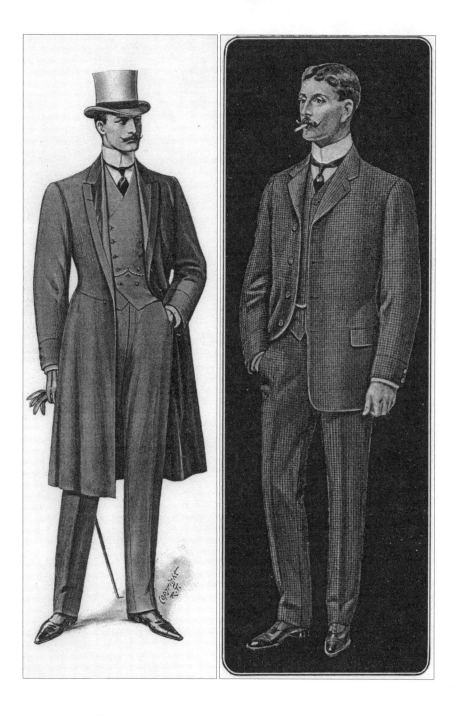

Figure 5.1. (left) Frock coat (*Master Tailor and Cutters' Gazette,* April 1907, n.p.); *figure 5.2. (right)* Lounge suit with jockey vest (*Master Tailor and Cutters' Gazette,* February 1907, n.p.)

or velvet fabric also helped to suggest informality and youth. By the mid-1860s, the lounge jacket was worn with matching waistcoat and trousers, forming the immediate precursor to the modern three-piece suit.

The dignified frock coat maintained its supremacy for some time against this sartorial upstart. Upper-class gentlemen and upscale tailors sneeringly referred to lounge suits as "dittoes" (Breward, *Hidden*, 34), associating them with livery or servants' uniforms (Martin and Koda, 149). Yet by the 1880s and '90s, the lounge suit, widely available at department stores (fig. 5.3), had become acceptable office wear and was then rapidly adapted into a range of variations for every activity, from sports to formal parties. Once the three-piece ready-to-wear lounge suit began to catch on, its adoption was radical and swift. Wanamaker declared in 1910, "A few years ago a man would never have dreamt of going to luncheon at the 'Ritz' or to pay a call in a lounge suit. Indeed he would never have appeared at all in town in such a costume in the height of the season. But now the lounge suit is all pervading and can be worn everywhere in the day time except to purely formal functions and very large and 'swagger' affairs" (7). In a relatively short time, the lounge suit had emerged from its humble beginnings as casual sportswear to usurp the frock coat and become all-purpose menswear for all but the most formal of occasions. By the First World War, the lounge suit had become universal (Laver, *Dandies*, 109–10).

The success of the lounge suit was part of a larger relaxation of long-held clothing conventions, as variety, informality, and flexibility crept into popular menswear. The men's monthly *Fashion* asserted, "English business men . . . are getting less and less formal every season" (Brummel, Dress News, April 1898, 15), and the *Tailor and Cutter* proclaimed in 1885, "At no period was the form or general character of the garments which compose the male dress more suitable for all kinds of occupations and occasions than they are now." A host of rigid sartorial rules that had previously distinguished classes and professions were bent or broken altogether. "The city clerk," Humphry explained in 1902, "once obliged to wear a black coat and silk hat, now enjoys comparative freedom in attire" (*Etiquette for Every Day*, 290). In 1895, George Augustus Sala analyzed and elucidated the changes in costume for many London trades, including the legal profession:

> A lawyer nowadays may wear any costume that he pleases; whereas, even
> as recently as the period when Dickens wrote *Bleak House* he described

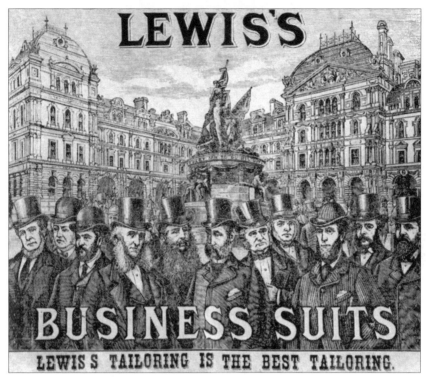

Figure 5.3. Lewis's Business Suits advertisement (Briggs, 49)

Mr. Tulkinghorn as being attired entirely in black, with knee-breeches tied up with ribbons, and black stockings. Nowadays the gentlemen who are kind enough to serve us with writs, or to serve others at our request with these documents . . . may wear without reproach any costume they choose. Dodson may appear in a suit of dittoes, and Fogg in a Newmarket cut coat and Oxford grey continuations; while nobody would quarrel with Mr. Perker if he donned a plaid ulster. (*London,* 337–38)

With ever-greater frequency, professionals abandoned the conventional business uniform of top hat and tailcoat—once "the only acceptable wear for City men" and what Charles Cavers, owner of the dressmaking firm Trenchard and Thomas Cavers, called "the very pinnacle of the English social system"—in favor of variations on the decidedly democratic and middle-class lounger (Harrods, 27; Cavers, 92). Cavers lamented that he observed only four top hats (including his own) on a day out in London in the late 1910s (92). The once-predominant frock coat faced a similar fate. Usurped by the lounger, the frock coat was worn with much less frequency after the 1880s, and it slipped gradually into obsolescence.[14]

Thus, the democratic, ready-to-wear lounge suit emerged as the distinctive business uniform of the rising bourgeois professional class.[15] Perfectly matched to the new technological conditions of mass production, the looser fit and uniform cut of the sack style made the lounge coat much cheaper to produce than the more fitted frock coat (Paoletti, 123). The increasingly sedentary nature of office work was also well suited to the loose style and more utilitarian design of the lounge suit. The rectangular cut and tubelike arms and legs tended to conceal both muscle and paunch, diverting attention away from the wearer's physical attributes and redirecting it to hallmarks of his economic and social status. Accessorized with gold watch and umbrella,[16] the ready-to-wear three-piece lounge suit served as the primary indicator of a man's membership in the professional middle class in late-nineteenth- and early-twentieth-century Britain. This is not to say that only the middle classes wore the business suit; indeed, the upper classes were quick to adopt it around the same time. To a certain extent, the path of the egalitarian lounger is not unlike that of denim blue jeans in the second half of the twentieth century, in that its function and meaning could be appropriated and adopted in a variety of ways: the lounge suit became popular country casual wear among the elite and was appropriated early on by London mashers. Yet the business suit and its accessories primarily represented a utilitarian uniform custommade for the work of the urban middle-class businessman; its design and style never reflected the lifestyle of the leisure classes. Iconographically speaking, the business suit was, and still is, associated with the bourgeois business class rather than with the aristocracy. While the upper-class gentleman often modifies his suit via custom tailoring, luxurious fabrics, and designer labels to distinguish it from the department store–bought variety worn by the masses, the generic image of the suit is still squarely associated with the middle-class businessman. This is significant not because it marks the first time that a sartorial style emerged from somewhere other than the upper classes, but rather because it was the first time that the upper classes adopted, but failed to fully appropriate, a fashion.[17] The lounge or business suit has remained a distinctively middle-class professional uniform, and the image of the Englishman in a smart lounge suit and bowler, clutching a tightly rolled umbrella, has become a universally recognized icon of quintessential Britishness.

Middle-Class Sartorial Freedom and the Move toward Informality

The versatile, practical, and ready-to-wear lounge suit distinguished the vigorous sartorial aesthetic of the middle-class City businessman from the confining, pretentious, occasion-specific styles of the fussy upper-class gentleman. Yet the lounge suit represented only one venue by which the middle classes rejected upper-class sartorial hegemony in an effort to create their own distinctive style. At the same time that the lounger emerged as the standard costume for the City, less formal, more recreational styles were also developing for the park, the country, and the expanding suburbs. The turn of the century witnessed the widespread adoption of informal menswear and a growing freedom and variety in men's sartorial choices. Laura Ugolini observes that recent fashion histories locate a "relaxation" of men's clothing only after the First World War, with the abandonment of the formal frock coat and starched collars and the adoption of lighter fabrics and more relaxed styles (429). But I counter that much of this change had begun decades earlier. The rigid formality and decorum of the office, church, and evening party were replaced by a sartorial aesthetic inspired by the energy and informality of the promenade and playing field. This was marked by the popular embrace of casual, recreational clothing and lighter fabrics formerly reserved for the country and sport. A great variety of informal hats (fig. 5.4) emerged beginning in the 1850s, including the sailor hat, Homburg, and boater (Foster, 15). The popular Trilby (which had taken its name from the title character for George du Maurier's wildly successful 1894 novel) was the first soft felt hat for men. The straw boater was the most popular informal hat of the final decade of the nineteenth century, "effectively destroying an age-old symbol of social rank, for this new kind of headgear had no 'class distinction'" (Cunnington and Cunnington, 341). In 1894 the *Tailor and Cutter* declared London "straw-hattier than ever." The Norfolk, a pleated woolen hunting and sporting jacket once worn exclusively in the country, had become increasingly popular for ordinary wear, especially with knickerbockers of the same material, by the 1890s (fig. 5.5; Cunnington and Cunnington, 318).[18] The Norfolk helped usher in other woolen and knitted outer garments for men, including the cardigan and the pullover sweater, often worn in place of a waistcoat (Adburgham, *Punch*, 213–15). Flannels were gradually adopted for suits in the second half of the nineteenth century, and by 1897, country tweeds had begun to appear in the city in the morning. Moreover, the unusually hot summers that plagued England around the turn of the century played a significant role in accelerating

Figure 5.4. Variety of men's hats in Thomas Townend and Co. advertisement (*Minister's Gazette of Fashion*, June 1889) (permission British Library)

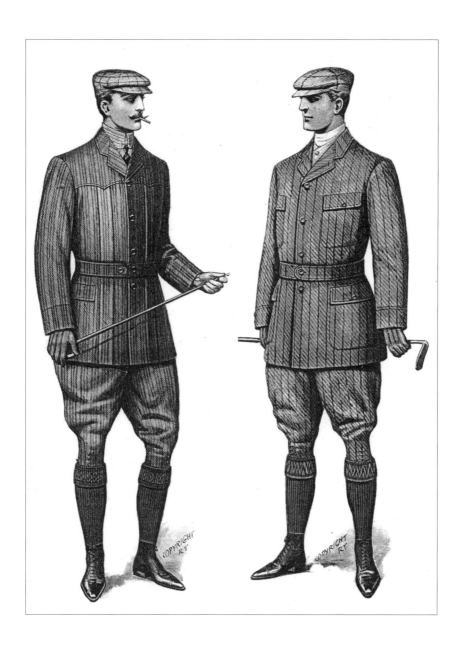

Figure 5.5. Norfolk jackets (*Master Tailor and Cutters' Gazette*, June 1907, n.p.)

the informality of men's apparel. *Fashion* reported that during the summer of 1900, "the coatless and waistcoatless man was by no means an uncommon object in London while the heat wave was passing over us" ("Shirt-Coat," 8).

The change to informal dress occurred relatively rapidly—in a matter of a few decades—and an indication of how fully accepted it had become socially can be found in the growing approval expressed in the historically conservative genre of conduct literature. In *Etiquette for Men* (1902), Devereaux heralded the new casual fashions and fabrics as a welcome change from the stuffy sartorial reserve of masculine London:

> In town just lately certain changes have begun to assert themselves, and the rigorous insistence on a black frock-coat and silk hat has had to give way, until it has become quite usual to see men in tweeds, short coats, and bowlers or straw hats. The fashion may be only temporary, but it looks uncommonly as though the thin end of the wedge has been inserted, and the change as it is is a very pleasant one, for it takes off something of the overwhelmingly business-like air London wears so much, and gives a pleasant impression that all men are not for ever catching the early train in and the fast train home.
>
> Somehow a man in tweeds wears quite a different expression on his countenance to the anxious, "must-be-upsides-with-everybody" look so common to the faces of his black frock-coated brother. There is an easy leisureliness in his walk too which is good to see amongst the hurrying, fussy London throngs. (22–23)

Comfort and convenience were repeatedly cited as the chief assets of the new informality in masculine dress. *The Glass of Fashion* celebrated the "simplicity, comfort, convenience" of the new male costume. "You may go anywhere and do anything in it. It is easily thrown off, easily put on; it is cleanly and neat, and sufficiently becoming" (169). "Our present dress . . . is adapted rather to the purpose of fitness than that of adornment," the author continued. "We do not wear our clothes with the view of dazzling or surprising others, but for our own convenience" (170). The popularity of the loose-fitting Norfolk jacket and blousing knickerbockers demonstrated to the *Tailor and Cutter* (in 1890) that the Englishman was "a lover of comfort," and a newspaper correspondent observed in 1906 that "men's dress is showing an increasing tendency to make comfort the first consideration" (Adburgham, *Punch*, 214–15). In his 1893 speech before the Sheffield Society, tailor T. Patterson asserted that "naturalness" and "utility" were the distinctive characteristics of both English dress and modern masculinity and concluded that "garments suitable to the pursuit of the individual tend more and more in the direction of use and simplicity" (165). Such discourse privileged comfort as a manly virtue unique to the middle-class male, positioning his relaxed and slightly rumpled informality in direct opposition with the stuffy, rule-bound polish of the aristocrat. With an implicit critique directed at the occasion-specific costume of the upper classes, the *Gazette of Fashion and Cutting Room Companion* simply stated, "People have not time now-a-days to change their dress three or four times a day" ("Thoughts," 1).

Sportswear and the Middle Classes

This newfound appreciation of sartorial comfort reflected a larger late-nineteenth-century cultural shift in social values that witnessed an exuberant celebration of a rugged, vigorous, athletic masculinity. This evolution had begun as early as the late 1850s with the rise of the Muscular Christianity movement, but not until the turn of the century did it reach a fever pitch—prompted in part by British imperial zeal and anxieties over the supposed feminization and "overcivilization" of English society (not to mention new suspicions regarding upper-class "effeminacy" in light of the 1895–96 Wilde trials)—with the popularity of fitness crazes, fad diets, vegetarianism, and the establishment of gymnasiums, athletic clubs, sporting leagues, and health spas.[19] In their most obvious, mainstream form, late-Victorian ideals of "rugged masculinity" manifested themselves in the explosive popularity of athletics and sport in England. At the turn of the century, the middle classes (of both sexes) embraced a variety of games and sporting pursuits that were new—or at least newly affordable thanks to mass production and the department store—including hockey, fencing, skiing, croquet, ping-pong, jujitsu, and roller-skating (Adburgham, *Punch*, 207–10, 215). Golf and tennis were particularly popular, and by the 1890s everyone was cycling—an unprecedented rage eclipsed only by the advent of the motorcar in the final years of the century.

Celebrated twentieth-century English fashion designer Hardy Amies may be overstating things a bit when he claims that sports are "the great engine" behind all fashion, but the emergence of a widespread mania for sports and recreation—what historian Hugh Cunningham calls "a national leisure culture"—helped fuel the radical transformation of men's fashions at the turn of the century, as well as of the entire cultural ideal of the male body (Amies, 69; Cunningham, 319). "The figure of the man of to-day is slim, athletic, but not burly," proclaimed Mrs. Burton Kingsland in *Etiquette for All Occasions* (1901). "His shoulders are broad (padding has been done away with), his limbs are sturdy, and he affects a quick, brisk walk. Anglomaniacs lengthen the step to a pronounced stride. All live much in the open air, and clothes are worn easier, looser, and more comfortable than heretofore. . . . It is a period of aesthetic athletes" (347). The athletic culture of the turn of the century was, to an extent, a kind of repudiation of fashion and commodities in favor of a celebration of the bare, unadorned manly body (Breward, *Hidden*, 252). But more often, it provided ample opportunities for these aesthetic athletes to adorn themselves in clothes derived from, or inspired by, the comfortable, loose-fitting, casual fit of sportswear (figs. 5.6 and 5.7). Cycling helped revive the wearing of knee breeches, and golf accelerated the popularity of knickerbockers, knitted pullovers, and waistcoats. *Punch* magazine, albeit with tongue undoubtedly planted

Figure 5.6. Fashion plate of four sporting costumes (*Gentleman's Magazine of Fashion,* July 1888, plate 247)

Figure 5.7. Fashion plate of female and male tennis costumes (*Minister's Gazette of Fashion,* June 1889, figs. 3235 and 3236) (permission British Library)

in cheek, nevertheless revealed the opportunities for male physical display and enhancement offered by golfing costume:

> The burning question which divides golfers into two hostile camps is the choice between knickerbockers and trousers . . . to a man with a really well-turned calf and neat ankles I should say, wear knickerbockers whenever you get a chance. Knickerbockers afford great scope for the display of stylish stockings. A very good effect is produced by having a little red tuft which should appear under the roll which surmounts the calf. The roll itself, which should always have a smart pattern, is very useful in conveying the impression that the calf is more fully developed than it really is. ("Golf," 160)

Department stores were eager to cater to the new demand for sportswear and casual clothing. Lewis's advertised football outfits in 1880 (fig. 5.8), Brown's of Chester offered ready-made lawn tennis costumes beginning in 1882, and Dickens and Jones' 1887 catalogue featured tennis flannels, boating jackets, and navy blazers (Adburgham, *Shops,* 197). Harrods' 1895 catalogue offered boxing gloves, dumbbells, fencing equipment, rugby balls, cricketing goods, lawn tennis equipment, croquet sets, golf clubs, and roller skates (*Victorian Shopping,* 1300–1301, 1307–19). In 1903 a new "Sports and Games Department" added to this list rowboats and canoes, exercise equipment and "developers," and supplies for football, badminton, croquet, archery, and billiards (*Harrods General Catalogue,* 1903, 1064–76). By 1900, men had begun to appear at the Goodwood Races and other outdoor summer occasions in white flannel suits, blazers, white trousers, and straw boaters—all items that had once been considered exclusively sportswear. "Things are more involved than ever in the sartorial line," observed Humphry, "since so many new sports and pastimes have sprung up for men" (*Manners,* 113). Sports undoubtedly provided the greatest opportunity, inspiration, and testing ground for late-Victorian middle-class men's burgeoning interest in fashionable consumption. Fiona Anderson contends that because sports were strongly associated with Victorian notions of manliness, they served as a publicly acceptable means by which men could experiment with fashion and new articles of clothing while avoiding ridicule and accusations of effeminacy (417). Sports-inspired clothing—because of its typically form-fitting nature and the activities often performed while in it—certainly permitted new opportunities for display, figure enhancement,

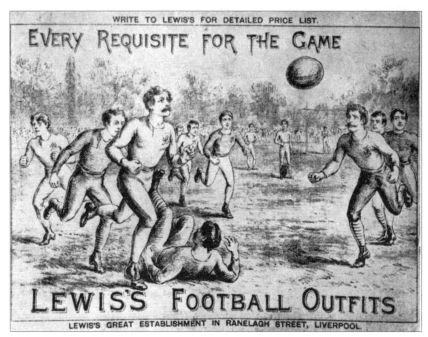

Figure 5.8. Advertisement for Lewis's Football Outfits, 1880 (Briggs, 50)

and sexual presentation that still fell safely under the guise of decidedly masculine behaviors.

While sports are often associated with the image of the wealthy and leisured elite, the late nineteenth century saw participation in athletics and the purchase of sporting equipment made affordable to the middle classes. The "sporting revolution," historian Helen Meller insists, "belonged, in the main, to the middle classes in their leafy suburbs" (236). Golf, for example, was at the turn of the century a decidedly middle-class pursuit, and cycling quickly became affordable to the bourgeoisie in the 1880s (Adburgham, *Shops*, 266). To be sure, sports have often served to maintain social and class distinctions in England, and certain sports—such as boating, riding, and mountaineering—were (and still are) very much upper-class diversions (Haley, 208–10). Yet the middle class's enthusiastic appropriation of both athletics and sports-related clothing during the late nineteenth century reflected the further obliteration of traditional class markers, for nearly everyone could afford to adopt the leisure clothing and consumable recreational pursuits once exclusive to the elite. For a time, conservative social commentators and traditionalists sought to maintain conventional class and sartorial borders: many turn-of-the-century conduct books added new rules regarding appropriate dress for each form of sport and popular recreation in a not-entirely-successful attempt to assimilate recreation into the system of rules that had guided all other forms of men's dress. Kingsland's *Etiquette for All Occasions,* for example, goes to great lengths to prescribe specific costumes for cycling, boating, swimming, golfing, riding, hunting, and driving.[20] Similarly, tailoring journals heavily promoted newly developed attire specific to each sport. In actuality, however, it was these new forms of affordable recreation and leisure that were guiding changes in how men dressed and what they wore. The middle-class men eager to adopt ready-made knockoffs of sport costume and sports-inspired clothing often chose to wear these items outside of the narrow bounds of their prescribed use.

The overt disregard increasingly demonstrated by middle-class men against conventional sartorial codes was often greeted with impotent hostility by the defenders of sartorial elitism. "We are threatened with a general decadence in dress," protested the trade journal *Tailor and Cutter* in 1894; "The contempt for time-honoured traditions which prescribed the proper costume for particular occasions is nowhere more openly expressed than in Rotten Row," Hyde Park's fashionable bridle path. The rapid popularity of the dinner jacket, with its informal shortness and tailcoatlike roll collar, in the final two decades of the nineteenth century caused the *London Tailor* to remark in disgust in 1898, "It is an error for gentlemen to go to public dinners or to assemblies where ladies are present, in dinner jackets; and yet they will do it" (quoted in Cunnington and Cunnington, 312). While fashion's dictates may still have been faithfully observed among the West End's elite, by the 1890s they were increasingly ignored nearly everywhere else. Members of the practical-minded middle class were often resistant to anything that suggested aristocratic pretensions designed to mystify and exclude. In 1890 *Etiquette for Gentlemen* advised, "Among the middle classes, evening dress is often considered an affectation, except on special occasions; it is well, therefore, to avoid it when it is not likely to be generally adopted" (19–20).[21] What was "not done" was precisely what *was* done by a growing number of middle-class males who disregarded upper-class dictums on dress and behavior. Because the middle classes did not know the formal rules of dress or simply did not bother to heed such rules, their sartorial transgressions helped to obliterate the conventions that governed "proper" dress and also to normalize their sartorial choices. In other words, what was once considered a sartorial faux pas became the norm through repetition.[22] Certainly, this was not always a political move; some men in the middle classes never consciously set out to revolt against upper-class codes of "fashionable" or "proper" dress—rather, they did not know, or did not care, or could not afford to follow the codes . . . and therefore simply didn't.

Nevertheless, middle-class males may be seen as engaging in a conscious and overt rebellion against the social hegemony of upper-class sartorial aesthetics, and the conflict between fastidious, occasion-specific dress and informal, all-purpose dress can be read as a struggle between upper- and middle-class masculinities for social legitimacy and sexual dominance. The open repudiation of sartorial rules— as well as the insistence by those of the middle classes that such rules were always inherently upper class and therefore undesirable—was undoubtedly fueled by related class-laden Victorian social issues, including the Muscular Christianity movement, late-nineteenth-century athleticism, and widespread quasi-medical concerns over the weakening of men within an "overcivilized" modern society. In a twist on the late-eighteenth- and early-nineteenth-centuries' "Great Masculine Renunciation," turn-of-the-twentieth-century Englishmen sought to assert the legitimacy of a vital middle-class masculinity not through sober dark-hued dress, but rather through the rejection of top hat and tailcoat and adoption of the more casual yet practical lounge suit and through the repudiation of rule-bound occasion-specific dress in favor of informal, sportier, all-purpose clothing. This was not the conventional image of the drab, mousy middle-class clerk, but rather the new paradigm of a vital, athletic bourgeoisie male. Middle-class men rejected established ideals and older models of fashion by asserting a sartorial display that they believed to be more energetic, more practical, and more casual—in short, more masculine—than the stuffy, fastidious, occasion-specific dress of the traditional upper-class gentleman.

The popular impression that the emerging middle classes, lacking birth and property, relied heavily on visual markers of conspicuous consumption—clothing, in particular—to assert their status and "keep up appearances" does not provide an entirely accurate or complete picture of nineteenth-century class dynamics. The widespread availability of both mass-produced and luxury items along with the increasingly visual, spectacularized nature of British culture elicited a growing reliance on consumable goods as indicators of social status by all classes. Clothing therefore played an ever-more-important role in the creation, presentation, and maintenance of social identity. The waning of traditional aristocratic socioeconomic power and the machinery of mass culture led to a splintering of the fashion market that opened it up to new influences and venues beyond the world of the elite. The emergence of a plurality of coexisting fashions served as a highly visual and immediate arena for the expression of multiple class-specific masculinities.

The conditions of late-nineteenth-century Britain—advances in mass production, widespread economic prosperity, the rise of the department stores, the growth in white-collar professions, the emerging suburbs, and the popularity of sports, recreation, and tourism—produced a middle class whose vocations, expenditures, shopping venues, domestic life, and leisure pursuits were often profoundly different from those of the elite. Thus, rather than renouncing fashion or simply aping the costume of social superiors, the middle classes adopted a sartorial aesthetic reflective of its own tastes and appropriate to its own emerging lifestyle. At the same time, the adoption by the upper-class gentleman of occasion-specific dress and ever-more-complicated sartorial rules rendered his fashion aesthetic increasingly irrelevant to middle-class masculinity. What Tim Edwards identifies as the two primary images of contemporary masculinity employed by the fashion industry in the 1980s and '90s—the "corporate power look" and "outdoor casual"—actually found their beginnings a century earlier in the business lounge suits and informal sportswear of the Victorian middle-class male (41–42). Together, the lounge suit and sports-inspired clothing marked the emergence of a new, distinctly middle-class masculinity—not the sober, reserved, dour style of earlier nineteenth-century middle-class masculinity or the stiff, overly elegant, fastidiously correct mode of upper-class masculinity, but rather a masculinity that was "correct" as well as practical, relaxed, sporty, and athletic. And it was a masculinity that emerged as one of the most enduring and dominant images of British manhood throughout the twentieth century.

Epilogue

Beauty has so long been considered the prerogative of the fair sex that it is time the mere man should look to himself, and consider in what way he can best improve his appearance.

— "Improving the Mere Man," *Fashion* (1904)

The lines are blurring between the men who work with their hands and the men who have their hands worked on.

— Jim Rendon, *New York Times* (2004)

IN 2003, THE "METROSEXUAL," A STRAIGHT URBAN MALE WITH A strong aesthetic sense who spends a great deal of his time and money on personal appearance and lifestyle,[1] burst onto the pop culture landscape. Seemingly overnight, the metrosexual became a popular buzzword and amassed widespread attention through national magazine cover stories, Michael Flocker's trendy best seller *The Metrosexual Guide to Style: A Handbook for the Modern Man,* and the Bravo cable network's hit series *Queer Eye for the Straight Guy,* in which a quintet of gay style experts offer grooming, dressing, and home decorating tips to clueless straight men. Widely celebrated as the poster boy for metrosexuality was British soccer sensation David Beckham, the strikingly handsome and muscular celebrity athlete who constantly changes his hairstyle and has been seen on various occasions in pink nail polish, a sarong, and even his wife's panties, and who acknowledges—even encourages—his gay fan base . . . but who is nonetheless unquestionably masculine and straight (Salzman, 125).

The metrosexual represents the quintessential personification of the new male consumerism at the turn of the twenty-first century, as today's popular and commercial cultures pay growing attention to men's beauty, fashionable display, and purchasing power. Increasingly, young, urban, professional middle-class men with disposable incomes and a heightened sense of style are driving clothing sales and setting fashion trends. They shop at a growing number of High Street stores, departments, and boutiques catering directly to males, but their preoccupation with fashionable display has expanded far beyond clothing. Today, male grooming in

Britain is a £685 million market, having surged by 20 percent in the past five years; the U.S. market is worth $5.5 billion (Groskop, 12). Department store makeup counters, drugstores, and online merchants that once peddled only shampoos, shaving creams, and colognes to men now enthusiastically offer an ever-widening variety of "male cosmetics," including antiwrinkle creams, concealers, and self-tanners. Surveys indicate that men increasingly believe such products are necessary for their professional, social, and sexual success, and industry analysts predict that the men's cosmetics market is "about to explode" (Siskos, 30; "Cosmetics," 34). More and more men are going to even greater extremes for beauty, as the number of cosmetic surgery operations in Britain rose more than 50 percent between 2003 and 2004 ("Plastic Surgery"). In the United States, men are the fastest-growing segment of cosmetic surgery patients, their overall number of patients having rocketed an astonishing 269 percent between 1997 and 2003 (Troy). Assisting this rising preoccupation with male consumption, beauty, and fashionable display are Britain's "lad" magazines, such as *Maxim*, *FHM*, and *Loaded*, which have met with overwhelming success on both sides of the Atlantic by glorifying a macho consumer lifestyle of fast cars, trendy gadgets, fashionable clothing, and grooming products.

The large-scale popularization of consumer masculinity in both Britain and the United States in recent decades has been carefully observed by cultural critics and scholars. The work of Peter Jackson, Frank Mort, Sean Nixon, Susan Bordo, Tim Edwards, and Jon Stratton has traced dramatic changes in the relationship among masculinity, consumerism, and the popular commercialized depiction of the male body since the 1970s. From the growing employment of male sexuality in advertising and the idealization of the "New Man" in the '70s and '80s emerged a highly marketable figure of the sexualized, fashionable male who defines and expresses his masculinity through consumer goods, becoming the dominant image of contemporary Western manhood—what Nixon calls "commodified masculinity" ("Exhibiting Masculinity"). Edwards conceives of modern masculinity as defined by consumption rather than production and argues that it is now socially acceptable for men "to be consumers of their own masculinity or, in short, to look at themselves and other men as objects of desire to be bought and sold or imitated and copied" (1–2, 73).

Throughout this study, I have called for a broader historical understanding of the complicated relationship between British middle-class masculinity and consumerism—not simply back to the late 1960s, but rather to the Victorian age, when the sophisticated machinery of modern mass commodity culture first began to emerge. The ready-made suits and newly affordable mass-produced goods, the soaring department stores with their elaborate window displays and decorative heaps of merchandise, the eye-catching advertisements from increasingly savvy marketers, and the conduct manuals and fashion periodicals with their promises of social advancement through proper dress all assisted in the creation of an irresistible and modern cultural landscape based on the cultivation and expression of consumer desires. Many of the characteristics of contemporary masculinity that have attracted popular and scholarly interest can be linked directly to the late Victorian age and are a large-scale realization of the small steps first taken then. The period between 1860 and 1914 gave birth to trends—the middle class's dominance of fashion, the increased acknowledgment and cultivation of male beauty as a commodity, the men's lifestyle periodical—that have continued unabated through the twentieth century and right up to our own time.

While popular fashion now emerges from a variety of sources, from Paris designers and Hollywood to sports and urban street culture, the middle class— facilitated by mass production and the department store—continues to serve as the primary arbiter of sartorial tastes, in much the same way that late-Victorian middle-class men asserted their own class identity, values, and aesthetic through the adoption of the lounger as business costume and the appropriation of sportswear as casual clothing. The business suit and sports-inspired casual wear remain the two most popular uniforms of contemporary Western masculinity. Indeed, Edwards correctly observes that modern manhood finds its primary sartorial expression in "two central images": the "corporate power look" of the busy city executive with his dark, broadly cut, double-breasted business suit, briefcase, and cell phone, and the "outdoor casual" look of the muscular hunk in T-shirt, jeans, and leather (41). With only minor variations, the lounge suit of the 1850s and '60s has become the business suit of the twentieth and twenty-first centuries. While often dressed up by haute couture for the elite, it always retains the same basic lines that first popularized it among Britain's middle-class professionals. The widespread adoption of linens, cottons, and other lightweight fabrics; the preference for light colors instead of drab; and the T-shirts, jerseys, polo shirts, ball caps, and sweatshirts ubiquitously worn as casual wear all trace their origins back to the athletic and recreational clothing designed in the late-Victorian and Edwardian ages.

The repeated assertions by *Fashion*, the first men's fashion periodical, that late-Victorian men were as interested in, and as responsible for, caring about fashion and personal appearance as women were reflect a radical transformation of nineteenth-century ideals regarding men's relationship to dress. The emphasis on men's responsibility to display themselves properly was echoed throughout the twentieth century and today finds its most common expression in the notion that a man's consumption is just as important to his identity as a woman's. "Men have become as much a part of modern consumerism as women," asserts Robert Bocock. "Their construction of a sense of who they are is accomplished as much through style, clothing, body image and the right look as is women's" (102). Significantly, three recent and popular men's lifestyle and shopping periodicals—*Nylon Guys*, *Vitals for Men*, and *Men's Vogue*—are offshoots of similarly titled women's lifestyle magazines, while *Cargo* sprang from its sister publication, *Lucky*.

Men's fashion and beauty concerns further merge with those of women in their growing use of skin-care and cosmetic products. As we have seen, cosmetic use by men was not unknown during the Victorian age, but the male cosmetics "explosion" that we now stand on the brink of reflects not simply the growing public acceptability of men's beauty concerns, but also the evolving acknowledgment of male beauty as a commodity and the public acceptance of goods that facilitate male beauty and sexual display. Branching out beyond the traditional soaps and shaving creams of the past, men are eagerly exploring an ever-expanding and increasingly affordable variety of grooming products, driving a 48 percent increase in cosmetics and toiletries between 1997 and 2003 ("In-Cosmetics"). According to one consumer goods research firm, sales of men's bath and shower products surged from $2 million in 1999 to $19.3 million in 2003; during that same period, sales of men's skin-care products grew from $3.9 million to $13.8 million (Rendon, 3.3). In recent years, both low-end drugstore and upscale department store brands have aggressively moved into the men's grooming market. XCD, an exclusive British line of products that combines skin care and cosmetics, peddles Reviver eye cream, an SPF-15 fortified moisturizer that "resembles foundation," and an overnight tanner (Howard, B3). In 2005, Aramis introduced a skin resurfacing scrub and skin revitalizer, and Origins debuted an expanded line of men's grooming products in 2006 (Thompson, S-6). Perhaps antiaging products promise the greatest growth potential. Since 2003, the beauty industry has rapidly opened the men's grooming and antiaging market through a combination of aggressive advertising, newly affordable pricing, male-friendly scents, no-nonsense names such as Circle Eraser and Stop Lines, and plain packaging in neutral colors (Rubin, G3). Not content with wrinkle creams and hair dyes alone,

many men are increasingly resorting to plastic surgery; the most popular procedures among both British and American men are nose jobs and liposuction (Fox;
"Top Cosmetic," D1). Britain leads all of Europe in the number of cosmetic procedures and in 2002 ranked third worldwide in plastic surgery operations ("UK
Tops"). The British Association of Aesthetic Plastic Surgeons reported that cosmetic surgery operations increased by more than 50 percent between 2003 and
2004, and in the United States, over 1.1 million men underwent plastic surgery in
2003 (Fox; Troy).

The surge in men's cosmetic sales and cosmetic surgery procedures reflects
the growing social and professional pressures, felt by many men, to appear young
and attractive. In 2002, the *New York Times* examined male professionals who opted
for cosmetic surgery to boost or rejuvenate their careers, and two years later, the
Wall Street Journal reported on a recent survey of senior executives that revealed that
82 percent regarded age bias as a "serious problem," while 94 percent of respon-
dents (mostly men in their forties and fifties) claimed that their age had cost
them job opportunities (Carr, 3.12; Hymowitz, B1). Men's antiaging potions now
outsell shaving products, and "cosmetic surgery, botox and other de-aging skin
treatments are becoming de rigueur for baby-boomer executives of both sexes
who fear being judged as over the hill" (Thompson, S-6; Hymowitz, B1). To be
sure, the cosmetics industry eagerly fans the growing flames of men's beauty and
aging anxieties. British magazine and television advertisements promoting L'Oréal's
Men's Expert skin-care line conspiratorially address women by declaring, "What
he thinks are great lines, you think are premature wrinkles"; and visitors to the
Men's Expert website are confronted with the dire warning, "Face it. You're getting older. Don't ignore it," accompanied by a chilling video simulation of a handsome young man's face sinking into the wrinkles, jowls, and liver spots of a with-
ered pensioner.[2]

Consumer masculinity has found its strongest voice in the emergence of the
men's lifestyle magazine since the early 1990s. While *Esquire*, *GQ*, and *Playboy* had
been around for decades on both sides of the Atlantic, the 1994 debut of *Loaded*
in Britain ushered in the age of "laddism"—an unapologetically primitive and
swaggering masculinity founded on the obsessive celebration of sport, beer, sex,
cars, and gadgets—not necessarily in that order. *FHM*, *Maxim*, and *Arena* soon
followed and met with similar success; today *FHM* is the top-selling British
men's magazine and the nineteenth-highest-selling magazine overall (Davidson;
Butcher). In 2004, *Nuts* and *Zoo Weekly* joined the macho orgy as the first British

men's weeklies. The premiere of the American version of *Maxim* in 1998 proved to be one of the most transformative successes of the decade. Now *Maxim* boasts a readership of 2.5 million, while its rivals *Stuff* and the American version of *FHM* each attract about half that number (Sanders). A wave of major men's lifestyle, fashion, and fitness titles debuted in the United States between 2003 and 2005; these magazines include *Vitals for Men, Cargo, T: Men's Fashion, Nylon Guys, Men's Vogue, Complex* (a young men's consumer bimonthly with a hip-hop sensibility, published by the clothing company Eckō Unlimited), *VMan* (a high-fashion biannual), *Giant* (a pop culture and entertainment magazine for men), *Sync* ("the first and only tech-tainment publication"), and *Sly* (a fitness magazine for men over forty, founded by action star Sylvester Stallone). Edwards notes that the triumph of lad and style magazines is in large part attributable to their success in selling fashionable consumption to men, and Alix Sharkey asserts, "For all its editorializing about boxing, football, and other so-called male pastimes, the men's magazine industry largely owes its expansion to the huge growth in sales of 'men's grooming products'" (Edwards, 74–76; Sharkey, 177).[3] The 208-page premiere issue of *T: Men's Fashion* in 2004, for example, featured 114 pages devoted to advertising, and sales for magazine advertising in the men's grooming category for 2005 were twice as large as those for 2004 (Lipke, 17; Thompson, S-6).

While *Playboy* is often credited with transforming the negative image of the nineteenth-century effeminate dandy, preoccupied with his looks and clothes, into the attractive image of the sexy, macho bachelor-consumer who wants the good life, we have seen how *Fashion* sought to achieve a similar purpose more than half a century earlier. Today's lad and men's lifestyle magazines carry on this project, glamorizing the construction of an attractive male identity through fashionable consumer goods. Nick Stevenson and colleagues' 2000 study of British lad magazine readership revealed that many readers "mainly saw the magazines as 'reflecting' the lifestyle which they most aspired to in terms of the forms of masculinity represented in the magazines and the consumptive concern with clothes, style and gadgets" (205). *Sync's* on-cover motto is "Stuff for a Man's Life," while promotional materials for *Cargo* featured the slogan "Shop like a man. Read it. Club it. Drag it home" ("Sync"; Frick, 38). Mort and Edwards have both observed that men's lifestyle magazines assist their readers in knowing just *what* to drag home, through the establishment of a "style cultural intelligentsia of experts disseminating their specialist know-how on matters of appearance" as a gateway into an elite world of fashion and prestige (Edwards, 74). Moreover, Edwards notes, these experts instruct readers on the value and significance of tailored suits, grooming products, and other goods and consequently encourage and perpetuate high spending, as invariably the most expensive option is the correct one (76, 74). *Fashion* likewise served as an advertiser and promoter of goods and positioned itself as an authority and final word on the correct selection, purchase, and use of masculine items. The late-Victorian monthly emphasized expensive items, always reasoning that cheap goods proved more costly in the long run, and it provoked men's sartorial, social, and sexual anxieties by promising to cure them through endless spending.

In this way, *Fashion* and the men's lifestyle magazines that have followed it perform a function similar to that of the conduct literature of the nineteenth century, advising male readers how to dress, how to groom, and how to behave in order to project a fashionable, sexually desirable, and professionally successful masculinity. Deborah Philips observes that men's style magazines are now regarded "as authoritative sources of information on the stylistic requirements for acceptable forms of masculinity" (246). As in the Victorian age, this is a masculinity that is assembled increasingly through the proper purchase of the proper goods. *Cargo*, one of the newest men's shopping periodicals, features the front cover slogan "The New Buyer's Guide for Men" and offers short blurbs about clothes, grooming products, and electronic items among advertisements for the same items. *Cargo*'s copy works hard—perhaps too hard—to sell male bikini waxing, collagen injections, and baubles to men, pointing out in one article, for example, that four out of five women claim they would date a man who wears jewelry (Frick, 38). Popular men's magazines such as *Esquire* frequently feature reassuringly prescriptive articles such as "There's No Shame In: A Good Moisturizer," in which "tough-skinned" William Sanderson of the HBO western *Deadwood* tests a variety of men's moisturizers, and "Grooming Advice (From a Guy Who Can Kick Our Ass)," in which former Australian football player and Ironman triathlete Rodney Cutler declares, "I am here to announce that it's now fully kosher for a man to wax his back" (Wrenn, 76; Cutler, 76). The hypermasculine tone of such articles resembles the same preemptive defensiveness *Fashion* assumed when celebrating male corset wear by highlighting its use by military officers, athletes, hunters, and other men of unquestioned masculinity.

Almost as soon as it had begun, the metrosexuality phenomenon was declared overexposed and played out. In December 2003, Lake Superior State University's annual "List of Words Banished from the Queen's English" declared *metrosexual* the "most misused, overused and generally useless word" of the year (Barker, D1). That same month, *Maxim* debuted a satirical ad campaign warning readers about the dangers of "Mantropy," a spiritual degeneration caused by men's embrace of metrosexuality, facials, wimpy sports, and feng shui (Ives, C10). The backlash from regular guys more interested in David Beckham's on-the-field talents than his off-the-field fashions inspired the term *retrosexual* to describe the unapologetically unsophisticated, macho man, proud of his slobbiness, and a 2004 survey of British men revealed that 10 percent did not shower or brush their teeth daily and a third did not regularly use deodorant (Groskop, 12). The continued muscle of lad magazine culture suggests willful defiance against the "New Man" and the metrosexual—"a shift away from a concern with style and grooming and towards more stereotypically masculine interests such as sport, gadgets and machines" (Attwood, 86).[4] Yet revealingly this backlash against metrosexuality is expressed not through a boycotting of consumer items altogether but merely through the consumption of other goods. Retrosexuals reject cosmetics and fashionable clothes and instead obsess over big stereos, fast cars, and tickets to sporting events. Indeed, one might wonder whether men in Western culture are even capable of defining their masculinity in any other way than through consumer goods.

While metrosexuality may have fallen out of fashion as a buzzword, what endures is an emphasis on male sexual display and the popularly accepted notion of masculinity constructed through the consumption of fashionable goods. The consumer behaviors and marketing onslaught led by men's clothing departments and boutiques, the cosmetics counter, the plastic surgeon's scalpel, and men's lifestyle magazines are gaining steam. Stratton asserts that Oscar Wilde "thought of himself as a commodity, transformed himself into a spectacle, and sold it" (139). The late-nineteenth-century Wildean dandy constructed himself as a spectacle by using consumable objects to produce "a total image which is necessarily more impressive than the person who is putting the image together" (183). Today we are all socialized to create our image out of consumable objects. Whether one embraces the contemporary dandyism of Armani suits, skin creams, and back-waxing or celebrates the loutish laddism of football jerseys, beer, and video games is immaterial. Indeed, since the late Victorian age, metrosexuality has been emblematic of the state of the modern "male as consumer," a man dependent on the purchase of a combination of goods out of which he assembles and displays his social status and masculinity.

Notes

Introduction

1. For histories of the development of the department store, see Pasdermadjian's *Department Store* and Miller's groundbreaking study *The Bon Marché*.

2. Men's acknowledged relation to consumption is predominantly limited to big-ticket items such as automobiles and stereos (Damon-Moore, 201).

3. In 1930, pioneering fashion theorist J. C. Flugel contended, "Men's dress is less 'modish' and more 'fixed' than women's. . . . [T]here is some small individual choice in minor details (the shape of a collar or the size and colour of a tie), but none at all as regards general cut, proportions, or design" (144). Nearly fifty years later, fashion historians Christina Walkley and Vanda Foster similarly maintained, "Men's clothes changed relatively little during the sixty-four years of Victoria's reign. It is true that their cut and construction showed a certain amount of variation, but while women's clothes ran through a dazzling succession of styles, fabrics and colours, men retained the same basic garments, the same colours and fabrics, and approximately the same outline. A coat, waistcoat and trousers, not necessarily matching, and a white shirt, were worn throughout the period. The coat and trousers, and increasingly the waist-coat, were usually made of a woollen cloth, and the shirt, which had above all to be washable, was always of linen or cotton. Nor did the colours vary: a study of the fashion plates of the 'forties and 'fifties shows a predominance of black and dark blue, with occasional ventures into brown and green, while *Complete Etiquette for Gentlemen*, published in about 1880, remarks that 'the four staple colours for men's wear are black, blue, brown, and olive.'" (127).

4. Several other important twentieth-century studies—including Laver's *Taste and Fashion*, Adburgham's *Shops and Shopping*, Wilson's *Adorned in Dreams*, Steele's *Fashion and Eroticism*, Bowlby's *Just Looking*, and Benson's *Counter Cultures*—examine nineteenth-century fashion solely or mainly in terms of female social history.

5. In her 1885 tract *The Science of Dress in Theory and Practice*, dress reform activist Ada Ballin attacked the "masher collar" as a preposterous excess of the current fashion, claiming that it caused "fainting, heat-stroke, and apoplexy" (259–61). The men's monthly *Fashion* warned in July 1898 of the danger of asphyxiation from high collars and reported the death of a wealthy Frenchman as a result of strangulation by his collar (Brummel, Dress News Collected and Dissected, 19).

6. Anne M. Buck notes that far fewer articles of men's clothing than of women's clothing from the Victorian era have survived (184).

7. Jo Barraclough Paoletti, Christopher Breward, and Frank Mort have all acknowledged that surviving primary sources pertaining to the appearance and consumption of Victorian (and twentieth-century) men are meager and spotty. Paoletti observes, "Compared with the avalanche of information of women's clothing that occurs [in nineteenth-century popular periodical literature] . . . , men's clothing seems hardly to have been noticed. The occasional article on men's dress which appeared in the newspapers or in ladies' magazines usually began with the remark that there had been little change before proceeding with the list of that season's variations in colours, fabrics, and cut. Larger changes are seldom mentioned, as are questions of changing usage" (127). As we shall see later, this is not entirely accurate.

8. Both Mort and Edwards analyze advertising imagery and particularly the recent advent of men's lifestyle magazines to explore how the new interest in men's consumer markets since the mid-1980s has transformed male consumerism, masculine identity, and sexual politics. Stratton's *Desirable Body* similarly examines representations of masculinity through the new attention paid to men in advertising during the 1960s and '70s, the cultivation of the men's fashion market in the 1980s, and the explosive popularity of the testosterone-heavy "New Lad" magazines in the 1990s.

9. I often use the term "Victorian" or "late Victorian" somewhat inaccurately to describe the period from 1860 to 1914.

10. Historians Neil McKendrick, John Brewer, and J. H. Plumb (1982) argue that a dramatic consumer revolution occurred in the eighteenth century in conjunction with the Industrial Revolution and that ready-made clothing, mass-manufactured goods, fashion magazines, social emulation of the upper classes, proliferation of London fashion to the provinces, rapid changes in fashion, and commerce's manipulation of fashion were all well established by 1800. Art historian Ann Bermingham goes even further, locating the birth of consumer society in the sixteenth century. And Claire Walsh contends that the Victorian era's greatest contribution to the modern commercial age—the department store—already existed (albeit on a smaller scale) throughout England by the second half of the eighteenth century.

11. Many of Britain's most famous department stores, including Debenham and Freebody's (founded in 1778), Dickens and Jones (1790), Swan and Edgar's (1812), Peter Robinson's (1833), Kendal, Milne and Faulkner (1836), Bainbridge's (1838), and Harrods (1849) began in the late eighteenth and early nineteenth centuries as small drapery or dry goods businesses staffed by only a handful of employees and carrying a highly specialized and limited line of merchandise. Many had grown by fits and starts into large-scale modern department stores by the late Victorian era,

though Bainbridge's and Kendal, Milne and Faulker had arguably achieved department store status by at least 1850 (Adburgham, *Shops*, 137; Lancaster, 7; Airey and Airey, 47).

12. Cunningham's "Leisure and Culture" offers an exhaustive, highly statistical overview of changes in Britain's leisure consumption between 1800 and 1945.

13. See Cott, "On Men's History and Women's History."

14. Brian Baker, customer liaison officer for Liberty's department store in London, remarked during a January 25, 2001, interview that no one knows what percentage of Liberty's nineteenth-century shoppers were men. Sales and clientele records for many London tailoring shops *do* still exist, but they only provide a window into the sartorial habits of Victorian England's most elite male shoppers. See Walker's *Savile Row* and Anderson's "Fashioning the English Gentleman."

15. See, for example, Langland's *Nobody's Angels*, Kimmel's *Manhood in America*, Tosh's *Man's Place*, and Vickery's *Gentleman's Daughter*.

16. According to Brian R. Mitchell, there were 15,596,000 males living in England and Wales in 1900 (*Abstracts*, 9). Of these, 5,566,100 were between the ages of 15 and 34 in 1901 (1,607,500 aged 15–19, which is 10.307% of the total male population; 1,472,600 aged 20–24, which is 9.442%; 1,328,300 aged 25–29, which is 8.517%; and 1,157,700 aged 30–34, which is 7.423%) (12). London's population in 1901 was 4,563,000; we can assume that males made up half of this number: 2,281,500 (22). Assuming that age distributions in London roughly reflected those for England and Wales more generally, we come up with 235,154 males between 15 and 19 living in London in 1901; 215,419 between 20 and 24; 194,315 between 25 and 29; and 169,356 between 30 and 34. Further, in 1901, 99.7% of males between 15 and 19 were single; 82.6% of males 20–24; 45% of males 25–29; and 25.4% of males 30–34 (Mitchell, *British*, 20). Applying these percentages to the individual age totals for London's male population, we come up with 234,449 single males between 15 and 19 living in London in 1901; 177,936 between 20–24; 87,442 between 25–29; and 43,016 between 30 and 34. This totals 542,843 single males between the ages 15 and 34 living in London in 1901.

Defining "middle-class," of course, is much more complicated and subjective. However, Dudley Baxter's 1867 estimate of the distribution of the National Income of England and Wales claims that 9.75% of families were middle class or lower middle class (annual earnings of £100–1000), or approximately 600,300 families (Perkin, 29). Fabian banker Sir Leo Chiozza Money estimated in 1904 that 8.7% were middle class—that is, living in "comfort," but not in "riches," with an annual income of £160–700 (Perkin, 30). If we apply these two percentages to the figure above, we come up with a final figure between 47,227 and 52,927—that is, roughly 50,000 single middle-class males between the ages of 15 and 34 residing in London in 1901.

Chapter One

1. The article continues: "Men's tailors display almost as much reticence as their customers. They indulge not, like women's tailors, in displayed advertisements or in the imaginative illustrations of fashion artists—or, if they pursue the latter course it must be confessed that they fail. The fashion-plate lady may not look as though she possessed head, heart, or mind; but she is almost always enchantingly pretty, and has sometimes quite an expression of her own. But the fashion gentleman has never been even fractionally human" ("Queen," 7).

2. For example, the author of *Best Dressed Man* writes, "What led up to the change I know not, but towards the latter part of George the Third's reign men's fashions in dress completely altered. Wigs, which had outlived the centuries, became gradually smaller and smaller, till they dwindled down to the proportions of a pigtail. . . . The colour of men's coats changed to plain black, brown, dark-blue, or green, save for military uniforms; and then fashion took the shape of tail-coats, frock-coats, short waistcoats, pantaloons or trousers, and beaver hats with narrow turned-up brims, which fashions, with certain modifications of style, but with comparatively little change, have held in their place to the present time" (68).

3. According to historian Michael Curtin, there is no record of any conduct book having been published in England between 1804 and 1828 (34).

4. See, for example, Armstrong's *Desire and Domestic Fiction*, Rose's "Conduct Books for Women," and Darby's "More Things Change."

5. Similarly, the long-running trade journal *London Tailor and Record of Fashion* assured readers in 1884 that "a man may . . . be very certain not to offend if he acts with a little caution by carefully selecting colours termed 'quiet,' and styles that are becoming, genteel, or elegant, according to the class of wearer" ("Hints on Dress," 28). The *Minister's Report of Fashion* noted in 1902, "With regard to patterns, it has been so long a cardinal virtue among well-dressed English gentlemen that the designs must be quiet and unostentatious; that for the home market anything loud, excepting perhaps a Harris Tweed—and even they are more subdued this season than for many years back—is absolutely tabooed" ("New Woollens," 1–2).

6. The *London Tailor* most likely lifted this tenet from one of the famous maxims for dandies listed in chapter 64 of Edward Bulwer Lytton's *Pelham* (1828), which reads, "Dress so that it may never be said of you, 'What a well-dressed man!'—but, 'What a gentlemanlike man!'" (183).

7. The image of the dandy as an ostentatious, flamboyant dresser who embraced the exaggerated extremes of fashion was one that developed only later, adopted by second- and third-generation dandies such as Benjamin Disraeli, Count D'Orsay, and the Aesthetes. I discuss this at greater length in chapter 4.

8. Another conduct manual, likewise entitled *Etiquette for Gentlemen* (1890), echoes, "It is often remarked that a man must have been well-dressed when, after spending an hour in his society, you cannot recal [*sic*] how he was dressed. In such a case the eye will neither have been caught by what is showy nor offended by what is mean. No shock will have been given to the sense of propriety, which is, after all, the great point to attain" (15–16).

9. *Routledge's Etiquette for Gentleman* notes, "The author of 'Pelham' has aptly said that a gentleman's coat should not fit too well. There is great truth and subtlety in this observation" (40).

10. Oliver Bell Bunce's *Don't* warns male readers, "Don't wear apparel with decided colors or with pronounced patterns. Don't—we address here the male reader, for whom this *brochure* is mainly designed—wear anything that is *pretty*. What have men to do with pretty things? Select quiet colors and unobtrusive patterns, and adopt no style of cutting that belittles the figure. It is right enough that men's apparel should be becoming, that it should be graceful, and that it should lend dignity to the figure; but it should never be ornamental, fanciful, grotesque, odd, capricious, nor pretty" (23–24).

11. The author of *Clothes and the Man* also speaks out against overzealous servility to exaggerated fashion plate styles: "There are . . . men who like trousers that should not be liked by well-dressed men. I refer to the fashion-plate style. I have known men to make absolute fools of themselves because of a fashion plate. They have seen a pair of trousers coloured in a set of fashion pictures, and they have said to themselves, 'Those are the trousers for me.' And then, when the tailor has come in, that young man has pointed casually to the fashion plate and said, 'I should like them cut something like that.' And the tailor, who cannot get the melancholy fact out of his mind that his mid-day joint is getting cold, has said, 'Yes, sir,' very nicely and politely, because he wants to get back to his dinner. He knows perfectly well that it is impossible for him or any other tailor to produce a pair of fashion-plate trousers. There never have been such trousers, never will be, and if it were possible to make them, they wouldn't look well. What man in his senses wants to look like a fashion plate? You must remember that if you had a pair of fashion-plate trousers on, you wouldn't be able to move a limb without spoiling the general effect. You would have to occupy yourself by standing rigidly still all day; otherwise the trousers wouldn't hang as perfectly straight as they do in the fashion plate" (80–81).

12. I discuss the growing popularity of less formal, casual dress among middle-class men at the close of the nineteenth century in chapter 5.

13. Anne Hollander contends that "long after high school," adults continue to conform to a particular "genre" of dress out of fear of ridicule and a desire "to join an available tribe" (185). In her study of Oxford students during the 1930s, Laura

Ugolini argues that the primary motive driving men's sartorial choices is to secure and maintain membership within a male group (444), and Jo Barraclough Paoletti asserts, "Fear or ridicule or criticism . . . influences male clothing behaviour far more than that of women" (124). All three writers were undoubtedly informed, in part, by the ideas of fashion theory pioneer George Van Ness Dearborn, who, in his foundational 1918 study, *The Psychology of Clothing*, claims that fear (of ridicule) drives people to dress "properly" (51–52).

14. So homogenized had black or dark dress become for urban men that in 1865 journalist and social investigator Henry Mayhew observed, "A gentleman of the present nineteenth century, attired for the gayest evening party, would apart from his jewellery, be equally presentable at the most sorrowful funeral" (63).

15. Here lies the discursive paradox at the heart of conduct literature: etiquette manuals purport to teach gentlemanly behavior but simultaneously imply that such behavior is knowable only by the true gentleman, for whom it comes so naturally that he does not need the aid of a manual. Flora Klickmann, for example, observes in *How to Behave* (1898), "There is a graceful way of holding the hat which every well-bred man understands, but which is incapable of explanation" (21). While conduct books promised to divulge the rules of Society, they repeatedly insisted that all their instruction was irrelevant if the reader did not possess a certain quality, that "indescribable something," "the art of knowing how to wear it" (Chenoune, 36–39). Proper behavior could never be fully explained but nevertheless was automatically understood by the true gentleman. For this reason, then, correct dress need never be explicitly acknowledged or talked about among gentleman; it was an inherent gift, a natural fact of their lives. Only bad, incorrect dress merited the attention of conduct authors.

16. Evidently, the practice of lifting sartorial observations and advice from earlier sources, unattributed, was rather common throughout the period. In this instance, text from *Habits of Good Society* (1859) reappeared verbatim in the article "Mr. J. Rae's Social Kaleidoscope" in an 1888 issue of a tailoring trade publication (3).

17. The *Glass of Fashion* similarly noted, "There is at least as much affectation in slovenliness as in over-dressing. . . . A man who does not dress well when he can afford to do so must either be mean and miserly, or a fool. An ill-fitting cloak is no mark of genius, but simply a sign that you do not or will not employ a good tailor" (166–67).

18. Michael Curtin elaborates, "To dress in an 'appropriate' way was, in a sense, to downgrade the independent importance of dress. That is, correct dress was a function of something else: time, place, occasion, rank, etc. To dress in a way that 'society pronounces as suitable to particular occasions' was a way of showing 'respect for society at large, or the persons with whom we are to mingle.' The gentleman was at

home in society and displayed a proper deference to its sartorial standards, whereas inappropriate dress indicated some disharmony between the wearer and his environment" (106–7). Appropriate dress for appropriate occasions displayed a gentleman's "stake in society, his participation in and endorsement of the values and activities of his class. Inappropriate clothing did just the reverse, and worse, stigmatized the wearer for expressing his rebellion in the superficial forum of dress" (107).

19. In 1892 a contributor to the journal *Pioneer of Fashion* going by the moniker "Alureda" echoed Lady Campbell's sentiments: "For people who dwell in glass houses to amuse themselves by throwing stones, has from time immemorial been regarded as a typical act of folly, and yet the masculine mind where it devotes itself to criticism of feminine conceits is only too apt to overlook the application of this most excellent adage. Man with his airs of superiority dogmatises about this or that fashion, in the most unblushing manner; he sneers at every quaint fancy that is devised to vary the monotony of our too uniform garments; he laughs at womankind as a collection of irresponsible beings, always ready to adopt any irrational device in dress, and swayed by nothing stronger than an insatiable craving for change at all costs. He altogether overlooks the fact that, were it worth the trouble, his own attitude towards fashion is every whit as deserving of derision as is that of the most bigoted of female devotees. His mental opinion is so obscured by his own self-satisfaction, that his own conventions, his own concessions to hard and fast rule, his own followings of unreasonable tradition, are hidden from him. Pick him to pieces and see how badly he will fare under examination" (14).

20. Oliver Bell Bunce similarly advised in 1883, "Don't go with your boots unpolished; but don't have the polishing done in the public highways. A gentleman perched on a high curb-stone chair, within view of all passers-by, while he is having executed this finishing touch to his toilet, presents a picture more unique than dignified. . . . Toilet offices are proper in the privacy of one's apartment only" (25–26).

21. Two other examples: "*May 5.* Bought a pair of lavender kid-gloves . . . and two white ties, in case one got spoiled in the tying" (36). And from August 3: "I bought a capital hat for the hot weather at the seaside. I don't know what it is called, but it is the shape of the helmet worn in India, only made of straw. Got three new ties, two coloured handkerchiefs, and a pair of navy-blue socks at Pope Brothers" (49).

22. If the notion of women shopping in the public arena of the department store initially seems antithetical to "separate spheres" ideology, Mona Domosh explains, "It was already clear in 1846 that women would be the store's major patrons, yet, under the reigning gender ideology of separate spheres, they could be allowed to do so only if they did not become too tainted with commercialism. In order not to disrupt established gender categories, the store had to build in the qualities associated

with nineteenth-century femininity and the domestic sphere: symbols of civic and cultural aspirations, well-ordered and arranged displays, services and amenities designed for women, and an environment in which one was safe and protected" (55).

23. Historian Elaine S. Abelson suggests that many women went to department stores out of boredom, because it was cheap entertainment. Thus shopping in the department store, to a degree, came to represent (female) aimlessness, idleness, purposelessness—the antithesis of male productivity (22).

24. Even in the 1930s and '40s, trade publications continued to assert that the associations between femininity and shopping were so strong that men avoided extensive excursions into department stores. It was therefore recommended that specially designed "men's shops" be located near a ground-floor entrance to "spare male customers an embarrassment which women would only consider as an attraction" ("Trend," 517; Levy, 87). I discuss this further in chapter 2.

25. In some instances, shop employees participated in the ridicule of male shoppers. Retail historian William Lancaster reports that female workers at some stores were widely known for the giggles and jeers they directed at "Molly Husbands"—men who accompanied their wives into the store. Lancaster suggests that such attacks were waged by female customers and employees to defend what they regarded as the uniquely "feminine terrain" of the urban department store (182).

26. Weiss's *Hell of the English* examines the relationship between popular fictional depictions of debt and the realities of debt in nineteenth-century Britain.

Chapter Two

1. By the early decades of the twentieth century, as William Leach explains, advertisers had developed a highly professionalized and sophisticated vocabulary of male-directed marketing strategies: "The display of men's wear was low-keyed, unassuming, connected with dark colors, always simple, muted, and undecorative in the 'masculine' manner. 'Simplicity should be the keynote in every display of men's clothing and furnishings' was a typical merchant's advice. 'Most men are averse to gay colors even in their ties. . . . The average man is inclined to look upon elaborate decorative effects as "useless frills."' It was one of the cardinal rules of early-twentieth-century display that men's wear never be shown in 'excessively animated' ways and never be visually reinforced by bright colors. Certainly no male mannequins in underwear appeared in windows. Nor were male mannequins used much at all, except as foils for other displays or to illustrate male dress in the most nonanimated way" (*Land*, 67).

2. Rita Felski's chapter "Imagined Pleasures: The Erotics and Aesthetics of Consumption" in her *Gender of Modernity* offers a revealing discussion on the negative portrayal of the all-consuming woman shopper.

3. Abelson's *When Ladies Go A-Thieving* provides a fascinating account of the female kleptomania "epidemic" as depicted by popular journalists, the medical and legal communities, and the stores.

4. That same year, an essay on London shopping in Sims's *Living London* echoed nearly the same sentiment: "Your wife can purchase her daughter's trousseau in one room, while in another you obtain the impedimenta incidental to a shooting expedition" (140).

5. Khaki was a significant innovation in military apparel, since its dull earth tones, ranging from drab olive greens to bilious yellow-brown hues, concealed the sand, dust, and mud stains of the British Empire's far-flung battlefields and provided far better camouflage than the brilliant reds and blues conventionally worn by European armies. The *London Tailor* claimed in 1900 that khaki had been recently developed by Belgian Colonel Dulier for military uniforms and popularized by the Boer War, despite the complaints of one critic who declared, "It makes a man look as if he suffered from chronic derangement of the liver" (77).

6. The Bon Marché of Paris, founded in 1851 and examined at length in Miller's fascinating study, often mistakenly receives recognition as the world's first department store, primarily because, according to Alison Adburgham, few American and French historians are aware of the British predecessors from smaller cities (*Shops*, 137). Adburgham, William Lancaster, and Angela and John Airey all suggest that Kendal, Milne and Faulker of Manchester (founded in 1836) and Bainbridge's of Newcastle (founded in 1838) were the first two department stores, Bainbridge's having divided its store into twenty-three departments by at least 1850 (Adburgham, *Shops*, 137; Lancaster, 7; Airey and Airey, 47).

Claire Walsh goes even further, rejecting conventional assertions that the department store and its innovative commercial and display techniques (e.g., offering fixed and clearly marked prices, making items visible in glass showcases rather than hiding them behind counters, selling ready-made goods) were uniquely Victorian inventions and instead locates their origins in the eighteenth century. She argues that by the second half of the century, many London shops had grown large enough to occupy several floors and cites evidence of "a few shops achieving massive proportions in the late 1700s, dwarfing the main body of retail outlets as did department stores" (63, 64). Maurice Corina agrees that "the foundations of department stores were laid by the turn of the eighteenth century" and identifies stores such as Bainbridge of Newcastle, Lewis of Liverpool, Browns of Chester, Andersons of Glasgow, and Debenham and Freebody's of London as pioneers (55).

7. Many department stores, including Debenham and Freebody's, manufactured some or all of the clothing items they sold, often in a workshop above the store (Chapman, 11).

8. First and foremost, Rappaport's "New Era of Shopping" and *Shopping for Pleasure* offer the best discussions of the transformation of London's West End into a female consumer's paradise at the turn of the century. Wilson's *Adorned in Dreams* notes that the reading rooms, tea rooms, and other female-friendly amenities provided by department stores to lure women customers marked "a major change at a period when it was improper for a woman to enter an ordinary restaurant unless accompanied by a husband, brother or father" (150). Leach's "Transformations in a Culture of Consumption" argues that the birth of the department store and consumer culture radically transformed the role of women and examines consumer culture's emancipatory power to move working- and middle-class women out of the home and into the public urban sphere. Tiersten's "Marianne in the Department Store" shows how the French department store successfully presented itself as a healthy profamily, pro-nation institution and "a staunch supporter of feminine domesticity and a bulwark of the Republic," by depicting women's shopping as an activity conducted for the benefit of the family (rather than as a compulsive selfish act) and by emphasizing "the department store's ability to bring satisfaction to everyone which made it a social progressive institution" (125). Chaney's "Department Store as a Cultural Form" briefly discusses women as primary consumers at the new department stores and the empowering effects of the department store on women (28–29); Domosh's chapter "Creating New York's Retail District" in *Invented Cities* portrays the department stores as an exclusively feminine space, a carefully constructed annex to the female sphere; and Barth's chapter on the American department store in *City People* repeatedly touches on the image of the department store as having created a world for women in city centers (111–47).

Hosgood's "Doing the Shops" examines some of the negative consequences of the close association between the department store and women's consumption, revealing that the popular portrayal of female consumers at the turn of the century shifted from that of naïve victims of manipulative store owners to overbearing and compulsive shoppers who took over the stores (109–10). Bowlby's *Just Looking* and Walkowitz's *City of Dreadful Delight* both examine the ways in which the controlled fantasy of the department store setting transformed women into empowered flaneurs who could observe without being obliged to buy, while at the same time leaving them vulnerable to seduction by men, who objectified them and formed their desires.

Finally, Abelson's fascinating *When Ladies Go A-Thieving* and Spiekermann's "Theft and Thieves in German Department Stores" both explore how female consumption in the department store was pathologized by social commentators and medical science into a so-called epidemic of female kleptomania.

9. Harrods' first catalogue appeared in 1870 and was 65 pages long (Ferry, 213). At 1,510 pages, the 1895 catalogue (reprinted as *Victorian Shopping: Harrod's Catalogue 1895; A*

Facsimile of the Harrod's Stores 1895 Issue of the Price List, etc. in 1972) is the earliest known edition to survive (ii).

10. According to Farid Chenoune, ready-made clothing—familiarly known in the clothing trade as "R.M." during the nineteenth century—had been available as early as the second half of the eighteenth century, when "certain merchant-tailors offered affordable, ready-made garments at set prices" (67). Factory-made clothing was first produced for the military in Britain, France, and the United States (Wilson, 73). Neil McKendrick claims that ready-made clothing was already common by 1800, but its appeal was undoubtedly limited to the lower and working classes until midcentury (83). Stanley Chapman goes further, claiming that a highly developed and heavily advertised ready-made market existed by the late eighteenth and early nineteenth centuries, making a full variety of clothing items available to all classes (5–7).

11. Ironically, at the same time the department store was helping shape the values and material desire of the middle class, its very existence was putting many middle-class owners of small shops out of business. Tailoring trade journals repeatedly decried the decline of both the business and the craftsmanship of their trade in the decades surrounding the turn of the century. In January 1888, the *Gentleman's Magazine of Fashion* reported that the tailors of Tooley Street had disappeared (3), in 1890 that "Ladies' Tailoring just now is at a terrible dead standstill" ("West," 8), and in 1891 that the trade had reached "a state of things not known, perhaps, in the memory of a living man" ("Bad," 3). Ten years later, the *Minister's Gazette of Fashion* still declared that the "outlook is discouraging" and eulogized the days "when tailoring *was* tailoring" (Leggatt, 234). The oft-repeated and racist accusation that much of the blame lay on East End Jewish tailors who undersold all competition by resorting to sweating reveals a multitude of larger binary tensions implicit in the competition between traditional tailoring and ready-mades: East End versus West End, Englishman versus Jew, upper class versus lower class, individually handmade versus machine-made/divided labor, quality versus quantity (Booth, *Poverty*, 40–61).

Christopher Breward contends, however, that most men purchased a combination of ready-made and made-to-order items, seeking out the best variety, cuts, and prices (*Hidden*, 28). In 1880 the *Tailor and Cutter* declared, "It is well known that while many, moving in the higher circles of society, have their coats and vest from our West End houses, they patronise without compunction those firms who advertise trousers made to measure for 13s. 6d." (155).

12. In contrast, the ladies departments—hairdressing, boots, millinery, furs, mantles, "toilet requisites," etc.—were located adjacent to one another in large rectangular rooms on Harrods' first floor (*Harrods General Catalogue*, 1909, 4).

13. The Levi's 501 television advertising campaign, aired both in Britain and the United States, showcased the bare-chested Kamen seductively slipping in and out of jeans. See Mort's "Boy's Own," Nixon's "Exhibiting Masculinity" (293–94), and Edwards's *Men in the Mirror* (51–54).

14. This is in large part attributable to the Major's chatty, rambling style. But when he does get down to business, his advice is specific and authoritative. For example, regarding the proper fit of trousers, the Major writes, "What is a well-cut pair of trousers? . . . A good pair of trousers should hang in straight lines from the hips and fork downwards. There should be no 'puckering' or surplus material about the fork. The seams should be made very neatly; otherwise they will cockle all the way down the leg, and trousers that have that fault are not worthy of the name trousers. The ends of the trousers should drop well over the boots in a small crease or two. I am told that one of the most difficult parts of the business is to cut the ends of a pair of trousers just so large that they shall cover a portion of the feet, but not so large that they shall appear sloppy and untidy. The trousers should not fit tightly at the seat, and yet they should not be loose at that part" (in *Clothes and the Man*, 84–85).

15. Men nevertheless continued to use cosmetics, lotions, and powder in increasing numbers—albeit covertly—throughout the period. Kathy Peiss's wonderful history of women's cosmetics briefly touches on their use by men in the nineteenth and early twentieth centuries. Peiss reports that men used their wives' skin creams or visited cosmetics studios to remove wrinkles and dye their hair, and some salesmen used subtle makeup—even eyeliner—to "enhance impression" (160). Ladies' mascara began as "mascaro" in the late nineteenth century and was sold to men to conceal gray hair and darken eyebrows and eyelashes (163). By 1900, men's use of hair and shaving products had spread, and "men of wealth, especially bachelors, conveyed a sense of sophistication and urbanity with the addition of aftershave powder or cologne" (159). All this, according to Peiss, went on in half secrecy, as "men interested in beautifying had to defend themselves against insinuations of frivolity, weakness, and homosexuality" (159). "When men 'come to the cosmetics counter and demand "just powder,"' observed a druggist, they want 'face powder, and the wise clerk will assume as much and ask no questions'" (160).

Chapter Three

1. At least 60 women's fashion magazines circulated in London after 1850 (Shaw, 31). Between 1880 and 1900, another 50 to 120 new women's magazines were founded (Rappaport, *Shopping*, 112), provoking George Augustus Sala to comment that women's fashion books "are as plentiful as peas" (*London*, 17). Beetham's *Magazine of Her Own?* explores the role of magazines in manipulating and cultivating women's consumer desires.

2. The sartorial conduct manual *Clothes and the Man* (1900) claims that the short-lived *Magazine à la Mode, or Fashionable Miscellany* of 1777—"adapted to the use of people of fashion of both sexes"—was the first non–trade periodical to offer fashion advice to men, though it provided only sporadic and incomplete information on fashion (3–7). Another quickly aborted attempt at a men's fashion periodical was the *Fashionable Magazine, or Ladies' and Gentlemen's Monthly Record of New Fashions, Being a Complete Universal Repository of Taste and Elegance for Both Sexes* (1786), featuring spotty news on fashion and padding its copy mainly with poetry and high-society gossip (7–14). Later trade periodicals that may have circulated beyond the tailoring shop were equally unsuccessful; for example, the *Gentleman's Gazette or, London Magazine of Fashion* lasted less than a year in 1832 (*Waterloo*, 416).

3. The *London Tailor* (1840–1910), the *Gazette of Fashion and Cutting Room Companion* (1846–1888), and the *Tailor and Cutter* (founded in 1866)—the "bible of British tailors"—are three noteworthy examples (Chenoune, 122).

4. In its first issue, *Fashion* remarked, "We are pleased to note an increasing attention given by the Public and by the Press to the subjects of Men's Modes. . . . We may observe that several newspapers now give notices of Masculine Fashions; for instance, the *Daily Telegraph*, the *City*, the *Field, Sporting and Dramatic News*, and other journals" (What, March 1898, 5). The author of the popular men's conduct book *Clothes and the Man*, who was also the editor of *To-Day*, declared, "We prided ourselves at *To-Day* upon the fact that we were the first paper to publish any details about men's fashions and men's clothes—I mean, of course, any paper other than a trade paper" (2–3). His sartorial advice, given under the moniker the "Major," was regularly cited and critiqued in the pages of *Fashion*.

5. *Ally Sloper's Half-Holiday* proclaimed, "Being a bit of a dandy himself, A. Sloper notes with considerable interest the appearance of the first men's fashion paper ever published in this or any other world," while *Stage* observed, "*Fashion* marks a new departure in journalism, being the first of its class—outside the trade papers—and as such should have a future to look to" ("In Praise of 'Fashion,'" 15).

6. The true identity of "Beau Brummel, Junr.," remains a mystery, though he claimed he was "already known" by this moniker "to a dress section of London Society" ("Introduction," 1). He also contributed the Well-Dressed Man column in the new magazine *Sphere* for a short while, writing as "Savile Rowe" (Godfrey-Turner, March 1900, 6–7).

7. Some confusion over the magazine's purpose and target audience must have remained, however, as its editor repeatedly ran a notice that "'FASHION' is not a trade paper" and therefore "cannot entertain the publication of cutters' designs for new coats, or anything bearing upon the purely technical" (Brummel, "Editorial," 25). Two

years later the monthly stated, "The Editor of Fashion would like to point out once more that his journal is not what is commonly known as a trade paper" but conceded that "it moves very freely among tailors (fifteen hundred copies represent roughly the subscribed circulation in this direction)" (Brummel, "Some," 5).

8. *Fashion* returned to the dilemma in February 1902, noting that "there ought to be some special sort of coat for Ping-Pong, since ordinary coats were too hot for so vigorous a game—pursued, generally in the heat of a gas-lit room—and the shirt-sleeves stage was hardly an appropriate one for a drawing-room pastime" ("Coat," 13).

9. These occasions included "For the River," "For the Links," "For the Cycle," "For the Motor," "For the Wedding," "For the Afternoon Call, Day Reception, or Matinee," "For Horse-Riding in the Park," "For Horse-Riding in the Country," "For Business and Morning Wear," "For Theatres, Formal Dinner, and Receptions," "For Informal Dinner and Club Wear in Evening," and "For the Races" ("Fashion" Dress Chart, June 1902, 21). A few of the categories alternated depending on the season; for example, "For the Seaside" appeared during the summer of 1903 ("Fashion" Dress Chart, June 1903, 17). In March 1904, the chart changed to a two-page spread featuring small fashion plate–style illustrations in each of the categories ("Fashion" Dress Chart, March 1904, 14–15). While it still appeared monthly, it began to be updated on a seasonal basis. By the final issue in February 1905, the "Fashion" Correct Dress Chart had been simplified to only six categories: "For Town Wear," "For West End Outdoor Wear," "For Country or Suburban Wear," "For Chilly Days in Town," "A Night in Town," and "A Day in the Country" ("Fashion" Correct, 22–23).

10. See bibliography for the specific issue and page number.

11. See bibliography for the specific issue and page number on which these advertisements appear. The April 1902 issue featured advertisements for fifteen merchants possessing royal warrants. This was the "coronation year" for Edward VII, a famous lifelong dandy; presumably he had been busy assigning new warrants, and, of course, clothiers would have been eager to display them in advertising.

12. For a detailed account of the scandal and its aftermath, see Hyde's *Cleveland Street Scandal.*

13. The Worth et Cie corset advertisement in *Fashion* is very similar to the ones that appeared in *Punch* between 1880 and 1905 (see figures 2.13 and 2.14).

14. *Fashion* notes another use of the male corset that seems unlikely to have earned it any additional credibility as a belt to maintain one's "male potency"—cross-dressing theatricals: "Worth et Cie . . . is not unfrequently, especially in the Winter Season, called upon to supply corsets of a very feminine shape for the officers, who, to the amusement of their relatives and friends, assume female characters in fashionable amateur theatricals and barrack entertainments. Mr. Worth drew my attention to a

most wonderful corset which had been worn in private theatricals by a slim, but noble captain in one of our bravest regiments, and assured me that, small as was the thing round the waist, the owner of it had no difficulty whatever in getting into it. But he, said Mr. Worth, was an exception to the general run of the society amateur 'female impersonators,' and he related many amusing experiences he had had this season, of amateur theatricals, with burly guardsmen who wished to appear before their 'sisters and their cousins and their aunt,' as delicate fairies with 22-inch waists" ("Corsets and Their Worth," 16).

15. "We are not of [the] opinion that men should be as free to dye their hair and 'fake' their complexion as women. That is going just a little bit too far" ("Our Friend," 23).

16. Ballin was also a dress-reform activist and author of *The Science of Dress in Theory and Practice* (1885).

17. The article also discussed the successfully treated cases of "a medical man who found it difficult to obtain practice because ladies would not engage him owing to a port wine stain on his face," who "after its removal has set up a flourishing West End practice," as well as that of "a schoolmaster whose pupils used to irreverently designate him 'monkey,' because the hair grew right up on the cheeks under the eyes" who "is now able to stand the scrutiny of his class with serene indifference as, the hairs from his cheeks have been removed by electrolysis, he is now adorned by a handsome beard and moustache" ("Improving," 13).

18. Starting with the September 1902 issue, this figure sporadically alternated with a top-hatted and mustachioed gentleman in hunting pink holding up a riding crop in the same pose (*Fashion*, September 1902, 1). A related cartoon featured in the header for the Coffee and Cognac column depicted an upper-class gentleman having just laid down his issue of *Fashion* to enjoy a cigar and take a refreshment from his manservant (Godfrey-Turner, April 1898, 3).

19. The application of social emulation theory is most explicitly displayed in the December 1903 issue, in which the contributor identified as "Beaunash" asserted, "Fashion undergoes three successive stages of development. First comes the exclusive stage when a mode is confined to the picked few, then the second stage when a mode is confined to the favoured many, and last, the final stage, when it becomes the toy of the great untubbed" (19).

20. A June 1902 photographic collage of readers' letters sent to *Fashion* claimed to demonstrate that "the Editor is in communication with gentlemen residing in Tokyo, Moscow, Valparaiso, Sierra Leone, Cairo, Johore, Warsaw, Naples, Toronto, Budapest, Paris, Cape of Good Hope, Buenos Aires, Leipzig, Cologne, Barbados, New York, Chicago, Aachen, Grefeld, Etoile, St. Louis, St. Petersbourg, Boston, Santiago, San

Francisco, Philadelphia, Vienna, Bruges, Finland, South Australia, Naggráradon, Calcutta, Lucerne, Turin, Barcelona, Berlin, Mainz, etc." ("Photograph," 20).

21. Apparently dozens of newspapers and magazines across England and America lifted extracts from *Fashion* and reprinted them in full, often without acknowledging their source. Beau Brummel, Junr., voiced frequent complaints that his reporting had been plagiarized whole cloth in other journals without proper credit or acknowledgment. Finally, in June 1900, the magazine printed a warning that any further plagiarism would be met with public exposure: "Against the impudent lifting of paragraphs from my columns, without the slightest mention of their source, I most strongly protest, as being unfair not only to myself and my contributors, but also to the Proprietors and Editors of journals who imagine, when publishing such dishonestly-manufactured articles as I have referred to, they are dealing with matter supplied first-hand. I hereby give warning to all who are in the habit of extracting information from FASHION without due acknowledgement, that if they continue to employ this means of 'writing' Men's Dress articles, I shall expose them individually in these columns" (Brummel, "Special," 7).

Fashion then offered side-by-side extracts from its own copy and that of the *Tailor and Cutter* to reveal how "they should simply alter the order of the title by placing the 'Cutter' before the 'Tailor'" ("How the 'Tailor and Cutter,'" 25). The protest evidently worked, as the following issue happily reported that the primary offenders had "promptly fallen back upon their own abilities in the direction of dealing with the subject of men's dress" (London Expert, July 1900, 13–14).

Chapter Four

1. See, for example, Moers's *Dandy*, Laver's *Dandies*, Adams's *Dandies and Desert Saints*, Garelick's *Rising Star*, and Fillin-Yeh's *Dandies*.

2. The term *dandy* entered the English language around 1780 (*Oxford English Dictionary*, vol. 4, 238–39), though dandies were known throughout the nineteenth century by many other names, including "bucks," "bloods," "exquisites," "fashionables," "dashers," "butterflies," and "exclusives" (Chenoune, 32).

3. Bulwer's novel *Pelham* (1828) "was seen as a manual for the behaviour of the new dandies" (Lambert, "Dandy," 62).

4. I might add here that both Regenia Gagnier and Alan Sinfield convincingly argue that the open hostility that Beerbohm and many other British writers expressed toward Wilde's Aesthetic form of dandyism was motivated—prior to his 1895 "gross indecency" conviction—primarily by class snobbery (Gagnier, 55–99; Sinfield, 96–99, 122–23). In the eyes of conservative critics, "he was a middle-class Irish subject who appropriated these upper-class signs, performing a gentility to which he had no right" (Schaffer, 40).

5. Max Beerbohm claimed that the term derived from the refrain of a popular music-hall song: "I'm the slashing, dashing, mashing Montmorency of the day" (Chenoune, 96).

6. Charles Booth associate James MacDonald reported, "In the matter of dress, tailors have always been considered the best off among working men, and certainly the younger members of the trade keep up their reputation in that respect. Many of the supposed West End mashers are nothing more or less than our friend the tailor" (143).

7. According to Christopher Breward, "He was not specifically working-class, but symbolised a pervasive celebration of caddishness and vulgarity that were assumed to have lowly social origins" (*Hidden*, 203).

8. Alison Adburgham outlines the specific characteristics of the "decadents" of the early 1890s, the "dilettantes" of the late 1890s and early 1900s, and the "bloods" of the 1900s and '10s (*Punch*, 167–204).

9. The *Oxford English Dictionary* describes the masher as "a fop of affected manners and exaggerated style of dress who frequented music-halls and fashionable promenades and who posed as a 'lady-killer'" (vol. 4, 424).

10. *Fashion*'s editors did not seem particularly concerned, responding, "It is quite possible that the similarity he notices between the coster's clothes and the 'Johnnie's' is purely accidental. Anyhow, it is interesting to notice how closely they resemble each other in many particulars" (11).

11. Wilde gladly welcomed this harmony of one's interior and exterior and prescribed free expression in dress that could serve as a visual lexicon readable by all. In an 1891 essay printed anonymously in the *Daily Telegraph*, Wilde playfully imagined that "the coat . . . of next season will be an exquisite colour-note, and have also a great psychological value. It will emphasise the serious and thoughtful side of a man's character. One will be able to discern a man's views of life by the colour he selects. The colour of the coat will be symbolic. It will be part of the wonderful symbolistic movement in modern art. The imagination will concentrate itself on the waistcoat. Waistcoats will show whether a man can admire poetry or not. That will be very valuable. Over the shirt-front Fancy will preside. By a single glance one will be able to detect the tedious" ("Fashions," 5). This is the dandy's own version of identity written on the body.

12. It might be noted here, ironically, that Dickens was well known for his dandified dress and was widely regarded as not quite a gentleman; while on his American lecture tour in the 1840s, he was criticized for wearing bright waistcoats "somewhat in the flash order" (Foster, 15).

13. Several evening-dress reformers recommended a return to the wearing of breeches that had distinguished menswear in the early decades of the nineteenth century, and

the *Monthly Record of Fashion* offered an illustration of such an ensemble in 1884 ("New Ideas," 29). Similarly, in 1891 Wilde suggested that the 1840s-era costume worn by Mr. Wyndham in the play *London Assurance* be adopted as a new model for modern evening dress ("Fashions," 5). The *Gazette of Fashion and Cutting Room Companion* made reference in 1888 to "talk of establishing a Society for the Improvement of Evening Dress for Men" ("Thoughts," 70). Despite repeated attacks against the "waiterly" or funeral appearance of men's black evening wear, the calls for reform resulted only in a handful of aborted attempts, as the dinner jacket ("tuxedo" in America) became all the more firmly ensconced as the official male formalwear with the turn of the century.

14. The *English Gentleman* offered a typical admonition: "There is . . . a great difference between following a fashion, and carrying it to an extreme. Directly you begin to be over careful and elaborate in your dress, and give yourself a finical and effeminate appearance, from that hour do you commence vulgarity" (102).

15. Miles Lambert notes, "A man who flaunted jewellery and scent, who wore dress designed to attract attention and comment, and who exalted his public image above all else, was as far from a gentleman as Thackeray could conceive" (69).

16. In the classic model of dandyism, described by Ellen Moers, the dandy counteracts the potentially feminizing effects of his interest in fashion by connecting it to the masculine ideals of restraint and discipline (33–36).

17. Significantly, *Patience* spoofs Aestheticism as a sham, a posture with which to attract girls. All the Aesthetes eventually abandon the lifestyle to become members of the consuming middle class, and the protagonist, Grosvenor, appears at play's end dressed as a traditional English businessman (Gilbert and Sullivan, 196).

18. Richard Ellmann notes that Wilde's costume was actually modeled on Masonic ceremonial attire, not Little Lord Fauntleroy (40).

19. The classification of particular sexual practices—including homosexuality, masturbation, incest, fetishism, sadomasochism, and bestiality—as pathological perversions became the preoccupation of medical science and the emerging field of psychology and served to exacerbate anxieties that many Victorians felt regarding what was socially accepted as "normal" sexuality.

20. Tim Edwards explains, "Various authors have raised an added question concerning the role or significance of men looking at other men, particularly in terms of consumption. . . . The point, put simply, is that in the process of encouraging men to look at other men as consumers of style, fashion and visual display, as opposed to producers of work and achievement, the distinction of heterosexual and homosexual is undermined as, historically, looking at other men is seen as the sole preserve of homosexuals" (116).

21. The *Oxford English Dictionary* identifies the first uses of *homosexual* in C. G. Chaddock's translation of Richard von Krafft-Ebing's *Psychopathia Sexualis* and in Havelock Ellis's *Studies in the Psychology of Sex* (1897) (*OED*, vol. 7, 345).

22. Alan Sinfield maintains that the suggestion of "same-sex passion" implicit in the Aesthetic movement's celebration of "decadence" was "only a minor and indeterminate element" (95). "To be sure," Sinfield writes, "the aesthete was regarded as effeminate—but not, as far as I can see, as distinctly homosexual" (90).

23. For detailed examinations of events and figures surrounding the Wilde trials, see Foldy's *Trials of Oscar Wilde* and Hyde's *Trials of Oscar Wilde*.

24. The article continued sardonically, "This is well worth knowing, and men who like pink underwear, and have hitherto been nervous about getting it, are clearly indebted to the 'Major' [*To-Day*'s editor] for his comforting information. But I should like to know all the same what men want with pants the colour of ballet girls' tights." The old association between effeminate dandyism and the upper classes was invoked, as *Fashion* suggested that upscale retailers were to blame for cultivating such overrefined tastes in men: "I know, of course, that there is a big demand for them in the West (I mean the pants), and that it is chiefly the very high-class shop that keeps them, but one cannot help feeling tempted to wish that these things were not displayed in fancy colours" (Brummel, Dress News, October 1898, 20).

Chapter Five

1. Laver's writings from the 1940s through the '60s rested on what he called the "Hierarchy Principle," in which "dress and adornment serve only to signal wealth and power" (Polhemus, 46). McKendrick maintained that social emulation was the key factor in the development of consumerism and that, as a marketplace of fashionable goods and consumer spectacle, London "served as a shopwindow for the whole country, the centre of forms of conspicuous consumption which would be eagerly mimicked elsewhere" ("Consumer," 21). Another historian has observed, "McKendrick argues that domestic servants played a crucial role in the transmission of consumer taste and behaviour from the dominant classes in the metropolis to other classes in the provinces. In this way, he maintains, social emulation flowed downward from the rich to their domestic servants, then to industrial workers, and finally to agricultural workers. Working in this way, he argues, social emulation 'became an engine for growth, a motive power for mass production'" (Storey, 9–10).

2. Diverging from Veblen and Simmel, Douglas and Isherwood maintain that consumption is not simply social emulation but rather acts as a symbolic means of communication that makes "visible and stable the categories of culture" (xiv). They argue that as "the visible part of culture," "goods are part of a live information system" (66, xiv).

3. Dudley Baxter's 1867 estimate of the distribution of the national income of England and Wales defines lower-middle class and middle class as annual earnings between £100 and £1000 (Perkin, 29). In 1904 Fabian banker Sir Leo Chiozza Money defined middle class—that is, living not in "riches" but in "comfort"—as an annual income of £160–£700 (30).

4. Grove wrote, "The story is told of the beautiful Duchess of Somerset that when some one asked her in a shop, 'Was that the gentleman who served you?' replied, 'No; it was that nobleman with the bald head.' But nowadays we are less high-handed and more democratic, perhaps also less witty" (116–17).

5. Diana De Marly notes, "The industrialist, the bankers, the shipbuilders, the railway magnates, the factory owners, were gaining on the aristocracy of land. Accordingly the Victorian era saw more books on etiquette and correct dressing being published than ever before" (100).

6. Also extremely popular were the "Silver Fork" novels of the 1830s–50s by such authors as Theodore Hook, Sir Edward Bulwer-Lytton, and Catherine Gore. With their emphasis on the minutiae of etiquette and graces of society, the novels served as do-it-yourself manuals for those with upper-class aspirations, and they continued to be read well into the second half of the nineteenth century.

7. These are all real conduct manuals: *Don't: A Manual of Mistakes and Improprieties More or Less Prevalent in Conduct and Speech* (1883), by "Censor" (a pseudonym for Oliver Bell Bunce), was published in multiple editions until 1938; *Manners and Rules of Good Society* (1897), by "a member of the aristocracy," was published in at least forty-eight editions until at least 1929; and *The Art of Conversing, or Dialogues of the Day*, purportedly by the same author, was published in 1897. John Ruskin's well-known collection of essays on Victorian ideals, *Sesame and Lilies*, was first published in 1864.

8. Frederick Willis notes the similar elitist consumption of tobacco: "Those were the days when you could have your cigarettes made to order with a blend of tobacco mixed by an expert to suit your taste, and your initials in gold on the paper. Assuming once again that you were out of the top drawer, you could have your crest instead of your initials engraved in gold on each cigarette. This wasn't considered pernickety. No man-about-town would dare to be seen smoking any popular brand of cigarettes. They were known as 'gaspers' and were considered fit only for the common herd" (173).

9. Art historian Ann Bermingham asserts that a top-down model of consumer influence reinforces the notion that culture is always the exclusive province of the elite. Feminist historian Amanda Vickery contends that McKendrick's use of social emulation theory implicitly trivializes female consumption as motivated by a "pathological desire to consume" and posits a reductive consumer model in which "envy and

wishful thinking are the norm" (277, 275). Loeb argues that middle-class consumers were attracted to the modernity and aesthetic value of goods rather than to their aristocratic characteristics and that "consumer demand . . . lay not so much in imitation of aristocratic (or even rich) behavior, as in a distinctively bourgeois pursuit of equal opportunity" (158).

10. To cite a few examples from groceries: "The consumption of tea . . . rose per head of the population from 2.7 lb. a year in 1860 to 6.1 lb. in 1900. That of sugar increased from 34.1 lb. to 87.1 lb. In the thirty years before 1900, the consumption of meat, bacon and ham rose from just over 100 lb. to just over 130 lb., and, to take a very different commodity, that of tobacco from 1.7 lb. to 2.1 lb." (Briggs, 121–12).

11. Roberts's *Classic Slum* discusses the working class's desire to achieve the appearance of middle-classness (32–41).

12. Admittedly, a small number of department stores made their reputation by appealing to an upscale crowd—Whiteley's and Liberty's of London being the best-known examples. Other department stores, such as Selfridges, were patronized by lower-middle-class consumers, while Marks and Spencer met its early success by catering to the working class (Crossick, 34; Rees, 7).

13. Asa Briggs's history of Lewis's provides a fascinating account of the London department store's aggressive 1910–14 campaign to win over tailoring customers (131–32).

14. The frock coat's fall can be traced in tailoring journals and conduct books; the *London Tailor and Record of Fashion* predicted as early as 1884 that the frock coat would die "slowly" yet "hard" ("Current," 26). In 1900, *Clothes and the Man* observed that young men preferred loungers and morning coats to frock coats, and ten years later, John Wanamaker concluded, "One might call the frock coat the badge of increasing years" (4). Indeed, by the 1910s and '20s, its wear was relegated mainly to old men and wedding ceremonies.

15. T. R. Gourvish defines the "professions" as white-collar occupations requiring education and proficiency in an esoteric body of knowledge that provides a service to the community and is regulated by a governing authority that maintains standards among all members within the occupation. This included, in Victorian times, clergy, barristers and solicitors, physicians and surgeons, midwives, dentists, teachers, authors, editors, actors, artists, musicians, architects, surveyors, civil and mining engineers, and accountants; it did not include industrial occupations or shopkeeping (20). According to Gourvish, "The professions, though growing, remained numerically small, about 4 per cent of the labour force by 1900. But there is abundant evidence to suggest that this group wielded a disproportionate amount of influence in late Victorian society" (33).

16. The turn-of-the-century lounger was invariably accompanied by two of the most familiar symbols of middle-class professional status. The first was a gold pocket

watch and chain, which was gradually replaced by the wristwatch at the very beginning of the twentieth century (Byrde, 222). The second was the umbrella, a descendent of the cane (and even earlier the sword) as a decorative dress accessory. In 1895 the *Tailor and Cutter* announced, "Closed rolled umbrellas will be seen more frequently than ever before. Fashionable men are already wedded to them," and Charles Cavers declared, "A good umbrella, neatly rolled, is the mark of a discreet gentleman" (210). The ideal umbrella was always rolled as tightly as possible and never suffered the ignominy of being opened, even in a downpour.

17. Two examples from the past in which the upper classes appropriated clothing from a lower class are the trousers and tailcoat, derived from the peasantry and the hunting attire of farmers and the gentry (De Marly, 87). Torn jeans, "hip-hop" couture, and "heroin chic" provide examples of "trickle-up" fasions at the turn of the twenty-first century.

18. In 1925, *Etiquette for Gentlemen* described the Norfolk as "democracy's reply to the frock coat" (26).

19. Rutherford's *Forever England* and Hall's *Muscular Christianity* offer valuable insights into the Muscular Christianity movement and its influence on late-nineteenth-century British masculinity. Green's *Fit for America* and Bederman's fascinating *Manliness and Civilization* both examine the health and fitness movement in the United States at the turn of the century.

20. A few examples from Kingsland:

> Golf has become so common an amusement that the golfer has settled down to the uniform costume, or to one which is simply "mufti," or general lounge-suits of light flannel with long trousers and "negligée" shirts. At club matches, however, the dress is more formal, and the coat of golfing "pink"—as it is the fashion to call scarlet—or green is worn with club buttons and knickerbockers of homespun or rough Scotch goods, with "quarter cuffs" of box cloth. The golf waistcoat is single-breasted, and usually of a rather violent pattern and color when worn with a sacque coat matching the trousers. Fashions vary so, no hard-and-fast rules can be given.
>
> The proper attire for a horseman consists of full riding breeches, usually of whipcoard [*sic*], and boots, or heavy boxcloth or leather leggings, buttoned up the front of the leg from ankle to knee, a high waistcoat, and cutaway coat with short tails, white stock tie, heavy-laced shoes, riding gloves, and a Derby or Alpine hat. The suit may be all of one color, or a dark coat may be worn with gray waistcoat and trousers. A Norfolk jacket is sometimes worn, with which riding boots are "de rigueur." A riding crop with

plain bone handle is carried. Men past their first youth often prefer to wear long trousers, with straps under the foot to keep them in place. A high silk hat or Derby is appropriately worn with this costume.

. . . For driving, there is less punctilio. The whip on the box-seat of a coach usually wears a suit of gray tweed with gray high hat, or if the weather permits, a top coat, which is usually of tan or gray cloth, box-shaped, the hat matching in general tone. In midsummer he may wear a soft felt hat, or even a panama, with a suit of light wool dittoes. The men of the party follow the same general rule.

A comfortable dress for summer driving is a dark serge coat with white linen or striped flannel trousers, with straw or panama hat, goatskin gloves, and russet shoes. (345–36)

21. Lady Colin advised in 1893, "It is the correct thing . . . for a man always to dress in the evening; if he is alone with his wife, and wishes to be economical, he may wear an old dress coat—but it must *be a dress* coat—and he must go to his dressing-room and put on a clean shirt with the same solicitude as if he were going out to dinner" (79). It seems unlikely that many men regularly observed such formalities in the privacy of their own homes. But some of the newer, more insecure members of the middle classes may have believed that this was an ideal they *should* follow. In his novel *Kipps*, Wells has his eponymous protagonist consult his more experienced friend Coote on "'whether I oughtn't to dress for dinner—when I'm alone 'ere.' Coote protruded his lips and reflected. 'Not full dress,' he adjudicated; 'that would be a little excessive. But you should *change*, you know. Put on a mess jacket, and that sort of thing—easy dress. That is what *I* should do, certainly, if I wasn't in harness—and poor'" (192).

22. This is not unlike the widespread wearing of athletic clothing today: although once considered to have been specifically designed for sports, such items as sweatshirts, sleeveless muscle shirts, jogging pants, and baseball caps have become acceptable, generic casual wear worn by all classes and ages for a wide variety of occasions—often without any conscious intent by the wearer to make a "fashion statement" or to appear in the mode.

Epilogue

1. The term *metrosexual* was coined by British journalist Mark Simpson in 1994 in his article "Here Come the Mirror Men" in *The Independent.* Simpson elaborated in 2002, "The typical *metrosexual* is a young man with money to spend, living in or within easy reach of a metropolis—because that's where all the best shops, clubs,

gyms and hairdressers are. . . . He might be officially gay, straight or bisexual, but this is utterly immaterial, because he has clearly taken himself as his own love object and pleasure as his sexual preference" (quoted in Safire, 30).

2. Bordo notes that even Viagra and other impotency drugs (with total sales of $2.7 billion in 2004) can be regarded as cosmetics that enable men to maintain heightened cultural expectations of male performance and stave off a fundamental male anxiety (Bordo, 42; Mullin).

3. While the unabashedly Neanderthal aesthetic of many lad magazines precludes articles on fashion or body maintenance, these titles nevertheless serve to promote a consumer masculinity preoccupied with cars, gadgets, beer, electronic equipment, video game systems, etc.

4. Many social commentators suggest that the age of laddism and the market for lad magazines is on the wane. Dave Hill of the *Weekly Guardian* asserts, "[T]he shoulder-swinging, lager-swigging scallywags who wielded such clout during the last decade are looking tired, as if suspecting that for 'lad' the world now just reads 'loser' or even 'lout'" (44).

Bibliography

Abelson, Elaine S. *When Ladies Go A-Thieving: Middle Class Shoplifters in the Victorian Department Stores.* New York: Oxford University Press, 1989.

Academician. "Hoods." *Fashion,* September 1899, 14–16.

Adams, James Eli. *Dandies and Desert Saints: Styles of Victorian Masculinity.* Ithaca, NY: Cornell University Press, 1995.

Adburgham, Alison. *A "Punch" History of Manners and Modes, 1841–1940.* London: Hutchinson, 1961.

———. *Shops and Shopping, 1800–1914: Where and in What Manner the Well-Dressed Englishwoman Bought Her Clothes.* London: George Allen and Unwin, 1981.

Advertising World, February 1913, 208.

Airey, Angela, and John Airey. *The Bainbridges of Newcastle: A Family History, 1679–1976.* Newcastle: Angela and John Airey, 1979.

Alureda. "Men's Dress." *Pioneer of Fashion,* December 1892, 14.

Amies, Hardy. *The Englishman's Suit: A Personal View of Its History, Its Place in the World Today, Its Future and the Accessories Which Support It.* London: Quartet, 1994.

Anderson, Fiona. "Fashioning the English Gentleman: A Study of Henry Poole and Co., Savile Row Tailors, 1861–1900." *Fashion Theory* 4 (December 2000): 405–26.

Andom, Robert. *We Three and Troddles.* Philadelphia: Henry Altemus, 1895.

Anglo-French. "Studholes." *Fashion,* September 1900, 21–22.

Armstrong, Nancy. *Desire and Domestic Fiction: A Political History of the Novel.* New York: Oxford University Press, 1987.

Artley, Alexandra, ed. *The Golden Age of Shop Design: European Shop Interiors, 1880–1939.* London: Architectural Press, 1975.

Art of Conversing, or Dialogues of the Day, The. By the author of "Manners and Rules of Good Society." London: Warne, 1897.

Attwood, Feona. "'Tits and Ass and Porn and Fighting': Male Heterosexuality in Magazines for Men." *International Journal of Cultural Studies* 8 (March 2005): 83–100.

Auslander, Leora. "The Gendering of Consumer Practices in Nineteenth-Century France." In *The Sex of Things: Gender and Consumption in Historical Perspective,* edited by Victoria de Grazia with Ellen Furlough, 79–112. Berkeley: University of California Press, 1996.

Baclawski, Karen. *The Guide to Historic Costume.* New York: Drama Book, 1995.

"Bad Season, A." *Gentleman's Magazine of Fashion,* August 1891, 3.

"Baggage Fashion." *Fashion*, January 1904, 17.

Baker, Brian [Liberty department store's customer liaison officer]. Personal interview.

Ballin, Ada. *The Science of Dress in Theory and Practice*. London: Sampson Low, 1885.

Baren, Maurice. *Victorian Shopping*. London: Michael O'Mara, 1998.

Barker, Olivia. "Regular Guys Cast a Jaded Eye at 'Metrosexual' Trend: Web Logs, Comedy Spoofs Feeding on a Backlash." *USA Today*, 22 January 2004, D1.

Baron. "The 'Beau' as Critic, and the Critic as 'Beau.'" *Fashion*, July 1899, 10–11.

———. "Colour in Male Dress." *Fashion*, October 1899, 8–9.

———. "Dressing: An Art?" *Fashion*, February 1900, 13.

———. "Full Dress." *Fashion*, November 1899, 20–21.

———. "How to Fail in Dress." *Fashion*, March 1900, 17–18.

———. "On Overdoing It." *Fashion*, October 1900, 20–21.

———. "The Personal Element: A Sermon on a Text." *Fashion*, January 1900, 19.

———. "Shams." *Fashion*, September 1899, 6–7.

Barth, Gunther. *City People: The Rise of Modern City Culture in Nineteenth-Century America*. Oxford: Oxford University Press, 1980.

Batterberry, Michael, and Ariane Batterberry. *Fashion: The Mirror of History*. New York: Greenwich House, 1977.

Baudelaire, Charles. "The Painter of Modern Life." 1863. In *Selected Writings on Art and Artists*, translated by P. E. Charvet, 390–435. Cambridge: Cambridge University Press, 1972.

Beaunash. Masculine Modes in America. *Fashion*, December 1903, 19–20.

———. Masculine Modes in America. *Fashion*, March 1904, 9–10.

———. Masculine Modes in America. *Fashion*, July 1904, 18–19.

Bederman, Gail. *Manliness and Civilization: A Cultural History of Gender and Race in the United States, 1880–1917*. Chicago: University of Chicago Press, 1995.

Beerbohm, Max. "Dandies and Dandies." 1896. In *Works and More*, 9–34. Grosse Pointe, MI: Scholarly Press, 1969.

Beetham, Margaret. *A Magazine of Her Own? Domesticity and Desire in the Woman's Magazine, 1800–1914*. London: Routledge, 1996.

Beeton, Samuel Orchart. *Beeton's Manners of Polite Society: For Ladies, Gentlemen, and Families*. London: Ward, Lock, 1879.

"Belts as Strength Economisers." *Fashion*, January 1903, 8–9.

Bennett, Arnold. *The Old Wives' Tale*. 1908. New York: George H. Doran, 1911.

Benson, Susan Porter. *Counter Cultures: Saleswomen, Managers, and Customers in American Department Stores, 1880–1940*. Urbana: University of Illinois Press, 1986.

Bermingham, Ann. "Elegant Females and Gentlemen Connoisseurs: The Commerce and Culture and Self-Image in Eighteenth-Century England." In *The Consumption of*

Culture, 1600–1800: Image, Object, Text, edited by Ann Bermingham and John Brewer, 489–513. London: Routledge, 1997.

Best Dressed Man: A Gossip on Manners and Modes. London: J. W. Doré, 1892.

Birbeck Bank. Advertisement. *Fashion,* March 1902, 27.

Blenkinsop, Adam. *A Shilling's-Worth of Advice on Manners, Behaviour and Dress.* London: n.p., 1850.

Blunders in Behaviour Corrected. London: Groombridge, 1855.

Bocock, Robert. *Consumption.* London: Routledge, 1993.

Booth, Charles. *Life and Labour of the People in London.* 1st series, *Poverty,* vol. 4. 1889, London: Macmillan, 1902.

———. *Life and Labour of the People of London.* 2nd series, *Industry,* vol. 3. London: Macmillan, 1903.

"Boots at McAfee's." *Fashion,* April 1902, 15–16.

Bordo, Susan. *The Male Body: A New Look at Men in Public and in Private.* New York: Farrar, Straus and Giroux, 1999.

Bovril. Advertisement. *Illustrated London News,* 2 February 1901, 173.

Bowlby, Rachel. *Just Looking: Consumer Culture in Dreiser, Gissing, and Zola.* New York: Methuen, 1985.

Bradley, H. Dennis. *Vogue: A Clothing Catalogue for Pope and Bradley.* London, 1912.

Breward, Christopher. *The Culture of Fashion: A New History of Fashionable Dress.* Manchester: Manchester University Press, 1995.

———. *The Hidden Consumer: Masculinities, Fashion and City Life, 1860–1914.* Manchester: Manchester University Press, 1999.

Briggs, Asa. *Friends of the People: The Centenary History of Lewis's.* London: Batsford, 1956.

Brown, C. W. Motor Notes. *Fashion,* January 1903, 9–13.

Brummel, Beau, Junr. "The Care of Clothes." *Fashion,* December 1898, 15.

———. Dress News Collected and Dissected. *Fashion,* April 1898, 13–18.

———. Dress News Collected and Dissected. *Fashion,* May 1898, 16–22.

———. Dress News Collected and Dissected. *Fashion,* June 1898, 19–25.

———. Dress News Collected and Dissected. *Fashion,* July 1898, 17–22.

———. Dress News Collected and Dissected. *Fashion,* September 1898, 19–25.

———. Dress News Collected and Dissected. *Fashion,* October 1898, 19–24.

———. Dress News Collected and Dissected. *Fashion,* February 1899, 20–25.

———. Editorial. *Fashion,* January 1900, 25.

———. From Head to Foot. *Fashion,* July 1898, 13–15.

———. From Head to Foot. *Fashion,* October 1898, 13–15.

———. From Head to Foot. *Fashion,* November 1898, 18–19.

———. From Head to Foot. *Fashion,* May 1899, 13–14.

———. From Head to Foot. *Fashion*, August 1899, 19.

———. From Head to Foot. *Fashion*, October 1899, 16–17.

———. From Head to Foot. *Fashion*, February 1900, 16–18.

———. From Head to Foot. *Fashion*, May 1900, 18–20.

———. From Head to Foot. *Fashion*, August 1900, 16–18.

———. From Head to Foot. *Fashion*, January 1901, 8–10.

———. From Head to Foot. *Fashion*, June 1901, 17–20.

———. From Head to Foot. *Fashion*, April 1902, 11–13.

———. "How to Clean Boot-Tops." *Fashion*, December 1898, 24.

———. "Introduction." *Fashion*, March 1898, 1.

———. "Notice." *Fashion*, August–September 1904, 5.

———. "Some New Year Remarks." *Fashion*, January 1902, 5.

———. "Special Statement." *Fashion*, June 1900, 7.

———. Untitled. *Fashion*, February 1899, 12.

———. Untitled. *Fashion*, February 1899, 15.

———. Untitled. *Fashion*, June 1900, 5.

———. "Valuable Discovery for the Hair." *Fashion*, July 1904, 22.

Buck, Anne M. *Victorian Costume and Costume Accessories.* London: Herbert Jenkins, 1961.

Bulwer Lytton, Edward. *Pelham: or, Adventures of a Gentleman / Eugene Aram.* Boston: Dana Estes and Co., 1828.

[Bunce, Oliver Bell.] By "Censor." *Don't: A Manual of Mistakes and Improprieties More or Less Prevalent in Conduct and Speech.* New York: D. Appleton and Co., 1883.

Butcher, Jim. "*FHM* Runs Away with Top Men's Mag Title." 12 February 2004. http://www.mad.co.uk/abc2004h2/story.aspx?uid=dc8fd031-2b1c-413d-9c46-0ac89fdcacfa&sguid=d2339767-e8cf-4c67-9f8d-faf19eea1b61 (accessed 5 August 2005).

Butler, Judith. *Gender Trouble: Feminism and the Subversion of Identity.* London: Routledge, 1990.

Byrde, Penelope. *The Male Image: Men's Fashion in Britain, 1300–1970.* London: Batsford, 1979.

Cadbury's Cocoa. Advertisement. *Illustrated London News*, 19 January 1901, 85.

———. Advertisement. *Punch*, 13 June 1885: n.p.

Callery, Sean. *Harrods, Knightsbridge: The Story of Society's Favourite Store.* London: Ebury, 1991.

Calloway, Stephen, and David Colvin. *The Exquisite Life of Oscar Wilde.* London: Orion, 1997.

Campbell, Colin. "Understanding Traditional and Modern Patterns of Consumption in Eighteenth-Century England: A Character-Action Approach." In *Consump-*

tion and the World of Goods, edited by John Brewer and Roy Porter, 40–57. London: Routledge, 1993.

Campbell, Gertrude Elizabeth, Lady. *Etiquette of Good Society.* London: Cassell and Co., 1893.

Camplin, Jamie. *The Rise of the Plutocrats: Wealth and Power in Edwardian England.* London: Constable, 1978.

Carlyle, Thomas. *Sartor Resartus: The Life and Opinions of Herr Teufelsdröckh.* 1833–34. Edited by William Savage Johnson. Boston: Houghton Mifflin, 1924.

Carr, Coeli. "Men Put Plastic Surgery on the Résumé." *New York Times,* 7 July 2002, 3.12.

Carreras, J. J. Advertisement. *Fashion,* April 1902, 2.

Cavers, Charles. *Hades! The Ladies! Being Extracts from the Diary of a Draper.* London: Gurney and Jackson, 1933.

"Century of Tailoring: Some Interesting Things about the Evolution of Clothes, A." *Minister's Gazette of Fashion,* July 1901, 123.

Chaney, David. "The Department Store as a Cultural Form." *Theory, Culture and Society* 1 (1983): 22–31.

Chapman, Stanley. "The Innovating Entrepreneurs in the British Ready-Made Clothing Industry." *Textile History* 24 (1993): 5–25.

Chenoune, Farid. *A History of Men's Fashion.* Translated by Deke Dusinberre. Paris: Flammarion, 1993.

Cleveland Bicycles. Advertisement. *Fashion,* July 1898, 25.

Clothes and the Man: Hints on the Wearing and Caring of Clothes. By the "Major" of *To-day.* New York: M. F. Mansfield; London: Grant Richards, 1900.

"Coat for Ping-Pong, A." *Fashion,* February 1902, 13.

Cobbett, William. *Advice to Young Men, and (Incidentally) to Young Women, in the Middle and Higher Ranks of Life.* 1830. Preface by George Spater. Oxford: Oxford University Press, 1980.

Cole, Hubert. *Beau Brummell.* London: Granada, 1977.

Colin, Lady M. *Everybody's Book of Correct Conduct, Being the Etiquette of Every-Day Life.* London: Saxon, 1893.

Collins, Wilkie. *The Woman in White.* 1860. Edited by Julian Symons. London: Penguin, 1985.

Colmore, G. "Eight Hundred a Year." *Cornhill Magazine,* June 1901, 790–800.

"Concerning the Snuff Fashion." *Fashion,* March 1902, 20.

Cook, Chris. *The Longman Companion to Britain in the Nineteenth Century, 1815–1914.* London: Longman, 1999.

Corina, Maurice. *Fine Silks and Oak Counters: Debenhams, 1778–1978.* London: Hutchinson, 1978.

Corisande. "Fashions for Men." *Warehouseman and Drapers' Trade Journal*, 16 August 1879, 386–87.

"Corsets and Their Worth." *Fashion*, January 1903, 16.

"Corsets in the Army." *Fashion*, January 1903, 8.

"Cosmetics, Where Vanity and Opportunities Meet." *Exposé*, July 2004, 34–37.

Cott, Nancy. "On Men's History and Women's History." In *Meanings for Manhood*, edited by Mark C. Carnes and Clyde Griffen, 205–11. Chicago: University of Chicago Press, 1990.

Cotton, J. T. "Tailoring Ancient and Modern, Part 2." *Gentleman's Magazine of Fashion*, June 1888, 3.

"'Court Journal' on 'Fashion,' The." *Fashion*, August 1898, 7.

"'Critic' on 'Fashion,' The." *Fashion*, August 1898, 7.

Crossick, Geoffrey. "The Emergence of the Lower Middle Class in Britain: A Discussion." In *The Lower Middle Class in Britain, 1870–1914*, edited by Geoffrey Crossick, 11–60. New York: St. Martin's Press, 1977.

Cunningham, Hugh. "Leisure and Culture." In *The Cambridge Social History of Britain, 1750–1950*, edited by F. M. L. Thompson, vol. 2, 279–339. Cambridge: Cambridge University Press, 1990.

Cunnington, C. Willett, and Phillis Cunnington. *Handbook of English Costume in the Nineteenth Century*. London: Faber and Faber, 1959.

"Current Styles." By "West-Ender." *London Tailor and Record of Fashion*, February 1884, 26.

Curtin, Michael. *Propriety and Position: A Study of Victorian Manners*. New York: Garland, 1987.

Cutler, Rodney. "Grooming Advice (From a Guy Who Can Kick Our Ass)." *Esquire*, March 2005, 76.

Cutter's Gazette of Fashion, April 1893, 48.

Damon-Moore, Helen. *Magazines for the Millions: Gender and Commerce in the "Ladies' Home Journal" and the "Saturday Evening Post," 1880–1910*. Albany: State University of New York, 1994.

Darby, Barbara. "The More Things Change . . : The Rules and Late Eighteenth-Century Conduct Books for Women." *Women's Studies* 3 (June 2000): 333–55.

Davidoff, Leonore, and Catherine Hall. *Family Fortunes: Men and Women of the English Middle Class, 1780–1850*. Chicago: University of Chicago Press, 1987.

Davidson, Darren. "*Zoo* Piles Pressure on *Nuts*." 17 February 2005. http://www.mad.co.uk/abc2004h2/story.aspx?uid=10468f49-f753–48f7–8a82–87bfd6de2304&sguid=7dbfbe60–6b9b-48f6–9ec0-c9e6ce1f647e (accessed 13 August 2005).

Dearborn, George Van Ness. *The Psychology of Clothing*. Princeton, NJ: Psychological Review Company, 1918.

"Decline of Good Tailoring, The." *Minister's Gazette of Fashion*, January 1901, 2.

"Defiance" Coach Stables. Advertisement. *Fashion*, March 1902, 4.

De Marly, Diana. *Fashion for Men: An Illustrated History.* New York: Holmes and Meier, 1985.

Devereaux, G.R.M. *Etiquette for Men: A Book of Modern Manners and Customs.* 4th ed. London: Pearson, 1902.

de Winton, Sydney. "A Dozen Collars." *Fashion*, July 1899, 18–19.

"Did you call the police, Sir?" Cartoon. *Punch* 24 (1853): 58.

Disraeli, Benjamin. *Endymion.* 1880. New York: M. Walter Dunne, 1904.

Domosh, Mona. *Invented Cities: The Creation of Landscape in Nineteenth-Century New York and Boston.* New Haven: Yale University Press, 1996.

Doré, Gustave, and Blanchard Jerrold. *London, A Pilgrimage.* 1872. Reprint, New York: Blom, 1968.

Douglas, Mary, and Baron C. Isherwood. *The World of Goods: Towards an Anthropology of Consumption.* London: Allen Lane, 1978.

Draper, The, 25 July 1903, 992.

Draper's Record, 28 April 1906.

"Dress and Character. III: City Types." *Fashion*, November 1898, 15–16.

"Dress as a Matter of Business." *Fashion*, June 1903, 25–26.

Dr. Tibbles' Vi-Cocoa. Advertisement. *Daily Mail*, 12 March 1900, 8.

Duke of Windsor (Edward VIII). *A Family Album.* London: Cassell, 1960.

du Maurier, George. "Inconvenience of Modern Male Attire." Cartoon. *Punch,* 21 February 1891, 95.

"Early Spring Fashions." *Master Tailor and Cutters' Gazette*, March 1900, 92.

Edwards, Tim. *Men in the Mirror: Men's Fashion, Masculinity and Consumer Society.* London: Cassell, 1997.

Eliot, George. *Middlemarch.* 1872. Edited by Gordon S. Haight. Boston: Houghton Mifflin, 1956.

Elliman's Universal Embrocation. Advertisement. *Illustrated London News*, 25 October 1890, 535.

Ellmann, Richard. *Oscar Wilde.* New York: Knopf, 1988.

Empire Theatre. Advertisement. *Fashion*, October 1898, 25.

English Gentleman: His Principles, His Feelings, His Manners, His Pursuits, The. London: George Bell, 1849.

Etiquette for Gentlemen, With Hints on the Art of Conversation. 6th ed. London: Charles Tilt, 1838.

Etiquette for Gentlemen. London: Black, 1864.

Etiquette for Gentlemen. London: Frederick Warne and Co., ca. 1890.

Etiquette for Gentlemen: A Guide to the Observances of Good Society. London: Ward, Lock and Co., 1925.

Etiquette of Modern Society: A Guide to Good Manners in Every Possible Situation, The. London: Ward, Lock, 1882.

Etiquette, Politeness, and Good Breeding. London: Ward, Lock and Tyler, 1870.

Expert Wrinkler, The. "Golf and Good Form." *Punch,* 2 March 1904, 160–61.

Fairchilds, Cissie. "The Production and Marketing of Populuxe Goods in Eighteenth-Century Paris." In *Consumption and the World of Goods,* edited by John Brewer and Roy Porter, 228–48. London: Routledge, 1993.

Fashion, March 1898, 1.

Fashion, July 1899, 18.

Fashion, September 1902, 1.

"Fashion." Advertisement. *Fashion,* April 1899, 26.

"Fashion." Advertisement. *Fashion,* September 1899, 3.

"Fashionable Jewellery." *Warehouseman and Drapers' Trade Journal,* 5 April 1879, 165.

"'Fashion' Correct Dress Chart for The Time, The." *Fashion,* February 1905, 22–23.

"Fashion" Dress Chart, The. *Fashion,* February 1902, 21.

"Fashion" Dress Chart, The. *Fashion,* June 1902, 21.

"Fashion" Dress Chart, The. *Fashion,* June 1903, 17.

"Fashion" Dress Chart, The. *Fashion,* March 1904, 14–15.

"Fashion's" Monthly Review. *Fashion,* April 1903, 19–23.

"Fashion's" Monthly Review of Gentlemen's Dress News. *Fashion,* May 1903, 19–22.

Felski, Rita. *The Gender of Modernity.* Cambridge, MA: Harvard University Press, 1995.

Ferry, John William. *A History of the Department Store.* New York: Macmillan, 1960.

Fillin-Yeh, Susan, ed. *Dandies: Fashion and Finesse in Art and Culture.* New York: New York University Press, 2001.

Flocker, Michael. *The Metrosexual Guide to Style: A Handbook for the Modern Man.* Cambridge, MA: Da Capo Press, 2003.

Flugel, J. C. *The Psychology of Clothes.* 1930. London: Hogarth, 1950.

Foldy, Michael S. *The Trials of Oscar Wilde: Deviance, Morality, and Late-Victorian Society.* New Haven: Yale University Press, 1997.

Foster, Vanda. *A Visual History of Costume in the Nineteenth Century.* London: Batsford, 1984.

Fox, Geoff. "More of Us Want Plastic Surgery: Breast Enlargements and Nose Jobs Are Top Choice." *Leeds Today Evening Post.* http://www.leedstoday.net/ViewArticle2.aspx?SectionID=39&ArticleID=928360 (accessed 13 July 2005).

Fraser, W. Hamish. *The Coming of the Mass Market, 1850–1914.* Hamden, CT: Archon, 1981.

Frick, Robert. "The Manly Man's Guide to Makeup and Metrosexuality: A New Periodical Smudges the Lines between the Sexes." *Kiplinger's*, June 2004, 38.

From Head to Foot. *Fashion*, February 1900, 18.

From Head to Foot. *Fashion*, January 1902, 23–26.

From Head to Foot. *Fashion*, April 1903, 10–14.

From Head to Foot. *Fashion*, June 1903, 8–10.

Gagnier, Regenia. *Idylls of the Marketplace: Oscar Wilde and the Victorian Public.* Stanford: Stanford University Press, 1986.

Galsworth, Frank. "The Fate of the Jam King." Illustration. *Fashion*, November 1898, 6.

Garelick, Rhonda K. *Rising Star: Dandyism, Gender, and Performance in the Fin de Siècle.* Princeton: Princeton University Press, 1998.

Garvey, Ellen Gruber. *The Adman in the Parlor: Magazines and the Gendering of Consumer Culture, 1880s to 1910s.* New York: Oxford University Press, 1996.

Gazette of Fashion and Cutting-Room Companion, May 1853.

Gazette of Fashion and Cutting-Room Companion, June 1853.

Gazette of Fashion and Cutting-Room Companion, July 1853.

Gazette of Fashion and Cutting-Room Companion, August 1853.

Gazette of Fashion and Cutting-Room Companion, October 1853.

Gentleman's Magazine of Fashion, 1884.

Gentleman's Magazine of Fashion, January 1888, 3, and plate 247.

"'Gentlewoman' Says, The." *Fashion*, March 1899, 23.

Gilbert, W. S., and Arthur Sullivan. *Patience, or Bunthorne's Bride.* 1881. In *The Complete Plays of Gilbert and Sullivan*, 157–97. Garden City, NY: Garden City Publishing, 1941.

Gilmour, Robin. *The Idea of the Gentleman in the Victorian Novel.* London: Allen and Unwin, 1981.

Glass of Fashion: A Universal Handbook of Social Etiquette and Home Culture for Ladies and Gentlemen. With Copious and Practical Hints upon the Manners and Ceremonies of Every Relation in Life, At Home in Society, and at Court, The. By the "Lounger in Society." London: Hogg, 1881.

Godfrey-Turner, L. Coffee and Cognac. *Fashion*, April 1898, 3–5.

———. Coffee and Cognac. *Fashion*, February 1899, 3–6.

———. Coffee and Cognac. *Fashion*, May 1899, 3–7.

———. Coffee and Cognac. *Fashion*, September 1899, 4–6.

———. Coffee and Cognac. *Fashion*, October 1899, 4–6.

———. Coffee and Cognac. *Fashion*, March 1900, 5–8.

———. Coffee and Cognac. *Fashion*, April 1900, 5–7.

———. Coffee and Cognac. *Fashion*, June 1900, 5–7.

———. Coffee and Cognac. *Fashion*, January 1901, 5.

"Good City Hosier, A." *Fashion*, March 1902, 15.

"Good Tailor, A." *Fashion*, April 1899, 15.

Gourvish, T. R. "The Rise of the Professions." In *Later Victorian Britain, 1867–1900*, edited by T. R. Gourvish and Alan O'Day, 13–35. New York: St. Martin's Press, 1988.

Green, F. W., and Alfred Lee. "The Bond St. Beau." Sheet music. London: J. Bath, 1873.

Green, Harvey. *Fit for America: Health, Fitness, Sport, and American Society.* New York: Pantheon, 1986.

Greenfield, Jill, Sean O'Connell, and Chris Reid. "Gender, Consumer Culture, and the Middle-Class Male, 1918–39." In *Gender, Civic Culture and Consumerism: Middle-Class Identity in Britain, 1800–1940*, edited by Alan Kidd and David Nicholls, 183–97. Manchester, England: Manchester University Press, 1999.

Groskop, Viv. "'Hair Coverage': The New Cellulite." *New Statesman*, 14 March 2005, 12.

Grossmith, George, and Weedon Grossmith. *The Diary of a Nobody.* 1892. London: Folio Society, 1969.

Grove, Lady (Agnes Geraldine). *The Social Fetich.* London: Smith, Elder and Co., 1907.

Grunfeld's Coat-Presser and Shape-Preserver. Advertisement. *Fashion*, October 1900, 24.

Grunfeld's Patent Brace Vest. Advertisement. *Fashion*, August 1901, 24.

Habits of Good Society: A Handbook of Etiquette for Ladies and Gentlemen, The. London: Hogg, 1859.

Haley, Bruce. *The Healthy Body and Victorian Culture.* Cambridge, MA: Harvard University Press, 1978.

Hall, Donald E., ed. *Muscular Christianity: Embodying the Victorian Age.* Cambridge: Cambridge University Press, 1994.

Hand-Book of Etiquette: Being a Complete Guide to the Usages of Polite Society, The. London: Cassell, 1860.

Harrison, C. "Which the Greater Torture—The 1837 Stock or the 1897 Collar?" Cartoon. *Punch*, 18 December 1897, 285.

Harrods. *A Story of British Achievement, 1849–1949.* London: Harrods, 1949.

Harrods General Catalogue. London: Harrods, 1900.

Harrods General Catalogue. London: Harrods, 1903.

Harrods General Catalogue. London: Harrods, 1909.

"Harrods Limited, The Shrine of Fashion, The World's Greatest Emporium." *Daily Mail*, 24 February 1904, 1.

Harvey, John. *Men in Black.* Chicago: University of Chicago Press, 1995.

Heath, Henry, Ltd. Advertisement. *Fashion*, December 1899, 1.

"Height of Masherdom, The." Cartoon. *Punch*, 4 February 1888, 57.

Hill, Dave. "The Elusive Mr. Right." *Weekly Guardian*, 17 November 2001, 44.

"Hints on Cleaning Riding Breeches." *Fashion*, December 1901, 15.

"Hints on Dress." *London Tailor and Record of Fashion*, February 1884, 28.

Holding, T. H. "Men's Clothes in Clubland." *Gentleman's Magazine of Fashion*, September 1890, 7.

Holland, F. "Four Recognised Types of Present Day Dress Waistcoats." *Fashion*, June 1899, 16.

Hollander, Anne. *Sex and Suits.* New York: Knopf, 1994.

Hosgood, Christopher P. "'Doing the Shops' at Christmas: Women, Men, and the Department Store in England, c. 1880–1914." In *Cathedrals of Consumption: The European Department Store, 1850–1939*, edited by Geoffrey Crossick and Serge Jaumin, 97–115. Aldershot, England: Ashgate, 1999.

Howard, Theresa. "Men's Skin Care Products Clean Up: As Prices Fall, Lotions, Scrubs Go Mainstream." *USA Today*, 19 November 2003, B3.

"How the 'Tailor and Cutter' Supplies Its Readers with News." *Fashion*, June 1900, 25.

How to Behave: A Pocket Manual of Etiquette, and Guide to Correct Personal Habits. Glasgow: Marr and Sons, 1883.

"How to Dress in the Latest Fashion for 7/6 a Year." Advertisement. *Fashion*, July 1899, 3.

"How to Put on Fox's Patent Puttee." *Fashion*, January 1899, 18.

Hughes, Thomas. *Tom Brown at Oxford.* 1861. London: Macmillan, 1889.

Humphry, Mrs. C. E. *Etiquette for Every Day.* London: Richards, 1902.

———. *Manners for Men.* London: Bowden, 1897.

———. *More Manners for Men.* London: Shaw, 1907.

Hyde, H. Montgomery. *The Cleveland Street Scandal.* New York: Coward, McCann and Geoghegan, 1976.

———. *The Trials of Oscar Wilde.* 1962. Reprint, New York: Dover, 1973.

Hymowitz, Carol. "Top Executives Chase Youthful Appearance, But Miss Real Issue." *Wall Street Journal*, eastern edition, 17 February 2004, B1.

"Ideal Husband, The." *Punch*, 18 December 1897, 285.

"Improving the Mere Man." *Fashion*, June 1904, 13.

"In-Cosmetics" Official Show Preview, Spring 2005, Herts, England. Showtime Media Services Ltd. http://www.in-cosmetics.com/files/in-cosmetics_2005_PreviewMag.pdf (accessed 13 August 2005).

"In Khaki Clad." *Outfitter*, 24 February 1900, 12–13.

"In Praise of 'Fashion.'" *Fashion*, May 1898, 14–15.

"In Praise of Waistcoats." *Tailor's Review*, November 1890, 88.

"Interesting to Advertisers." Advertisement. *Fashion*, March 1901, 17.

Ives, Nat. "A Men's Magazine Seeks to Swap a 'Laddie' Sensibility for a Prosperous Macho Sophistication." *New York Times*, 9 November 2004, C10.

"I will say this for Bill, 'e *do* look the Gentleman!" Cartoon. *Punch,* 15 March 1905, 190.

Jackson, Peter. "The Cultural Politics of Masculinity: Towards a Social Geography." *Transactions of the Institute of British Geographers* 16 (1991): 199–213.

Jaeger Military and Sporting Pure Wool Tailors. Advertisement. *Fashion,* January 1900, 2.

"Jaeger's Catalogue." *Fashion,* August 1900, 21.

Jefferys, James Bavington. *Retail Trading in Britain, 1850–1950: A Study of Trends in Retailing with Special Reference to the Development of Cooperative, Multiple Shop and Department Store Methods of Trading.* Cambridge: Cambridge University Press, 1954.

Jerrold, Douglas. "The Linen-Draper's Assistants." In *The Writings of Douglas Jerrold,* vol. 5, 235–42. London: Bradbury and Evans, 1853.

Jeune, Lady. "The Ethics of Shopping." *Fortnightly Review,* January 1895, 123–32.

Johnson, Herbert. Advertisement. *Fashion,* May 1898, 2.

Kelly, J. E. "You Hold Yourself Like This." Illustration from the souvenir program for *Patience, or Bunthorne's Bride,* by W. S. Gilbert and Arthur Sullivan. The 250th Performance at the Savoy Theatre, London, and the 100th Performance at the Standard Theatre, New York, by the D'Oyly Carte Opera Company, December 29, 1881. New York: Art Interchange Press, 1881.

Kimmel, Michael. *Manhood in America: A Cultural History.* New York: Free Press, 1996.

Kingsland, Mrs. Burton. *Etiquette for All Occasions.* London: Doubleday, Page and Co., 1901.

Klickmann, Flora, ed. *How to Behave: A Handbook of Etiquette for All.* London: Ward, Lock and Co., 1898.

Kropp Razors. Advertisement. *Fashion,* May 1899, 17.

Kuchta, David. "The Making of the Self-Made Man: Class, Clothing, and English Masculinity, 1688–1832." In *The Sex of Things: Gender and Consumption in Historical Perspective,* edited by Victoria de Grazia with Ellen Furlough, 54–78. Berkeley: University of California Press, 1996.

Kyle, G. W., and Co. Advertisement. *Fashion,* March 1901, 4.

Lady Province. "Man's Attire." *Fashion,* February 1905, 25–26.

Lambert, Miles. "The Dandy in Thackeray's 'Vanity Fair' and 'Pendennis': An Early Victorian View of the Regency Dandy." *Costume: The Journal of the Costume Society* (1988): 60–69.

Lambert, Richard S. *The Universal Provider: A Study of William Whiteley and the Rise of the London Department Store.* London: George C. Harrap, 1938.

Lancaster, William. *The Department Store: A Social History.* London: Leicester University Press, 1995.

Langland, Elizabeth. *Nobody's Angels: Middle-Class Women and Domestic Ideology in Victorian Culture.* Ithaca, NY: Cornell University Press, 1995.

Laver, James. *Dandies*. London: Weidenfeld and Nicolson, 1968.

————. *Taste and Fashion, from the French Revolution to the Present Day*. London: G. G. Harrap, 1945.

Leach, William. *Land of Desire: Merchants, Power, and the Rise of a New American Culture*. New York: Pantheon, 1993.

————. "Transformations in a Culture of Consumption: Women and Department Stores, 1890–1925." *Journal of American History* 71 (September 1984): 319–42.

Leggatt, W. E. "Is the Sewing Tailor Doomed?" *Minister's Gazette of Fashion*, December 1901, 234.

Leigh, Leonard. Advertisement. *Fashion*, July 1899, 1.

"Lever" Wardrobe. Advertisement. *Fashion*, September 1902, 3.

Levy, Hermann. *The Shops of Britain: A Study of Retail Distribution*. London: Routledge and Kegan Paul, 1947.

Lewin's. Advertisement. *Fashion*, April 1904, 10.

Linton, Eliza Lynn. "The Girl of the Period." Originally published 14 March 1868 in the *Saturday Review*. In *Prose by Victorian Women: An Anthology*, edited by Andrea Broomfield and Sally Mitchell, 356–60. New York: Garland, 1996.

Lipke, David. "T: Men's Fashion Debuts." *Daily News Record*, 13 September 2004, 17.

Loeb, Lori Anne. *Consuming Angels: Advertising and Victorian Women*. New York: Oxford, 1994.

London Expert. What the World Is Wearing. *Fashion*, July 1898, 10–11.

————. What the World Is Wearing. *Fashion*, October 1898, 8.

————. What the World Is Wearing. *Fashion*, December 1898, 10.

————. What the World Is Wearing. *Fashion*, February 1899, 8–10.

————. What the World Is Wearing. *Fashion*, March 1899, 10–11.

————. What the World Is Wearing. *Fashion*, August 1899, 8–10.

————. What the World Is Wearing. *Fashion*, September 1899, 8–9.

————. What the World Is Wearing. *Fashion*, January 1900, 10.

————. What the World Is Wearing. *Fashion*, July 1900, 12–14.

————. What the World Is Wearing. *Fashion*, September 1901, 8–11.

"London Notes." *Outfitter*, 3 February 1900, 5.

London Tailor, 30 September 1899, 305.

London Tailor, May 1900, 77.

Lucchesi, Joe. "'The Dandy in Me': Romaine Brooks's 1923 Portraits." In *Dandies: Fashion and Finesse in Art and Culture*, edited by Susan Fillin-Yeh, 153–84. New York: New York University Press, 2001.

Ludlow, Hal. "Smoke!" Illustration. *Fashion*, December 1898, 3.

Lunt, Peter K., and Sonia M. Livingstone. *Mass Consumption and Personal Identity: Everyday Economic Experience*. Buckingham: Open University Press, 1992.

Macdonald, James. "West End Tailoring (Men)." 1889. In *Life and Labour of the People in London*, edited by Charles Booth. 1st series, *Poverty*, vol. 4, 142–49. London: Macmillan, 1902.

Major, The. "Especially Clothes." *Fashion*, January 1901, 12–15.

Manners and Rules of Good Society, or Solecisms to Be Avoided. By a member of the aristocracy. 22nd ed. London: Frederick Warne and Co., 1897.

Mantalini, Mr. "Concerning Cravats: Their Past and Future." *Fashion*, October 1900, 14–16.

———. "Other-Class Fashion." *Fashion*, February 1900, 18–20.

Manual of Etiquette for Ladies and Gentlemen: Revised and Rewritten from the Work by the Countess of —— *by M.H.E., A.* London: Routledge, 1907.

Martin, Richard, and Koda, Harold. *Jocks and Nerds: Men's Style in the Twentieth Century.* New York: Rizzoli, 1989.

Masculine Modes in America. Fashion, July 1901, 18–23.

Masculine Modes in America. Fashion, August 1901, 19–24.

Masculine Modes in America. Fashion, August 1903, 13–16.

Master Tailor and Cutters' Gazette, February 1907.

Master Tailor and Cutters' Gazette, April 1907.

Master Tailor and Cutters' Gazette, June 1907.

Mathias, Peter. *Retailing Revolution: History of Multiple Retailing in the Food Trades Based upon the Allied Suppliers Group of Companies.* London: Longmans, 1967.

Mayhew, Henry, ed. *The Shops and Companies of London, and The Trades and Manufactories of Great Britain.* Vol. 1. London, 1865.

McAfee, Alan. Advertisement. *Fashion*, January 1902, 6.

McDowell, Colin. *The Man of Fashion: Peacock Males and Perfect Gentlemen.* London: Thames and Hudson, 1997.

McKendrick, Neil. "The Commercialization of Fashion." In *The Birth of a Consumer Society: The Commercialisation of Eighteenth-Century England*, edited by Neil McKendrick, John Brewer, and J. H. Plumb, 34–99. Bloomington: Indiana University Press, 1982.

———. "The Consumer Revolution of Eighteenth-Century England." In McKendrick et al., *Birth of a Consumer Society*, 9–33.

Meller, Helen Elizabeth. *Leisure and the Changing City, 1870–1914.* New York: Routledge, 1976.

"Memo for Buyers." *Outfitter*, 24 February 1900, 11.

"Men's Fashions in Fiction." *Fashion*, May 1904, 23–24.

Meredith, George. *The Egoist.* 1879. New York: Modern Library, 1951.

Miller, Michael B. *The Bon Marché: Bourgeois Culture and the Department Store, 1869–1920.* Princeton: Princeton University Press, 1981.

Mills, C. Wallis. Cartoon. *Punch,* 24 March 1909, 207.

Minister's Gazette of Fashion, June 1889, figures 3235 and 3236.

Mitchell, Brian R. *Abstracts of British Historical Statistics.* Cambridge: Cambridge University Press, 1962.

———. *British Historical Statistics.* Cambridge: Cambridge University Press, 1988.

Mixing in Society. A Complete Manual of Manners. By the Right Hon. The Countess of _____. London: Routledge, 1870.

Modern Etiquette in Private and Public. London: Warne, 1870.

Moers, Ellen. *The Dandy: Brummell to Beerbohm.* London: Secker and Warburg, 1960.

Montagu. Masculine Modes in America. *Fashion,* July 1902, 14–16.

———. Masculine Modes in America. *Fashion,* September 1903, 12–14.

Morphing Sequence. "L'Oréal Men." http://www.lorealparisusa.com/men/ (accessed 28 July 2005).

Mort, Frank. "Boy's Own? Masculinity, Style and Popular Culture." In *Male Order: Unwrapping Masculinity,* edited by R. Chapman and Jonathan Rutherford, 193–224. London: Lawrence and Wishart, 1988.

———. *Cultures of Consumption: Masculinities and Social Space in Late Twentieth-Century Britain.* London: Routledge, 1996.

Moses, E., and Son. *The Growth of an Important Branch of British Industry, The Ready-Made Clothing System.* London, 1860.

Moss, Michael, and Alison Turton. *A Legend of Retailing: House of Fraser.* London: Weidenfeld and Nicolson, 1989.

"Mr. J. Rae's Social Kaleidoscope." *Gentleman's Magazine of Fashion,* July 1888, 3.

Mullin, Rick. "Viagra." *Chemical and Engineering News,* 20 June 2005. http://pubs.acs.org/cen/coverstory/83/8325/8325viagra.html (accessed 29 July 2005).

"Necessity of the Hat, The." *Fashion,* July 1904, 20–21.

"New Ideas for Gentlemen's Evening Dress." *Monthly Record of Fashion,* February 1884, 29–30.

"New Woollens, The." *Minister's Report of Fashion,* February 1902, 1–2.

Niagara Hall. Advertisement. *Fashion,* March 1902, 4.

Nixon, Sean. "Exhibiting Masculinity." In *Representation: Cultural Representations and Signifying Practices,* edited by Stuart Hall, 291–330. Thousand Oaks, CA: Sage, 1997.

———. "Have You Got the Look? Masculinities and Shopping Spectacle." In *Lifestyle Shopping,* edited by Rob Shields, 149–69. London: Routledge, 1992.

"Notice." *Fashion,* June 1898, 16.

"Notice." *Fashion,* February 1900, 25.

"Observations." *Gentleman's Magazine of Fashion,* November 1888, 3.

O'Connor, Bessie. "Man and Dress." *Fashion,* February 1905, 5–7.

"On Velvet." *Fashion*, July 1904, 10–11.

"Our Friend, the 'Rival.'" *Fashion*, July 1898, 23.

Oxford English Dictionary, The. 2nd ed. Oxford: Clarendon Press, 1989.

Paoletti, Jo Barraclough. "Ridicule and Role Models as Factors in American Men's Fashion Change, 1880–1910." *Costume: The Journal of the Costume Society* 19 (1985): 121–34.

Pasdermadjian, Hrant. *The Department Store: Its Origins, Evolution and Economics.* New York: Arno, 1954.

Pater, Walter. *The Renaissance: Studies in Art and Poetry: The 1893 Text.* 1877; 1893. Edited by Donald L. Hill. Berkeley: University of California Press, 1980.

Patterson, T. Transcript of paper read before the Sheffield Society. *Cutter's Gazette of Fashion.* November 1893, 165.

Peiss, Kathy. *Hope in a Jar: The Making of America's Beauty Culture.* New York: Owl, 1998.

"'Pelican' and 'Fashion,' The." *Fashion*, September 1899, 10.

Perkin, Harold. *The Rise of Professional Society: England since 1880.* London: Routledge, 1989.

Philips, Deborah. "Shopping for Men: The Single Woman Narrative." *Women: A Cultural Review* 11 (Winter 2000): 238–51.

"Photograph of the Circulation of 'Fashion,' A." *Fashion*, June 1902: 20.

"Plastic Surgery Industry Faces Tightening-Up." *Daily Telegraph*, 28 January 2005. http://www.telegraph.co.uk/news/main.jhtml?xml=/news/2005/01/28/ucosmetic.xml&sSheet=/portal/2005/01/28/ixportaltop.html (accessed 13 August 2005).

Polhemus, Ted. "The Invisible Man: Style and the Male Body." In *Material Man: Masculinity Sexuality Style*, edited by Giannino Malossi, 44–51. New York: Harry N. Abrams, 2000.

"'Queen' on Fashion, The." *Fashion*, August 1898, 7.

"Queer Customers." *Master Tailor and Cutters' Gazette*, February 1900, 46.

Rappaport, Erika Diane. "'A New Era of Shopping': The Promotion of Women's Pleasure in London's West End, 1909–1914." In *Cinema and the Invention of Modern Life*, edited by Leo Charney and Vanessa R. Schwartz, 130–55. Berkeley: University of California Press, 1995.

———. *Shopping for Pleasure: Women in the Making of London's West End.* Princeton: Princeton University Press, 2000.

Reed, David. *The Popular Magazine in Britain and the United States, 1880–1960.* Toronto: University of Toronto Press, 1997.

Rees, Goronwy. *St. Michael: A History of Marks and Spencer.* London: Weidenfeld and Nicolson, 1969.

Regent's Park Riding School. Advertisement. *Fashion*, April 1901, 4.

"Reminder for the Traveller, A." *Fashion*, July 1903, 15.

Rendon, Jim. "Now, a Man's World Is at the Spa or Salon." *New York Times*, 28 March 2004, 3.3.

Reviews of *Fashion*. *Fashion*, April 1899, 26.

Richards, Thomas. *The Commodity Culture of Victorian England: Advertising and Spectacle, 1851–1914*. Stanford: Stanford University Press, 1990.

"'Road' on Fashion, The." *Fashion*, August 1898, 25.

Roberts, Robert. *The Classic Slum: Salford Life in the First Quarter of the Century*. Harmondsworth: Penguin, 1973.

Rose, Jane E. "Conduct Books for Women, 1830–1860: A Rationale for Women's Conduct and Domestic Role in America." In *Nineteenth-Century Women Learn to Write*, edited by Catherine Hobbs and Carroll Smith-Rosenberg, 37–58. Charlottesville: University Press of Virginia, 1995.

Ross, Adrian, and Percy Greenbank. *Our Miss Gibbs*. London: Chappell and Co., 1909.

Ross, C. H., ed. *The Comic Album of Folly and Fashion*. London: n.p., 1870.

Rotundo, E. Anthony. *American Manhood: Transformations in Masculinity from the Revolution to the Modern Era*. New York: Basic, 1993.

"Round the London Shops." *Pall Mall Gazette*, 22 April 1889, 7.

Routledge's Etiquette for Gentlemen. London: Routledge, Warne, and Routledge, 1864.

Rubin, Peter. "Man Stands at a New Frontier: Vanishing Cream." *New York Times*, 5 May 2005, G3.

Ruskin, John. *Sesame and Lilies*. New York: Wiley and Sons, 1884.

Rutherford, Jonathan. *Forever England: Reflections on Race, Masculinity and Empire*. London: Lawrence and Wishart, 1997.

Safire, William. "On Language: *Metrosexual*; New Word for the New Narcissism." *New York Times Magazine*, 7 December 2003, 30.

Sala, George Augustus. *London Up to Date*. London: Adam and Charles Black, 1895.

———. *Twice Round the Clock or the Hours of the Day and Night in London*. 1858. Reprint, New York: Leicester University Press, 1971.

Salzman, Marian. "David Beckham: Soccer's Metrosexual." *Time*, 26 April 2004, 125.

Sanders, Lorraine. "Coming Shakeout in Men's Magazines: Too Many Titles to Survive; Guessing Who Will Go." *Media Life*, 9 March 2005. http://69.20.6.242/News2005/mar05/mar07/3_wed/news2wednesday.html (accessed 20 July 2005).

Sarony, Napoléon. "Portrait of Oscar Wilde, January 1882." Photograph. George Eastman House. GEH NEG: 1404 13431.

Schaffer, Talia. "Fashioning Aestheticism by Aestheticizing Fashion: Wilde, Beerbohm, and the Male Aesthetes' Sartorial Codes." *Victorian Literature and Culture* 28 (2000): 39–54.

Sharkey, Alix. "New Media, New Men: The Lost Paradigm of Male Normality." In *Material Man: Masculinity Sexuality Style*, edited by Giannino Malossi, 171–77. New York: Harry N. Abrams, 2000.

Shaw, Gareth. "The European Scene: Britain and Germany." In *The Evolution of Retail Systems, c. 1800–1914*, edited by John Benson and Gareth Shaw, 17–34. Leicester: Leicester University Press, 1992.

"Shirt-Coat for Summer, The." *Fashion*, April 1901, 8.

Shugaar, Antony. "The Comedy of Errors: Gender Icons as Modular Components of Identity." In *Material Man: Masculinity Sexuality Style*, edited by Giannino Malossi, 64–71. New York: Harry N. Abrams, 2000.

Simmel, Georg. "Fashion." *International Quarterly* 10 (October 1904): 130–55.

Sims, George R., ed. *Living London: Its Work and Its Play, Its Humour and Its Pathos, Its Sights and Its Scenes.* Vol. 3. London: Cassell, 1904.

Sinfield, Alan. *The Wilde Century: Effeminacy, Oscar Wilde, and the Queer Moment.* New York: Columbia, 1994.

"Sir Robert Peel, Bart., as a Leader of Fashion." *Fashion*, August 1899, 10–12.

Siskos, Catherine. "Cover Boys." *Kiplinger's*, April 2000, 30.

Slaters Detectives. Advertisement. *Fashion*, October 1899, 25.

"Some Well-Dressed Americans." *Fashion*, July 1900, 8–9.

"Special Notice to Advertisers." *Fashion*, July 1900, 14.

"Special Notice to Readers." *Fashion*, October 1902, 8.

Spiekermann, Uwe. "Theft and Thieves in German Department Stores, 1895–1930: A Discourse on Morality, Crime and Gender." In *Cathedrals of Consumption: The European Department Store, 1850–1939*, edited by Geoffrey Crossick and Serge Jaumin, 135–59. Aldershot, England: Ashgate, 1999.

"Sporting Garments at Lovegrove's." *Fashion*, March 1902, 11.

Stallybrass, Peter, and Allon White. *The Politics and Poetics of Transgression.* Ithaca: Cornell University Press, 1986.

"Standing No Nonsense." Cartoon. *Punch*, 8 May 1880, 215.

Steele, Valerie. *Fashion and Eroticism: Ideals of Feminine Beauty from the Victorian Era to the Jazz Age.* New York: Oxford University Press, 1985.

Stevenson, Nick, Peter Jackson, and Kate Brooks. "Ambivalence in Men's Lifestyle Magazines." In *Commercial Cultures: Economies, Practices, Spaces*, edited by Peter Jackson, Michelle Lowe, Daniel Miller, and Frank Mort, 189–212. Oxford: Berg, 2000.

Stohwasser and Co. Advertisement. *Fashion*, February 1900, 1.

Storey, John. *Cultural Consumption in Everyday Life.* London: Arnold, 1999.

Stratton, Jon. *The Desirable Body.* Manchester: Manchester University Press, 1996.

"Sync Magazine Promotes All-Stars." Press Release. *Yahoo! Finance*, 7 July 2005. http://biz.yahoo.com/prnews/050707/nytho88.html?.v=17 (accessed 1 August 2005).

Tailor and Cutter, 8 April 1880, 155.

Tailor and Cutter, 1885.

Tailor and Cutter, 1890.

Tailor and Cutter, 1894.

Tailor and Cutter, 1895.

Tailor and Cutter, 1896.

Tailor and Cutter, 20 May 1897.

Tailor's Review, June 1890, 108.

Thackeray, William Makepeace. *Vanity Fair, A Novel without a Hero*. 1848. Edited by John Sutherland. Oxford: Oxford University Press, 1983.

"Things We Have Borrowed." *Fashion*, March 1898, 4.

Thompson, Stephanie. "Nowhere But Up for Male Grooming: Boys Get Serious; Magazines, Supplements Are Lining up for a Piece of the Marketer Action." *Advertising Age*, 13 June 2005, S-6.

"Thoughts on Fashion." *Gazette of Fashion and Cutting Room Companion*, May 1888, 1.

"Three Men in a Cap." Cartoon. *Fashion*, May 1898, 22.

Tiersten, Lisa. "Marianne in the Department Store: Gender and the Politics of Consumption in Turn-of-the-Century Paris." In *Cathedrals of Consumption: The European Department Store, 1850–1939*, edited by Geoffrey Crossick and Serge Jaumin, 116–34. Aldershot, England: Ashgate, 1999.

"Top Cosmetic Surgeries for Men." *USA Today*, 27 May 2003, D1.

Tosh, John. *A Man's Place: Masculinity and the Middle-Class Home in Victorian England*. New Haven: Yale University Press, 1999.

Townend, Thomas, and Co. Advertisement. *Minister's Gazette of Fashion*, June 1889, n.p.

"Trends Towards Informality in Men's Wear." *Manchester Guardian Commercial*, 2 December 1938, 517.

Trollope, Anthony. *The Struggles of Brown, Jones, and Robinson By One of the Firm*. 1861–62. London: Penguin, 1993.

———. *The Way We Live Now*. 1875. New York: Knopf, 1950.

"Trousanger, The." *Fashion*, July 1901, 18.

Troy, Bill. "Numbers Soar for Male Surgery Patients; They're Willing to Talk about It, Too." *Cosmetic Surgery Times*, June 2004. http://www.cosmeticsurgerytimes.com/cosmeticsurgerytimes/article/articleDetail.jsp?id=102227 (accessed 1 August 2005).

Trumbach, Randolph. "Gender and the Homosexual Role in Modern Western Culture." In *Homosexuality, Which Homosexuality?* edited by Dennis Altman, Carole Vance, Martha Vicinus, and Jeffrey Weeks, 149–64. London: Gay Men's Press, 1989.

"Tyranny of Attire, The." *Fashion*, October 1902, 15–16.

Ugolini, Laura. "Clothes and the Modern Man in 1930s Oxford." *Fashion Theory* 4 (December 2000): 427–46.

"UK Tops Euro Plastic Surgery League." 11 March 2002. http://news.bbc.co.uk/1/
     hi/health/1867098.stm (accessed 13 August 2005).

Untitled. Advertisement. *Fashion*, March 1901, 18.

Untitled. *Fashion*, January 1899, 16.

Untitled. *Fashion*, October 1899, 24.

Untitled. *Fashion*, August 1902, 7.

"Up-to-Date Window Dressing." *Outfitter*, 17 March 1900, 17–18.

Veblen, Thorstein. *The Theory of the Leisure Class: An Economic Study in the Evolution of Insti-
     tutions.* New York: Macmillan, 1899.

Vickery, Amanda. *The Gentleman's Daughter: Women's Lives in Georgian England.* New Haven:
     Yale University Press, 1999.

*Victorian Shopping: Harrod's Catalogue 1895; A Facsimile of the Harrod's Stores 1895 Issue of the
     Price List, etc.* Introduction by Alison Adburgham. London: David and Charles, 1972.

Viyella. Advertisement. *Fashion*, May 1901, 15.

Voyager. "Fashions in Sticks." *Fashion*, August 1899, 14–15.

Walker, Richard Anderson. *The Savile Row Story: An Illustrated History.* London: Multi-
     media, 1988.

Walkley, Christina, and Vanda Foster. *Crinolines and Crimping Irons: Victorian Clothes; How
     They Were Cleaned and Cared For.* London: Peter Owen, 1978.

Walkowitz, Judith R. *City of Dreadful Delight: Narratives of Sexual Danger in Late-Victorian
     London.* Chicago: University of Chicago Press, 1992.

Walsh, Claire. "The Newness of the Department Store: A View from the Eighteenth
     Century." In *Cathedrals of Consumption: The European Department Store, 1850–1939*, edited
     by Geoffrey Crossick and Serge Jaumin, 46–71. Aldershot: Ashgate, 1999.

Wanamaker, John. *The Etiquette of an Englishman's Dress.* New York: John Wanamaker,
     1910.

"War Window, A." *Outfitter*, 19 May 1900, 11.

Waterloo Directory of Victorian Periodicals, 1824–1900, The. Compiled by Michael Wolff.
     Waterloo, Ontario: Wilfrid Laurier University Press, 1976.

Weeks, Jeffrey. *Sex, Politics and Society.* 2nd ed. London: Longman, 1989.

Weiss, Barbara. *The Hell of the English: Bankruptcy and the Victorian Novel.* Lewisburg, PA:
     Bucknell University Press, 1986.

Wells, H. G. *Kipps: The Story of a Simple Soul.* 1900. London: W. Collins Sons, 1925.

Wernick, Andrew. *Promotional Culture: Advertising, Ideology and Symbolic Expression.* Lon-
     don: Sage, 1991.

"West End Notes." *Gentleman's Magazine of Fashion*, March 1890, 8.

"What a miwackulous tye, Fwank." Cartoon. *Punch* 25 (1853): 18.

What the World Is Wearing. *Fashion*, March 1898, 5–6.

What the World Is Wearing. *Fashion*, April 1898, 5–7.

White, Percy. *The West End: A Novel*. London: Sands and Co., 1900.

Wilde, Oscar. "Fashions in Dress." *Daily Telegraph*, 3 February 1891, 5.

———. "House Decoration." 1882. In *Essays and Lectures*, 157–71. 1909. Reprint, New York: Garland, 1978.

———. *The Picture of Dorian Gray*. 1891. Edited by Donald L. Lawler. New York: Norton, 1988.

Williams, Rosalind H. *Dream Worlds: Mass Consumption in Late Nineteenth-Century France*. Berkeley: University of California Press, 1982.

Williams' Shaving Soaps. Advertisement. *Punch*, 23 February 1895, n.p.

Willis, Frederick. *A Book of London Yesterdays*. London: Phoenix House, 1960.

Wilson, Elizabeth. *Adorned in Dreams: Fashion and Modernity*. Berkeley: University of California Press, 1985.

Winstanley, Michael J. *The Shopkeeper's World, 1830–1914*. Manchester: Manchester University Press, 1983.

Wonderful Development of Harrods in Twenty-One Years, The. London: Harrods, 1911.

Worth et Cie. Advertisement. *Punch*, 31 July 1880.

———. Advertisement. *Fashion*, January 1903, 21.

Worth's Corsets. Advertisement. *Punch*, 4 January 1905, v.

Wrenn, Penny. "There's No Shame In: A Good Moisturizer." *Esquire*, March 2005, 76.

Zola, Emile. *The Ladies' Paradise. (Au bonheur des dames.)* 1883. Introduction by Kristin Ross. Berkeley: University of California Press, 1992.

Index

class (cont.)
162–66; consumption and class identity, 172–74; emulation of upper-class appearance by the lower classes, 4, 124–25, 129, 137, 144, 146–54, 162–68, 214n4, 219n9, 221n; waning of old wealth and/or conventional markers of upper-class status, 4, 147–48, 164–65, 168, 169, 218nn4–5

Cleveland Street scandal, 114, 212n12

Clothes and the Man, 67, 78–79, 146, 150, 167, 203n11, 210n14, 211n2, 211n4, 219n14

clothing: accessories for the care and storage of, 67, 68, 108–10; conservatism and repression, 16, 24–26; as conveyer of social identity, 13–14, 101, 148, 159, 161, 162, 166, 189, 194, 217n; eighteenth-century clothing, 23–25; emphasis on plain, drab, quiet clothing, 4, 6, 22, 23–25, 27–28, 38, 39, 51, 77, 96, 113, 152, 169, 170, 189, 202n2, 203n10; as expression of gender, 9, 14; growing popularity of informal and recreational clothing, 17, 163, 164, 174, 176, 179–89, 203n12; growing variety of men's clothing and accessories, 66–67, 85–89, 179–89; as marker of class, 14, 28; as means of male sexual display, 25, 80–84; men's presumed lack of interest in, 5, 21, 95–96, 99; and men's vanity, 35–36, 83; occasion-specific clothing, 102–3, 137, 168–69, 179, 183, 187–88, 190, 212n9; as reflection of culture, 14; as reflection of inner qualities, 23–27, 101; sexually revealing clothing, 25, 82–84; women's clothing, 2, 147. *See also* fashion

clubs, men's, 71, 73, 110, 114, 121, 126, 161

Cobbett, William, 81

Colin, Lady, 168, 170, 221n21

collars, 5–6, 12, 24, 66, 78, 80, 82, 98, 104, 108, 114, 125, 140, 141, 148, 152, 167, 179, 188, 199n5

college. *See* university life

Collins, Wilkie, 154

coat. *See* jacket

color, in men's clothing, 6–7, 8, 25, 27, 28, 38, 39, 40, 78, 95, 97, 102, 111, 114–15, 135, 144, 152, 154, 169, 193, 199n3, 200n7, 202n2, 203n10, 217n24, 220n20; bright colors, 7, 25, 38, 40, 78, 144, 154, 169, 206n1, 215n11, 217n24; emphasis on black and dark colors, 6, 7, 17, 24–28, 34, 51, 189, 193, 199n3, 202n2, 204n14, 206n1, 220n20

comfort, in clothing, 5, 174, 182–84

Complex, 196

conduct literature, 15, 17, 22, 26–40, 50, 51, 67, 79, 81, 128, 146–47, 152, 159, 162, 166–68, 169–70, 176, 182, 184, 187–88, 197, 202n2, 203n10, 204nn15–17, 205n20, 218n7; advice regarding dress, 26–40, 162; advice stressing adherence to fashion, 32–37; advice stressing appearance of paying little concern to one's dress, 29–31, 36–37, 125; advice stressing importance of clothing and appearance, 32–27; warnings against overdressing, 29, 124–25; warnings against preoccupation with fashion and appearance, 29–31, 125; warnings against underdressing, 146–47, 204n17

conformity, in men's fashion, 33, 35, 36, 52–53, 55, 113

conspicuous consumption, 2, 10, 54, 121, 129, 132, 135, 150, 164, 172, 189, 217n1; "inconspicuous consumption," 23

consumer culture, 10, 11, 19, 51, 54, 80–90, 166, 171; beginnings of, 12–13; as Victorian development, 13, 19

consumption, 17, 41–50, 55, 104, 110, 121, 128, 134–37, 172–74, 191–98, 201n12; as feminine, 4, 11, 12, 41–43, 45–46, 56–58; as gendered act, 4, 41, 56–57; by men at the turn of the twenty-first century, 191–98, 200n8; men's consumer desires, 46–50, 90, 136; men's consumption distinguished from women's, 56–58, 74; as opposite of production, 31, 58. *See also* shopping

Cornhill Magazine, 41

corset, men's, 7, 84–85, 86, 115–20, 212n14

cosmetic surgery, 120, 213n17; growth in men's market in the twenty-first century, 20, 192, 195

cosmetics, growing men's market in the twenty-first century, 20, 192, 194–95, 198; male use of, 12, 20, 90, 120–21, 129, 210n15

cotton, 67, 169, 170, 193, 199n3

counterculture, 163, 171

country wear, 146, 168, 169, 171, 174, 178, 179, 212n9

Craik, Dinah Mulock, 1

Curtin, Michael, 202n3, 204n18

Cutter's Gazette of Fashion, 55

cycling, 59–60, 64, 183, 184, 187, 188

D. H. Evans (department store), 3

D'Orsay, Count, 132, 202n7

dandy, 3, 7, 9, 10, 11, 18, 22, 24, 26, 27, 28, 30, 31, 34, 35, 40, 44, 45, 49, 87, 78, 79, 84, 102, 114, 115, 118, 128–60, 163, 196, 198,

fashion (*cont.*)
tight or form-fitting fashions, 29, 81–83, 129, 135; Victorian silence regarding men's fashion, 2, 9, 22; warnings against appearing too fashionable, 29, 102, 104, 203n11

Fashion (men's periodical): 1, 17–18, 21–22, 67, 68, 79, 82, 91–127, 136, 146, 152, *153*, 158, 176, 182, 191, 193, 196, 197, 199n5, 211–14nn4–21, 215n10, 217n24; advertising, 105–6; attitudes toward middle-class fashion, 123–24; celebration of expanding sartorial freedom, 102, 110–11; and class, 121–26; concealing the effort devoted to correct dress, 100; concerns regarding homosexuality, 113–15; condemnation of men's corset, 115–16; criticism of other periodicals' fashion reporting, 103–4; demise, 127; description, layout, and departments, 91, 93–94; difficulties in attracting readership, 126; dress charts, 103, 212n9; first issue, 91, 99; as a "gentlemen's club," 99–101; positive reviews, 92–93, 96–97, 127; as a promoter of goods and services, 68, 197, 105–10; promotion and legitimization of men's interest in fashion, 82, 95–101, 110–11, 193–94; promotion of hair dyes, cosmetics, and plastic surgery, 120–21; promotion of men's corset, 116–20, 197; purpose and goals, 91, 94–95; reaction by public and press, 92–93, 94, 96–97, 211n5; readership, 123; success and growth, 126; tips and how-to advice for men, 99–100

fashion plates, 7, *8*, 15, 93, 104, 156, 174, *184*, *185*, 199n3, 203n11, 212n9

femininity, 5, 11, 14, 16, 26, 56, 86, 118, 206n24; shopping and clothing as feminine interests, 4, 11, 12. *See also* effeminacy; women

FHM, 127, 192, 195, 196

flannel, 78, 100, 153, 169, 179, 186, 220n20

Flocker, Michael, 191

Flugel, J. C., 23, 25, 80, 163, 199n3

football (soccer), 66, 196, 197, 191; football costume, 186, *187*

footwear: boots, 7, 26, 39, 72, 100, 104, 105, 124, 130, 140, 205n20, 209n12, 210n14, 220n20; shoes, 9, 74, 93, 220n20; slippers, 23, 25; socks, 66, 78, 104, 111, *112*, 144, 167, 169, 205n23

fop, 30, 31, 79, 81, 116, 124–25, 130, 215n9. *See also* dandy; masher

Foucault, Michel, 36, 156, 159

France, 2, 3, 91, 209n10; French fashions, 2, 5, 30, 93, 118, 199n5

Fraser's, 43

French Revolution, 23–24

frock coat. *See under* jackets

Gagnier, Regenia, 214n4

Gazette of Fashion and Cutting-Room Companion, 6, 7, 8, 150, 183, 211n3, 216n13

gender: and clothing, 9, 14, 16; defined by a system of opposing attributes, 30, 41–42, 56–57, 81, 83; men as gendered, 14, 16; performative nature of, 4, 14, 15

gender-commerce bond, 40–43, 46, 51

Gentleman's Magazine of Fashion, 35, 52, 77, 135, *184*, 209n11

Giant, 196

Gilbert, W. S., and Arthur Sullivan, 155, 216n17

Gilmour, Robin, 24

Glass of Fashion, 1, 27, 28, 32, 33, 146, 148, 161, 167, 170, 182, 204n17

gloves, 44, 45, 46, 66, 108, 124, 169–70, 186, 205n21, 220n20

golf, 183, 187, 188; golf costume, 64, 184–86, 220n20

Gore, Catherine, 218n6

Gourvish, T. R., 219n15

Great Masculine Renunciation, 4, 5, 16, 22, 23–26, 27, 36, 37, 51, 52, 53, 54, 76, 79, 90, 130, 156, 164, 189, 202n2; as assertion of middle-class political legitimacy, 23–26; middle-class values reflected by, 23–26, 189; as renunciation of male sexuality, 25; sartorial characteristics, 24; as sartorial system based on gender, 25

Green, Harvey, 220n19

Greenfield, Jill, Sean O'Connell, and Chris Reid, 12, 93, 97–98, 113

grooming, men's, 19, 37; growth in men's market in the twenty-first century, 191–92, 194, 196–97; products, 13, 55, 80, 85–89

Grossmith, George, 15, 38–39

Habits of Good Society, 29, 30, 32, 35, 37, 85, 132, 146, 204n16

hair dye, 19, 85, 120–21, 194, 210n15, 213n15

hair products, 19, 20, 74, 85, 120–21, 194, 210n15

Hall, Donald E., 220n19

Hand-Book of Etiquette, 29

Harrods, 2, 42, 43, 52, 61, 65, 172, 186, 200n11, 208n9; catalogue, 66–67, 85, 87, 88; floor plan, 72–74, 209n12; male-directed

McKendrick, Neil, 163, 200n10, 209n10, 217n1, 218n9
Meller, Helen, 187
Men Only, 12, 93, 98, 114
men: male shopper as a figure of ridicule, 57–58; men's bodies, 17, 25, 81–85, 186; men's bodies used in advertising, 59–61, 62, 74–76, 77, 210n13; responsibility for performing and displaying class status; shopping habits, 43, 56, 71–72
men's departments (in stores). *See* department store
Men's Vogue, 194, 196
metrosexuality, 19, 191, 197–98
middle class: and the department store, 64, 164, 172–74; fashion aesthetics of, 10, 18, 22, 23–26, 38–40, 51, 123–24, 160, 162–90, 193; growing affluence of, 171–72; growing influence of middle-class fashion, 10, 162, 174–90, 193; identity based on consumption, 48, 164, 171–72; middle-class identity, 23–26, 48, 51
Middlemarch (Eliot), 46–48
military: dress, 67, 69, 70, 91, 93–94, 118, 197, 202n1, 209n10; images used in advertising, 60–63; khaki as a civilian spin-off of, 63–64, 207n5
Miller, Michael B., 173, 199n1, 207n6
Minister's Report of Fashion, 202n
Modern Etiquette in Private and Public, 35
Modern Man, 93
Moers, Ellen, 214n1, 216n16
Money, Leo Chiozza, 201n16, 218n3
More Manners for Men, 35
Mort, Frank, 12, 18, 19, 74, 75, 192, 196, 200n8, 210n13
Muscular Christianity, 31, 183, 189, 220n19

neckwear: cravat, 37, 97, 125; neckcloth, 5–6, 29, 78, 130, 133; necktie, 5–6, 9, 38, 39, 63, 66, 97, 133, 152, 169
Nixon, Sean, 19, 75, 192, 210n13
Norfolk jacket. *See under* jacket
Nuts, 195
Nylon Guys, 194, 196

Our Miss Gibbs (Ross and Greenbank), 42, 52, 57
Outfitter, 61–63
Oxford University, 11, 48–50, 203n13

Paoletti, Jo Barraclough, 16, 31, 200n7, 204n13
Pasdermadjian, Hrant, 199n1
Pater, Walter, 136

Patience, or Bunthorne's Bride (Gilbert and Sullivan), 155, 216n17
patterned fabrics, 7, 8, 28, 38, 64, 78, 111, 114, 135, 144, *145*, 169, 202n5, 203n10, 220n20
Peiss, Kathy, 12, 210n15
Pelham (Bulwer Lytton), 202n6, 203n9, 214n3
periodicals: men's, 93, 127, 211n; tailoring trade, 15, 52, 55, 93, 188, 204n16, 209n11, 211n3, 211n7, 219n14; women's fashion, 93, 96, 210n1. *See also Fashion* (men's periodical)
Peter Robinson's, 200n11
Philips, Deborah, 197
Picture of Dorian Gray, The (Wilde), 53, 136
pink, 78, 97, 104, 115, 158, 169, 217n24, 220n20
Pioneer of Fashion, 205n19
plastic surgery. *See* cosmetic surgery
Playboy, 101, 121, 127, 195, 196
pocket watch, 24, 67, 130, 178, 219n16
Pope and Bradley, 34
Punch, 57, 74, 76, *77*, 84, *85*, 86, 94, 96, *133*, *134*, *138*, *139*, *140*, 144, 150, 184, 212n13

Queer Eye for the Straight Guy, 191

Rappaport, Erika Diane, 5, 41–43, 46, 65, 208n8
ready-made clothing, 3, 10, 13, 66, 67–68, 124, 137, 139, 152, 169, 170, 174, 186, 188, 193, 200n10, 207n6, 209n10; department store's role in the success of, 17, 67–70, 169, 174, 186, 207n6
Reed, David, 172
reserve, in men's fashion, 17, 27, 29, 30, 31, 33, 39, 49, 51, 52, 53, 83, 132, 172, 183, 190
Roberts, Robert, 219n11
Rose, Jane E., 202n4
Ross, Adrian, and Percy Greenbank, 42, 52
Rotundo, E. Anthony, 16
Routledge's Etiquette for Gentlemen, 28, 30, 169, 203n9
royal warrants, 105, 212n11
rugby, 59, 118, 186
Ruskin, John, 167, 218n7
Rutherford, Jonathan, 220n19

Sala, George Augustus, 44, 143, 150–52, 176, 210n1
Sartor Resartus (Carlyle), 1, 52
satin, 104
Schaffer, Talia, 155
Selfridges, 71–72, 74, 219n12
separate spheres, 4, 16, 17, 22, 40–43, 205n22
servants, 123, 149–50, 153, 166, 176, 217n1; as ciphers for men's purchases, 17, 48–50
Sesame and Lilies (Ruskin), 167, 218n7

West End (London), 64, 65–66, 71, 95, 121, 144, 161, 166, 168, 170, 188, 208n8, 209n11, 215n6

West End, The (White), 21

White, Percy, 21

Whiteley's, 3, 44, 69, 71, 219n12

Wilde, Oscar, 35, 132, 133, 135, 136, 144, *145*, 155–59, 198, 214n4, 216n18; comments on fashion, 53, 78, 215n11, 216n13; gross indecency trials, 113–14, 157–59, 183, 217n23

William Whiteley's. *See* Whiteley's

Willis, Frederick, 170, 218n8

Wilson, Elizabeth, 199n4, 208n8

window displays, 61–63

Woman in White, The (Collins), 154

women: attention to men's appearance, 52, 81–83; as ciphers for men's purchases and/or consumer desires, 45–48; and department store, 45, 65, 71; female shopper as a figure of ridicule, 42, 57–58, 206n23, 207n3; as primary consumers and domestic managers, 11, 22, 41, 50, 166; shopping for men, 45–46; shopping habits, 42; women's consumption and shopping, 4, 5, 42, 45–46, 136; women's fashions, 2, 147

working class, 4, 11, 12, 24, 27, 35, 40, 54, 80–81, 129, 133, 139, 144, 147, 150, 152, 153, 159, 164, 165, 166, 167, 171, 209n11, 215n7, 218n3, 219n11

World War I, 11, 12, 13, 78, 144, 176, 179

World War II, 12, 18, 19, 23

Worth, Charles Frederick, 84–85, 118, 119, 212n13, 212–13n14; Worth's corsets ad, *85, 86, 117,*

youth fashions and culture, 12, 30, 48–50, 55, 84, 144

Zola, Emile, 65, 173

Zoo Weekly, 195